"In *The Young Crusaders*, V. P. Franklin reveals that the entire history of civil rights protest has depended in large measure on activism by children and teenagers. Covering events in nearly fifty cities, the book is stunning in its breadth and proves the undeniable impact and courage of these youthful activists. Their voices and stories resonate powerfully today and should energize and inspire a new generation of young activists in their fight for reparations and equality."

MARY FRANCES BERRY
*Geraldine R. Segal Professor of American Social Thought
and professor of history and Africana studies, University of Pennsylvania,
and author of* History Teaches Us to Resist

"Filling a void in our understanding of the Civil Rights Movement, V. P. Franklin presents the remarkable and largely untold story of young peoples' central role in the movement. *The Young Crusaders* reveals the unheralded work of children and teens, showcasing the incredible power of youth activism for our time, for all time."

IBRAM X. KENDI
*National Book Award–winning and #1 New York Times
best-selling author of* How to Be an Antiracist

"Few make history jump off the pages like V. P. Franklin, one of the field's most prominent and thoughtful historians. *The Young Crusaders* will stand as the definitive untold history of young people getting into 'good trouble' for racial justice. Franklin documents the relentless history of young people resisting and launching social justice campaigns for civil rights, educational justice, Black Power, and reparations. Both revelatory as well as a joy to read, it is a profound reflection on the power of young crusaders to change the world."

BETTINA LOVE
author of We Want To Do More Than Survive:
Abolitionist Teaching and the Pursuit of Educational Freedom

The Young Crusaders

OTHER WORKS BY V. P. FRANKLIN

New Perspectives on Black Educational History (COEDITOR)

The Education of Black Philadelphia

Black Self-Determination:
A Cultural History of African-American Resistance

Living Our Stories, Telling Our Truths:
Autobiography and the Making of the
African-American Intellectual Tradition

Martin Luther King, Jr.: A Biography

African Americans and Jews in the Twentieth Century:
Studies in Convergence and Conflict (COEDITOR)

My Soul Is a Witness: A Chronology of the
Civil Rights Era, 1954–1965 (COAUTHOR)

Sisters in the Struggle: African American Women
in the Civil Rights–Black Power Movement (COEDITOR)

Cultural Capital and Black Education: African American Communities
and the Funding of Black Schooling, 1860 to the Present (COEDITOR)

Message in the Music: Hip Hop, History, and Pedagogy (COEDITOR)

The Journal of African American History, 2002–2018 (EDITOR)

THE YOUNG CRUSADERS

THE UNTOLD STORY OF THE CHILDREN AND TEENAGERS WHO GALVANIZED THE CIVIL RIGHTS MOVEMENT

V. P. FRANKLIN

Beacon Press
Boston

BEACON PRESS
Boston, Massachusetts
www.beacon.org

Beacon Press books
are published under the auspices of
the Unitarian Universalist Association of Congregations.

24 23 22 21   8 7 6 5 4 3 2 1

This book is printed on acid-free paper that meets the uncoated paper
ANSI/NISO specifications for permanence as revised in 1992.

Text design by Wilsted & Taylor

Library of Congress Cataloging-in-Publication Data

Names: Franklin, V. P. (Vincent P.), author.
Title: The young crusaders : the untold story of the children and teenagers
    who galvanized the civil rights movement / V. P. Franklin.
Description: Boston : Beacon Press, [2021] | Includes bibliographical
    references and index.
Identifiers: LCCN 2020030880 (print) | LCCN 2020030881 (ebook) | ISBN
    9780807040072 (hardcover) | ISBN 9780807040096 (ebook)
Subjects: LCSH: Students—Political activity—United States—History—20th
    century. | Civil rights movements—United States—History—20th century.
Classification: LCC LB3610 .F73 2021 (print) | LCC LB3610 (ebook) | DDC
    371.8/1—dc23
LC record available at https://lccn.loc.gov/2020030880
LC ebook record available at https://lccn.loc.gov/2020030881

To Young Freedom Fighters—
Past, Present, and Future

Contents

The Young Crusaders

Introduction

Children and Teenagers

Foot Soldiers for Democracy

The day we were arrested, one of the Negro trusties
sneaked us a newspaper. We discovered that over four
hundred high school students had also been arrested.
We were so glad we sang freedom songs for an hour or so.

Anne Moody (1968)[1]

IT MAY SURPRISE many readers to learn that the largest civil rights demonstration in United States history was *not* the August 1963 March on Washington, but the system-wide school boycott in New York City on February 3, 1964, when over 360,000 elementary and secondary school students went on strike and thousands attended the "freedom schools" opened throughout the city. Civil rights activist Bayard Rustin, who had organized the March on Washington, was recruited by local leaders to head up the mobilization for the Freedom Day protests in New York City. The day after the strike Rustin declared, this was "the largest civil rights protest in the nation's history."[2] It was the participation of hundreds of thousands of African American, Puerto Rican, and white children and teenagers in the public school boycotts in New York, Boston, Chicago, and other cities in the 1960s that made them successful. Indeed, children and teenagers were on the front lines at nonviolent protests and demonstrations throughout the 1950s and 1960s, but their major contributions to civil rights activism has generally gone unacknowledged.

1

We have witnessed children and teenagers taking center stage in twenty-first-century protests and demonstrations aimed at arresting the deterioration in our physical environment and ending the unnecessary slaughter associated with gun violence. Yet decades earlier, children and teenagers often took the lead in challenging the disparities in educational resources between rich and poor, Black and white public schools; opposing Jim Crow practices in public accommodations; and protesting the unprovoked violence carried out by law enforcement officials. When civil rights organizers came to town to recruit participants in nonviolent direct-action campaigns to challenge racially discriminatory practices, children and teenagers were often the first ones to show up on the picket lines in large numbers, and oftentimes they were attacked, brutalized, and arrested by the police.

Anne Moody was born in Centreville in Wilkinson County, Mississippi, in 1940, and before graduating from Tougaloo College in 1964, she worked as a civil rights organizer for the Congress of Racial Equality (CORE) and the Student Nonviolent Coordinating Committee (SNCC). In May 1963, Moody was sent to Jackson, Mississippi, to work with SNCC's Robert Parris Moses and other civil rights organizers in conducting workshops "where potential demonstrators, high school and college students mostly, were taught to protect themselves."[3] Moody's *Coming of Age in Mississippi*, published in 1968, became a best seller, especially after it was reviewed in the *New York Times Book Review* by Massachusetts senator Edward "Ted" Kennedy.[4] The book soon became a "classic autobiographical account" and brilliant narrative not just of Black life in the Deep South in the first half of the twentieth century but also of the civil rights campaigns mounted there and her work in "The Movement."[5]

In June 1963, Moody and four others from Tougaloo decided to stage a sit-in at the Woolworth's lunch counter in Jackson. As the Black and white protesters sat there for several hours, angry whites gathered and started smearing them with ketchup, mustard, sugar, and everything on the counter. Adam D. Beittel, president of Tougaloo College, soon arrived and was finally able to convince the policemen who were standing around outside to allow him to lead the protesters out of Woolworth's. "When we got outside, the policemen formed a single line that blocked the mob from us. However, they were allowed to throw at us anything they had collected."[6]

The sit-in led to a rally that night at the Pearl Street Church attended by hundreds of adults and teenagers and where the Woolworth's sit-inners were introduced by Medgar Evers, the National Association for the Advancement of Colored People (NAACP) leader for the state of Mississippi. Plans were made for a "pray-in" at the local post office the next day. Fourteen demonstrators, seven Blacks and seven whites, managed to make it inside, but outside "the whites standing there had murder in their eyes," and the police came and arrested protesters. The same day Moody and the others were taken to jail, the students at all-Black Lanier High School started singing freedom songs in the cafeteria during their lunch hour. When the bell rang to return to class, they just kept singing. The principal, fearing a riot, panicked and called in the police, who brought dogs and then turned them loose. "The students fought them off for a while," and mothers who arrived at the scene and saw what was happening "joined in fighting off the dogs. They had begun to throw bricks, rocks, and bottles." Several students and their mothers were arrested.[7]

The day after that unprovoked attack, over four hundred students from Lanier, Jim Hill, and Brinkley high schools gathered at the church on Farish Street. SNCC, CORE, and NAACP youth council organizers briefly instructed the teenagers on how to protect themselves when attacked and then led them into the street. After marching two blocks they were met by a squadron of police who ordered the teenagers to disperse. When they refused, they were arrested and herded into "paddy wagons, canvas-covered trucks, and garbage trucks. Those moving too slowly were jabbed with rifles."[8] The police brought dogs, but they were not used. The high school students were taken to the fairgrounds and held there. Moody and other civil rights workers also got themselves arrested hoping to join the teenagers at the fairgrounds, but these "professional agitators" were kept at the city jail.

While the teenagers were being held, mass protest rallies took place every night in Jackson, and every day that week people were taken to jail. Despite court injunctions prohibiting street demonstrations, they continued, and even NAACP officers Roy Wilkins and Medgar Evers were arrested on the picket line in front of Woolworth's. In and out of jail several times, Moody was again arrested during this protest, and this time she was taken to the fairgrounds where the high school students were being held. As the place where cattle were held and then auctioned off during the annual state fair, the fairgrounds were enclosed in barbed wire. "It reminded me of a concentration camp. . . . I imagined myself in Nazi Germany, the policemen Nazi soldiers." There were still about 150 high school girls there. "It was hot and sticky and girls were walking around half dressed all the time." The food provided was not fit for human consumption. "The sight of it nauseated me." Over the next few days, "many were taken from the fairgrounds sick from hunger."[9]

Then, on June 12, 1963, Medgar Evers was shot outside his home and later died. The next day when people learned of the shooting, huge demonstrations were mounted in the streets of Jackson. Moody was arrested again, and the police brought dogs, billy clubs, and fire trucks and used hoses to disperse the crowds. Protesters and bystanders who threw bottles, rocks, and other debris at the police were being arrested. Then, John Doar stepped out from the police barricade and identified himself as being from the US Department of Justice. He came over and talked with the demonstrators, suggesting "this wasn't the way" to respond to Evers's death. Several ministers present agreed and started asking people to return to their homes, and soon the crowd dispersed.[10]

The protests in Jackson, Mississippi, in which Anne Moody participated and described in detail in her celebrated autobiography, included many of the elements that would characterize children and teenagers' contributions to civil rights activism before and after 1963.[11] Prior to 1963 and the events in Jackson, young people in the NAACP youth councils and other civil rights groups participated in nonviolent direct-action campaigns mounted by the adult leaders in the organizations; however, as in Jackson, Mississippi, children and teenagers soon began organizing and leading their own protests. Part 1 of this book, "Freedom on Their Minds," covers this early period, from 1935 to 1964. "Youth and Civil Rights Activism Before the *Brown* Decision," chapter 1, examines the work of Juanita Jackson, the NAACP youth director, in establishing youth councils in cities and on college campuses in the 1930s, and documents young people's activism in "Don't Buy Where You Can't Work" campaigns and for the freedom of the Scottsboro Nine, teenagers who were falsely accused of rape, tried, and sentenced to death in Alabama. Members of the youth councils also marched in support of antilynching legislation that had been introduced into the US Congress almost every year between 1920 and 1950. Historians Charles Kellogg, Robert Zangrando, Patricia Sullivan, and others have documented the numerous unsuccessful attempts to get a law passed that would make lynching and other vigilante violence a federal crime.[12] The successful school boycotts organized by Black teenagers in Lumberton, North Carolina, in October 1946 and Prince Edward County, Virginia, in April 1951 are also discussed in chapter 1 within the context of NAACP youth activism and the litigation leading to the US Supreme Court's 1954 *Brown v. Board of Education* decision.[13]

Similar to crusaders in earlier eras, the children and teenagers' religious beliefs provided a cultural justification for their social engagement. The young crusaders learned of the need for social activism at rallies and meetings held in their churches, as took place in Jackson, Mississippi, in 1963. Before going off to march or picket, the adults and the young people prayed for themselves and their opponents hoping that their religiously motivated social activism would result in meaningful change in racially biased policies and practices. After the *Brown* decision, children and teenagers came to the forefront of civil rights activism through their determination to desegregate all-white educational institutions.[14]

Women in general and female college students in particular, like Anne Moody, served in many leadership roles and led successful civil rights campaigns. Early accounts of civil rights activism focused primarily on the activities of Martin Luther King Jr., Ralph Abernathy, Roy Wilkins, A. Philip Randolph, Andrew Young, Robert Parris Moses, Stokely Carmichael, Bayard Rustin, and other male figures. However, when the contributions of women and girls to the civil rights campaigns began to be documented in the late 1980s, it changed our understanding and overall interpretation of "The Movement." These women not only were "bridge leaders," serving as the liaisons between the national civil rights organizations and local movements, they also mobilized people, developed strategies, led civil rights campaigns, and were arrested, jailed, and sometimes brutalized. These courageous women have narrated their personal stories in published memoirs and unpublished interviews, and their enormous contributions have been documented in numerous historical works.[15] Rachel Devlin's 2018 book *A Girl Stands at the Door: The Generation of Young Women Who Desegregated America's Schools* includes individual portraits of the girls and young women who were the first to enroll in all-white schools, and it was teenage girls and boys who individually and collectively decided to put their bodies on the line to advance African Americans' rights, often paying a heavy price.[16]

When we document children and teenagers' contributions to protests organized by adult activists and by the young people themselves, it also changes our overall understanding of the Civil Rights Movement and better explains how and why it was successful in ending legal segregation — American apartheid. Focusing on the young crusaders' crucial and multifaceted roles reveals entirely new dimensions and previously unexplored aspects of the most important social movement in the United States in the twentieth century.

"Grace Under Pressure: Children, Teenagers, and School Desegregation," chapter 2, documents the experiences of the Milford Ten in Delaware, the Clinton Twelve in Tennessee, the Little Rock Nine in Arkansas, and other African American children and teenagers who integrated all-white schools in the 1950s and early 1960s. The voices of the teenagers themselves are used to explain what happened and the positive and negative consequences of their activism. Tens of thousands of African American, Hispanic, and white children and teenagers demonstrated their support for equal educational opportunity and the implementation of the *Brown* decision in the (largely overlooked) "Youth Marches for Integrated Schools" in October 1958 and April 1959.[17]

With the launching of the student sit-in movement in February 1960, the emerging Civil Rights Movement entered a new, more expansive phase. The four teenagers who carried out the nonviolent direct-action protest at the Woolworth's lunch counter in Greensboro, North Carolina, had recently enrolled at North Carolina A&T State University. Yet before that, they had participated in, and even led, civil rights protests as high school students and members of NAACP youth councils. In chapter 3, "High School Students and Nonviolent Direct-Action Protests," the civil rights demonstrations launched by secondary school students in Greensboro; Chattanooga, Tennessee; Baton Rouge, Louisiana; Atlanta and Americus,

Georgia; and Orangeburg and Rock Hill, South Carolina, are examined. In many instances the teenagers' activism led to the participation by local adults who earlier had remained on the sidelines.

In McComb, Mississippi, the arrest of 16-year-old Brenda Travis in October 1961 for sitting in at the Greyhound bus terminal and her suspension from Burgland High School led to a walkout and march by hundreds of her fellow classmates. As the teenagers descended on city hall, they came under attack by the police, and over a hundred were arrested. NAACP leader Medgar Evers declared that the high school students' sit-in, protest march, and arrest "focuses the spotlight on the terrible conditions by dramatizing the situation . . . and forces the parents to take a firm stand."[18] In Albany, Georgia, the bus terminal sit-in and arrest of three high school and two college students on November 22, 1961, sparked the Albany Movement, in which Dr. King and SCLC and SNCC organizers participated over the next year and thousands of children and adults were arrested.

The brutality meted out to children and teenagers in Birmingham, Alabama, in May 1963 appalled people around the world who saw the film footage. The violent attacks on nonviolent students had a galvanizing effect on children and teenagers throughout the country, especially among southern youth.[19] "The Birmingham Children's Crusade and Southern Student Activism," chapter 4, provides the personal perspectives of Bernita Roberson, Annetta Streeter Gary, Larry Russell, Willie A. Casey, and others who were children or teenagers at the time and participated in the Birmingham campaign. Rufus Burrow Jr., in *A Child Shall Lead Them: Martin Luther King Jr., Young People, and the Movement*, notes that "it was children and young people who boldly led the way in many civil rights campaigns, who energized the movement at strategic moments. They asserted themselves, making it clear once and for all that they were fully aware of racial discrimination and its adverse effects on them." Tracing youth activism associated with Dr. King's campaigns in Montgomery and Birmingham, Alabama, the 1964 Freedom Summer in Mississippi, the 1965 Selma to Montgomery March, and other SCLC and SNCC demonstrations, Burrow concluded that "Martin Luther King never lost faith in young people and their ability and determination to help move this society in the direction of the beloved community."[20]

While young people did play important roles in the civil rights campaigns organized or led by Dr. King during that period, hundreds of thousands of children and teenagers engaged in sit-ins, school boycotts, marches, and demonstrations in which Dr. King played little or no part. On the heels of the Birmingham confrontation, more and more young people in the South began to join the civil rights campaigns. In June 1963 in Fayetteville, North Carolina, it was the students at E. H. Smith High School and Washington Drive Junior High who joined the NAACP youth Commandos in the march on the downtown, seeking to "crush Segregation in North Carolina." Indeed, many teenagers who attended the historic March on Washington on August 28, 1963, had already participated in civil rights campaigns in their hometowns and many returned from the march to organize numerous protests that took place in 1963 and 1964 in cities and towns throughout the South.[21] Chapter 4 focuses specifically on junior and senior high school student activism in Greenville, Hammond, Clinton, and Plaquemine, Louisiana; Memphis, Tennessee; and Orangeburg, South Carolina. After Anne Moody organized the civil rights protests in Jackson, she moved on to Canton, Mississippi, where she found that "so far mostly teenagers were involved in the Movement." Despite opposition coming from parents and school administrators, Moody was able to recruit high school students for the voter registration drives and found "they were more energetic than any bunch of teen-agers I had known or worked with before."[22]

In part 2, "The Quality Integrated Education Movement," the analysis shifts to the northern and midwestern states and the organized campaigns to bring about the desegregation of the public school systems in Boston, Chicago, New York, and other cities. In the 1950s and early 1960s there was extreme overcrowding in urban public schools due to the postwar baby boom and African American in-migration from the South. The public schools in Black neighborhoods were not just overcrowded, they also tended to be older and in poor condition. After the 1954 *Brown* decision, African American and Puerto Rican parents and NAACP attorneys petitioned northern school officials to allow children of color to transfer to underutilized public schools in predominantly white neighborhoods. When school official after school official refused to allow Black or other children of color to enroll in all-white schools, the integration of the public schools became an important objective of civil rights activism. Indeed, in some places quality integrated public schooling became *the* major civil rights issue, and the campaigns' effectiveness depended on the broad participation of children and teenagers.

Chapter 5, "Freedom Day Boycotts: Chicago, Boston, and New York City," describes children and teenagers' participation in the largest civil rights demonstrations to take place in the United States. In Chicago, public school officials dealt with overcrowding by having students attend one of two shifts, one in the morning and the other in the afternoon, and through the construction of mobile classrooms on school grounds. Black parents and community leaders' complaints were to no avail, even after protests and individual school boycotts were organized. Similar conditions in the Boston public schools led to the first system-wide school boycott by secondary school students. On June 22, 1963, thousands of junior and senior high students in Boston decided to "Stay Out for Freedom" and instead attended the "freedom schools" opened throughout the city where the teenagers learned how their actions contributed to the advancement of the civil rights campaigns in the city.

A system-wide school boycott was organized in Chicago in October 1963 in which over 224,000 Black, Puerto Rican, Mexican American, and white students participated, and thousands attended the freedom schools. In February 1964, a second boycott took place in Chicago, and 170,000 school children stayed home or attended the freedom schools. The largest civil rights demonstration in United States history, the system-wide school boycott in New York City on February 3, 1964, involving over 360,000 Black, Puerto Rican, and white students, was followed by a second strike on March 16, 1964, in which over 165,000 students participated. The backlash from white parents and community leaders in New York City who opposed school officials' antiracist policies is also discussed in the fifth chapter, including the two-day public school boycott by over 170,000 white students in September 1964.

The district-wide school strikes for quality, integrated education were organized by community leaders and parents, but it was the participation of the children and teenagers that was crucial. Chapter 6, "Every Child a

Freedom Soldier: Cleveland, Milwaukee, and Mississippi," discusses the unique circumstances behind the system-wide school boycotts in Cleveland and Milwaukee. Given the extreme overcrowding in public schools in Black neighborhoods in Cleveland, school officials decided to bus some African American students and teachers to all-white schools, but did not allow the Black students to interact with the white children at the receiving schools. Indeed, the practice of "intact busing" meant that the African American children and teachers were segregated *within* the all-white public schools.

The intact busing practiced in the Milwaukee public schools was even worse than in Cleveland because the African American students were bused to the white schools, then taken back to their old school for lunch, and then returned to the white schools for the afternoon session, and then bused back to their old school in the late afternoon. Black parents and leaders complained bitterly about the "lost classroom time" due to the busing, and they organized a school strike. In Cleveland, the boycott took place on April 20, 1964, and an estimated 55,000 children and teenagers participated in the antiracist activism with hundreds attending the freedom schools. In Milwaukee, the first of three strikes was mounted on May 18, 1964; freedom schools were opened, and an estimated 12,000 Black students participated, 60 percent of the Black student enrollment. While the lawsuits filed by the NAACP and local leaders eventually led to some public school desegregation in Cleveland and Milwaukee, children and teenagers, through their participation in the school boycotts, demonstrated their commitment to African Americans' demands for equal educational opportunity. In 1964, the most famous Freedom School Program was launched by SNCC during its Freedom Summer campaign in Mississippi. Chapter 5 discusses where the forty-one schools were opened, the students who attended, what they learned, and the impact this program had on children and teenagers' subsequent social activism.

Part 3, "From Civil Rights to Black Power," describes the changes in the avowed objectives of high school student activism from 1965 to 1970. Chapter 7, "Police Brutality, Black Self-Defense, and Student Activism," examines civil rights activism in Alabama, the famous Selma to Montgomery March, and the pivotal roles played by children and teenagers before, during, and after this major voting rights campaign. The attack on peaceful marchers on the Edmund Pettus Bridge on March 7, 1965, "Bloody Sunday," was the tragic climax of civil rights protests that had been taking place for the previous three months. And during that period, hundreds of children and teenagers were marching in the streets, getting arrested and jailed, and being brutalized by law enforcement officers. Black self-defense groups emerged during the civil rights protests in the South to protect the nonviolent activists, in keeping with the cultural value of resistance that has defined African Americans' ongoing response to unjust oppression.[23] Chapter 7 describes what occurred in Tuscaloosa, Alabama, and Jonesboro, Louisiana, when teenagers who had organized their own nonviolent direct-action protests came under attack.

In northern and midwestern cities beginning in the 1930s, once a critical mass of Black residents existed, the unrestrained police violence perpetrated against African American men, women, and children sparked rioting, and in many instances, it was the teenagers who fought back against the police attacks. Chapter 7 describes the participation of young people in the riots in Harlem in 1935, 1943, and 1964, the first year of the long, hot summers of the 1960s. Investigations of the rioting in 1964 in Jacksonville, Florida; Brooklyn, New York; Philadelphia, Pennsylvania; and several cities in New Jersey revealed that the major cause was police brutality, and that most of the rioters were teenagers and young adults. This was also the case in the violence and rioting in the Watts neighborhood of Los Angeles in July 1965; Chicago and Cleveland in July 1966; in Cincinnati and Tampa in June 1967; and Detroit and Newark in July 1967.

The extreme white backlash and opposition to civil rights demands and public school desegregation provided some justification for increasing demands in the late 1960s by African American parents and leaders for "Black Power" and community control of public schools in Black neighborhoods. Chapter 8, "Civil Rights, Black Power, and Increasing Youth Militancy," examines the shifts in children and teenagers' activism between 1965 and 1970. In Philadelphia, Chicago, and Memphis, teenage gang members were recruited by civil rights leaders to serve as marshals for the large and ongoing protests and demonstrations. With the advent of Black Power, however, the major educational changes that Black high school students demanded were the introduction of Black History courses and an increase in the number of African American teachers, staff, and administrators, especially in predominantly Black schools.

In 1967, in Philadelphia, Chicago, and other cities, thousands of high school students participated in walkouts and protests over the implementation of their Black Power demands. And with the assassination of Martin Luther King Jr. on April 4, 1968, teenagers not only engaged in rioting in cities and towns across the United States, they also organized their own memorials and special programs to honor the slain leader. In the 1968–69 school year, Black high school students in Chicago and other cities, Mexican American students in California and other western states, and white students throughout the country organized walkouts, strikes, and demonstrations demanding educational change, contributing to the emerging Student Rights Movement, which continued into the 1970s.

The 1980s and 1990s witnessed a decrease in social movement activism compared to the 1950s and 1960s, and there were fewer youth-oriented antiracist campaigns during those decades. However, the twenty-first century has seen a resurgence in social activism among teenagers and young adults. The epilogue, "Keep Stirring Up 'Good Trouble,'" highlights the ongoing climate strikes among high school students inspired by 16-year-old Swedish activist Greta Thunberg and the campaign against gun violence launched by the survivors of the mass shooting in February 2018 at Marjory Stoneman Douglas High School in Parkland, Florida. The students organized the March for Our Lives on March 24, 2018, that brought hundreds of thousands to Washington, DC, and 1.2 million people all over the world into the streets.

Black Lives Matter and other youth-oriented protest organizations emerged in the 2010s following the deaths of innocent African Americans at the hands of police. Thousands of children and teenagers participated in demonstrations launched by the Movement for Black Lives, and in 2020, following the police murder of George Floyd in Minneapolis, teenagers organized and led large-scale antiracist protests in cities and towns across the country. Black Lives Matter and other social justice groups are seeking not only an end to unprovoked police violence against African Americans and other people of color but also reparations from the US government and multinational corporate capitalists for slavery, slave trading, Jim Crow discrimination, mass incarceration, and the destruction of the physical environment.

Many believe the reparations campaigns that have reemerged in the Caribbean, Africa, and the United States will be the major social justice movement in the twenty-first century. Children and teenagers must engage in their own "reparatory justice" campaigns to pursue reparations not just for African Americans and other people of color but also for environmental degradation, escalating gun violence, the negative impact of pervasive high-stakes testing on elementary and secondary education, and crushing student debt, especially in the era of COVID-19. National and multinational corporations, enabled by the political establishment, have contributed greatly to the extreme economic inequality in American society and done great damage to the land, air, and water primarily for the financial benefit of the 1 percent. In the 1960s the rallying cry was "Freedom Now!"; in the twenty-first century it needs to be "Reparations Now!" Civil rights icon John Lewis emphasized that young people will have to "keep stirring up good trouble" if they want to improve their lives and the prospects for future generations of children and young people.

PART I
Freedom on Their Minds

Chapter 1

Youth and Civil Rights Activism Before the *Brown* Decision

If it wasn't for the church, what would we do? It was the social center, the meeting place, where we met to protest wrongs against our people. It was the support that raised funds for all of our civic efforts and backed us.

Juanita Jackson Mitchell[1]

"BALTIMORE WAS MEAN." In the summer of 1931, 18-year-old Juanita Jackson had just graduated from the University of Pennsylvania and returned home. "In Baltimore we were completely segregated. We lived in court-enforced racial ghettos."[2] The national economy was depressed with unemployment approaching 20 percent, and even "college-bred Negroes" found it difficult to find a job. Jackson attended a town hall discussion at the home of Elizabeth Coit Gilman, daughter of Johns Hopkins University president and prominent socialist Daniel Coit Gilman, focusing on the socioeconomic challenges facing Baltimore. Jackson proposed a similar meeting among Black youth, many of whom were unemployed and in need of counsel about how to find employment. She shared the idea with Clarence Mitchell, a recent Lincoln University graduate returning to the city, and they organized a planning session in September with her sisters, Virginia and Marian Jackson. What became known as the City-Wide Young People's Forum held its first public meeting at Sharpe Street Memorial Methodist Episcopal Church on October 2, 1931, with over a hundred young people in attendance. The participants decided to mobilize around three specific objectives: to provide public lectures by prominent leaders on the pressing issues of the time; to promote equal rights for all US citizens; and to pursue equal employment opportunities.[3]

In Baltimore at that time African Americans were not only excluded from employment in most state offices and private businesses but also "couldn't even buy articles in department stores," as Jackson recalled. When she was in high school, Jackson and her friends made use of what they learned in their French classes: "We would put turbans on our heads and go down to Stewart's Department Store and speak French." They were served because they were perceived as "black foreigners" and exotic. African Americans born in the United States, however, "were unwelcome."[4]

SOCIAL PROTEST AND AFRICAN AMERICAN YOUTH

Among the speakers at the weekly young people's forums in Baltimore were leaders and organizers from various cities where Don't Buy Where You Can't Work campaigns had been mounted. These urban boycott campaigns can be traced to the early twentieth century, especially following the implementation of Jim Crow laws in the southern states. In the nineteenth century, Frederick Douglass, Ida B. Wells, and other African Americans protested against the policies of railroad companies after having been physically removed from passenger trains. Wells ultimately sued the railroad officials, but lost after the US Supreme Court in 1883 nullified the provisions in the Civil Rights Act of 1875, which called for nondiscrimination in public accommodations. In 1887, Florida was the first state to pass a law requiring racial segregation on railways within the state. This was followed by Mississippi in 1888, Texas in 1889, and Louisiana in 1890. It was the Louisiana law that Homer Plessy challenged and the Supreme Court upheld in *Plessy v. Ferguson* in 1896.[5]

When southern states began passing laws calling for segregation on streetcars and other public transit, however, African Americans responded with organized boycotts. Protests took place in all the southern states, especially in the major cities, following the passage of statutes mandating segregation on streetcars. In 1905, the *Mobile Daily Register* reported, "In every city where it has been found advisable to separate the races in the street cars the experience has been the same. The [N]egroes . . . have invariably declared a boycott."[6] When alternative transportation systems were put in place by African Americans themselves, the operators were usually fined and forced to close down by the local police. Some earlier historians suggested class divisions within African American communities as the reason these campaigns to end Jim Crow practices on public transit failed. However, more recent research has challenged that view. Historian Blair L.M. Kelley documented the boycotts in twenty-three southern cities and concluded, "Efforts to contest segregation became more notable precisely because African Americans of all walks of life participated." He noted the protests of African Americans were not simply "class-based attempts at bourgeois respectability; protesters recognized that segregation was not only a daily inconvenience and public humiliation but also part of a focused attack on the citizenship of *all* black southerners."[7]

During the 1920s, boycotts of separate and under-resourced all-Black public schools occurred in at least fourteen cities and towns and were somewhat effective.[8] Chicago politician Oscar DePriest told the young people attending Baltimore's City-Wide Young People's Forum about the campaigns launched in the Windy City, beginning in 1930, against chain stores dependent on African Americans as customers. Woolworth and other chain stores were picketed and boycotted, and initially there was significant success resulting in an estimated three hundred jobs for Black workers. City-Wide Forum participants also heard about what happened at the Kroger stores in Toledo, Ohio, where the local NAACP branch organized picketing and a boycott led to an agreement that included hiring African Americans as clerks and managers. At times, store owners sought and obtained injunctions against picketers, accusing them of disrupting the flow of business, and the police were summoned to arrest the protesters.[9]

The Great Atlantic and Pacific Tea Company, better known as the A&P, was the first grocery store chain in the United States, and by 1930, there were an estimated sixteen thousand stores. At the same time, the A&Ps operating in predominantly Black neighborhoods in northern and midwestern cities had no African American employees. With the onset of the Depression, the A&Ps became a highly visible and somewhat vulnerable target for Black neighborhood improvement associations and NAACP youth councils. In Washington, DC, in 1933; Columbus, Ohio, in 1934; and Cleveland, Ohio; Richmond, Virginia; Gary, Indiana; and Plainfield, New Jersey, in 1936, picketers replaced customers; and even after injunctions ended picket lines, the boycotts remained in place.[10]

In pursuit of its stated objective of improving employment opportunities for Black youth, the City-Wide Young People's Forum targeted the A&Ps in Baltimore. Juanita Jackson, Clarence Mitchell, William Dorsey, and other forum members initially contacted store managers and asked that they begin hiring African Americans as clerks and managers. When none were hired, picket lines were set up on November 18, 1933, in front of every A&P store in Black neighborhoods. News of the boycott was spread among religious congregations whose members then joined the picket lines. Estimates indicate that up to five hundred people participated in the picketing each week. Store managers gradually began to hire Black workers. Up to fifty African Americans were hired soon afterward, and an agreement was reached to train some of these Black workers for management positions.[11]

The declining incomes of Black and white Americans following the onset of the Depression meant that the NAACP began to experience a significant drop in membership. Walter White, who became NAACP executive secretary in 1930, soon realized that the organization would be even more dependent on large donations from wealthy benefactors such as board member William Rosenwald, son of Sears, Roebuck and Company founder Julius Rosenwald. As part of its successful "Jobs for Negroes" and Don't Buy Where You Can't Work campaigns, the Chicago NAACP sought to address racial discrimination at Sears department stores. A. C. MacNeal, president of Chicago's NAACP branch, forwarded these charges to Walter White, pointing out that the local members wanted to begin picketing and boycotting Sears. White confronted William Rosenwald about this but was told that there was no discriminatory policy at any Sears store in Chicago. White replied to MacNeal and told him not to picket or boycott Sears, because Rosenwald "had taken up the charges of discrimination."[12]

This was but one example of Walter White's actions discouraging NAACP branches from organizing protest marches and picket lines against NAACP donors and recommending instead that they pursue petitioning and lobbying for antidiscrimination legislation at the local and state level. He feared a loss of contributions from large businesses and corporations in the midst of the Depression. This meant that NAACP branches and local groups committed to direct action campaigns could not expect to receive any financial support or legal counsel from the national office. White was aware of the increasing competition coming from local direct-action groups as well as the absence of programming being made available to the so-called junior branches. Therefore, at the NAACP's annual convention in July 1935 in St. Louis, he obtained the passage of a resolution calling for the restructuring of the organization's "youth work."[13]

JUANITA JACKSON AND THE NEW YOUTH COUNCILS

Given the success of the City-Wide Young People's Forum, Walter White decided to ask Juanita Jackson to join the NAACP staff in New York City in September 1935. She did. "For three years I traveled all over this country, but mainly in the South, organizing young people, challenging young people." Among other things, Jackson got rid of the junior branches and began establishing "youth councils, junior youth councils, and college chapters." Historian Thomas L. Bynum found that the NAACP's new youth department encouraged activities in several specific areas: equal educational and employment opportunities, voting rights and civil liberties, and antilynching legislation.[14]

Lillie Jackson, Juanita's mother, had been lobbying for the association's annual meeting to be held in Baltimore even before she was elected president of the local branch in 1935. Her persistence was rewarded, and in July 1936 at the NAACP's annual meeting at Sharpe Street Memorial Methodist Episcopal Church, Juanita Jackson recruited members of the City-Wide Young People's Forum to highlight youth activities. In their presentations at the convention the young people showcased their projects and sang "The Challenge Song."

> *Should we sit idly by and sigh,*
> *While lynching rules the land*
> *And thousands suffer agony*
> *From Jim Crow's cruel hand?*

Shall we allow rank prejudice
To thwart our destiny?
With the NAACP
We'll fight for victory.[15]

Before and after this annual convention, the NAACP youth council organized by Juanita Jackson took up the cause of African American teenagers in Baltimore County who were being deprived of secondary education.
There were many public high schools for white students in the county, but
none for African Americans. If they wanted to attend high school, Black
children had to pass a special examination—made purposely difficult—to
receive tuition assistance to attend one of the all-Black high schools in the
city. Protests at the school district office in the county were followed up
with a lawsuit on behalf of Margaret Williams and Lucille Scott, 13-year-
olds whose parents attempted to enroll them in (all-white) Catonsville
High School in September 1935, but were turned away by the principal.
NAACP attorney Thurgood Marshall filed the lawsuit against Catonsville's principal, David Zimmerman, demanding Williams's and Scott's
admission, but really hoping to get a separate and equal high school for
African American teenagers built in Baltimore County. At the *Williams v.*
Zimmerman trial in March 1936, Judge Frank Duncan, a Southern Demo-
crat, did not even address Marshall's argument about the lack of secondary
schools for African Americans living in the county, and instead dismissed
the suit on the grounds that Margaret Williams had not passed the "special
examination."[16]

Despite this setback, Juanita Jackson's efforts to organize young people
in Detroit were more successful, especially after she appointed Gloster
Current as chair of the youth council's central committee. The NAACP
annual convention was scheduled for the Motor City in 1937 and Current
was tasked with organizing youth participation. Current, a musician, had
recently graduated from West Virginia State University and returned to
his hometown. He was tapped to form NAACP youth councils throughout Detroit in the midst of the union organizing by United Auto Workers
(UAW) at Ford's River Rouge plant. Once the UAW launched its strike on
April 1, 1937, NAACP youth council members, led by 16-year-old Horace
Sheffield, joined the strikers on the picket lines and focused their efforts on

convincing Black strikebreakers, or "scab workers," to support the union. Members of the NAACP senior branch joined the young people in urging African American support for the striking workers. Walter White came to Detroit in June 1937 and was able to secure assurances from the UAW's leaders that the interests of Black workers would be protected under any new collective bargaining agreement.[17]

SOUTHERN AND NORTHERN YOUTH MOBILIZATION

When the first New Deal programs were launched in 1933 and 1934, information soon surfaced that African Americans were being excluded from various relief and recovery projects, especially in the South. A group of young Black leaders—John P. Davis, Abram Harris, Ralph Bunche, and Robert C. Weaver—organized a conference in Washington, DC, in May 1935 called "The Position of the Negro in the Present Economic Crisis." The participants not only called for organized efforts to address this exclusion but, in light of the passage of the Wagner Act guaranteeing workers the right to bargain collectively with employers for wages and working conditions, they also formed the Joint Committee on National Recovery, which soon issued a report calling for the formation of an "umbrella organization" to forge closer ties between African Americans and the organized labor movement.[18]

Shortly afterward, in Chicago in February 1936, the National Negro Congress (NNC) was founded to work specifically with labor unions to organize Black workers and to protest racial discrimination in employment. A. Philip Randolph, the head of the Brotherhood of Sleeping Car Porters (BSCP), was elected NNC president. Members of the Communist Party were supportive of and active in the NNC, and Randolph was sometimes criticized for this connection. But Randolph responded, "Since when can Negroes, the victims of the . . . Ku Klux Klan and Negro-phobists, North and South, afford to raise the 'red scare' bogey?" He emphasized that the Communist Party was "a legitimate political party whose members need make no apology for it." The Communists were willing to "fight for human and race rights" and "if we Negroes are so yellow, so cringing . . . and childish to permit the 'red label' to halt our march toward the true status of men, [then] God help us!"[19]

At that inaugural meeting in Chicago, plans were also made for the formation of an NNC youth division. The NNC delegates passed a resolution emphasizing that "it is the indubitable duty and right of all Negro youth to fight for the eradication of the evil from which they suffer." To avoid possible conflicts between youth and adult leaders, it was agreed to form NNC "youth councils" that would be independent of local branches and responsible only to the national secretary and executive board.[20] Attorney John P. Davis, NNC executive secretary, recruited James J. Jackson Jr. and Ernest Strong to begin working with the youth. James Jackson was born in Richmond, Virginia, and had engaged in organizing Black tobacco workers. He enrolled in Howard University and graduated with a degree in pharmacology in 1936. He returned to Richmond that year to work in his father's pharmacy. After attending the NNC's founding conference in Chicago, Jackson helped to lead the formation of a new youth organization to be affiliated with the NNC. Ernest Strong had been a member of the NAACP youth council in Flint, Michigan, and moved to Chicago to attend Central YMCA College. There he helped to organize the predominantly white National Student League's Negro Youth Conference held in June 1933. Following the NNC meeting in 1936, Jackson and Strong organized a conference in Richmond for young people, and over 530 delegates from twenty-three states attended and agreed to seek "the right to creative labor, to be gainfully employed with equal pay and employment opportunity—economic security. We have met for freedom, equality, [and] opportunity." At that July 1936 conference, the Southern Negro Youth Congress (SNYC) was formed, and Frederick Patterson, president of Tuskegee Institute in Alabama, was chosen chair of the Adult Advisory Board; and Charlotte Hawkins Brown, NNC vice president and founder of the Palmer Memorial Institute, a private secondary school in Sedalia, North Carolina, became the group's principal advisor. In February 1937, Jackson and Strong set up the SNYC headquarters in Richmond, Virginia.[21]

In the former Confederate capital, Jackson and Strong immediately began working with Congress of Industrial Organizations (CIO) leaders who were attempting to organize Black and white tobacco workers in the city. While the majority of its members were in their twenties, over the next few years the SNYC not only helped to organize tobacco workers, the members also participated in the formation of a Negro community theater, recruited students for national defense training programs, and mounted Negro history celebrations. After moving the offices to Birmingham, Alabama, in 1938, the SNYC launched the Right to Vote Campaign under the leadership of James Jackson and his wife, Esther Jackson, who opened a youth center that offered classes in first aid, sewing, Negro history, and Spanish and organized sports tournaments, art shows, and other social activities. SNYC branches also worked with NAACP youth councils to organize marches and rallies in support of antilynching legislation.[22]

In North and West Philadelphia, beginning in 1930, Don't Buy Where You Can't Work campaigns were organized by neighborhood improvement organizations. The North Philadelphia Youth Movement, led by Sam Evans, was an offshoot of the North Philadelphia Civic League. In August 1937 the Youth Movement targeted stores along Columbia Avenue, where African Americans shopped but none were employed. After picket lines were set up in front of several stores, Leon Steinberg, president of the Columbia Avenue Businessmen's Association, swore out warrants for the arrest of the young people, accusing them of "disorderly conduct," while Evans was charged with "breach of the peace and inciting to riot."[23] NAACP lawyers were able to get the charges dropped against Evans. In 1938, the US Supreme Court upheld African Americans' right to picket businesses engaging in racially discriminatory hiring practices in a case brought against the New Negro Alliance, a social protest group in Washington, DC. Historians August Meier and Elliott Rudwick concluded that "the Alliance's 1938 Supreme Court victory in the Sanitary Grocery case upheld the right of a racial group to picket against job discrimination. . . . This ruling encouraged direct action across the country, bringing a renaissance of job campaigns in Washington, New York, Philadelphia, Chicago, Cleveland, . . . and St. Louis."[24]

YOUTH AND THE ANTILYNCHING CAMPAIGNS

After a low of ten in 1929, the number of known lynchings in the United States increased to twenty-one in 1930, and twenty-eight in 1933. Throughout the 1920s the NAACP worked for the passage of the Dyer Anti-Lynching

Bill, which would make these murderous acts federal crimes, but it never emerged from the US Congress's legislative committee. Then in October 1933 in Princess Anne County, Maryland, a mentally ill Black man, George Armwood, who had been accused of raping an 82-year-old white woman, was taken from the local jail, hung from a tree, and his body burned in what the *New York Times* considered "the wildest lynching orgy the state has ever witnessed."[25] Given that comparatively little mob violence had taken place in the past in Maryland, NAACP leaders believed that the time was right for the introduction of a new antilynching bill, which was drawn up by the organization's legal committee. In January 1934 Senators Edward Costigan of Colorado and Robert Wagner of New York introduced the bill in Congress, calling on federal officials to prosecute state and local authorities who participate in or fail to prevent lynchings. Although it failed to get out of the legislative committee, the Costigan-Wagner bill was reintroduced in each session of Congress throughout the decade. Historian Patricia Sullivan declared that "the antilynching fight became the cornerstone of the NAACP's program in the 1930s and shaped its broader effort to influence the spirit of New Deal reform."[26]

Juanita Jackson decided that the NAACP youth councils and college chapters should mobilize to support the antilynching bill beginning on February 12, 1937. Throughout the entire year, the youth councils, often working with the SNYC and the predominately white American Student Union and American Youth Congress, organized marches, rallies, demonstrations, and other protests to draw attention to the barbarous practice. The NAACP youth council in Chicago organized a mass march through the downtown in February 1937. In New York City that month, the United Youth Committee Against Lynching was organized among several youth groups and a parade and rally was held, with Walter White and Rev. Adam Clayton Powell Jr. as the main speakers. In January 1938, the United Youth Committee organized another march, this time in Harlem, with Black and white youths "wearing black armbands as a sign of mourning for the eight victims lynched in 1937."[27]

One of the most famous *causes célèbres* of the 1930s was the arrest, speedy trial, conviction, and death sentences for nine Black teenagers falsely accused of raping two white women in Paint Rock, Alabama, in April 1931.

The NAACP was slow in coming to the assistance of the Scottsboro Nine, and lawyers from the Communist Party's International Labor Defense (ILD) oversaw the defense and subsequent appeals following the unjust conviction, labeled a "legal lynching." The Communists mounted "Free the Scottsboro Boys" rallies and petition drives throughout the United States and abroad. While NAACP attorneys were pushed to the sidelines in the appeal proceedings, Juanita Jackson urged youth councils around the country to mount petition drives and participate in marches and demonstrations to protest this "Alabama horror." "Ours is an immediate task," she declared. "Lynchers strike without warning. . . . We cannot lose a moment. We must not falter a step. We must march forward!"[28]

In her final year as director of the Youth Department, Juanita Jackson set up "citizenship training schools" in several southern cities through which the youth councils and college chapters offered a series of programs to educate African American citizens about their voting rights and to prepare those who sought to exercise the franchise. In the late 1930s teenagers fanned out in various locations canvassing residents about their willingness to register. They met with some positive responses, but in many places, especially in rural areas of the Deep South, Black voting power was viewed as a potential threat to white supremacy. Intimidation and obstructionism by whites were used against Black southerners attempting to register, and as a result few were added to voting rolls.[29] In September 1938, when Juanita Jackson married Clarence Mitchell, who was then working for the National Youth Administration in Maryland and later headed up the NAACP's Washington Bureau, she decided to give up her position in the NAACP. She later explained that "I resigned my post to marry my prince," and reminded those who later questioned her decision, "in those days . . . women left [jobs] to marry and raise a family."[30]

Juanita Jackson was succeeded by James Robinson, who had recently graduated from Union Theological Seminary and was an associate minister at Morningside Presbyterian Church in New York City. While NAACP youth director, Robinson kept his ministerial position and continued to work with neighborhood groups in Harlem. His major challenge came in 1939 after the Greenville, South Carolina, NAACP branch and the local youth council, led by 19-year-old William Anderson, launched a voter registration drive. In July 1939, Anderson had led a large group of African Americans to the local courthouse to obtain voter registration certificates. Historian Peter Lau reports that "in the days and months that followed, the response of Greenville's white residents to the voter registration drive showed the degree to which the black insurgency represented a challenge to a world ordered by hierarchies of race and gender—that is white male supremacy." Anderson was soon arrested on the trumped-up charge that he had telephoned a white girl for a date. While in custody he was beaten by the police. Placed under a five-thousand-dollar bond, he was subsequently sentenced to serve thirty days in prison or pay a thousand-dollar fine.[31]

When the news spread about Anderson's arrest, NAACP youth councils mounted fund-raising campaigns to help pay the fines. "Across the nation," Peter Lau reported, "the black struggle for voting rights in Greenville and the violent efforts to suppress it served as a rallying cry." In South Carolina, the voting rights movement in Greenville helped to provide a crucial impetus for the formation of a statewide NAACP chapter that would coordinate protest activities across the state and "spur the massive growth of branch memberships during the 1940s."[32]

Following the outbreak of war in Europe in September 1939, NAACP youth director James Robinson organized a series of Annual NAACP Student Conferences. Meeting at Virginia Union University in March 1940, the students issued the "Peace Proclamation of Negro Youth" and called on "the Negro youth of the nation to join in the fight for peace as a concrete contribution to the campaign against war-makers." Thomas Bynum notes that once the United States entered the war in December 1941, the young NAACP leaders supported the US involvement, and "these youth . . . believed that the war against Fascism and Nazism would illuminate the nation's peculiar democracy and force the United States to do right about its race problems at home."[33] At these annual student conferences, workshops were held that provided youth council members "the ABC's of Mass Pressure" and Gloster Current explained how they could use "dramatic demonstrations, parades, picket lines, . . . words, symbols, ideas, and the like" to confront racist practices.[34]

The outbreak of war in Europe spurred national defense mobilization in the United States and created potential employment opportunities for

African American youth. Unfortunately, most defense contractors continued to exclude Black workers, and federal officials refused to require nondiscrimination in hiring in defense industries. A. Philip Randolph resigned as NNC president in 1940 in a dispute over the Communists' influence in the organization. But to generate support for a federal mandate for nondiscrimination in defense industries, Randolph called for a "march on Washington" to obtain fair employment legislation. The March on Washington Movement (MOWM) soon gained support from all the major Black social and cultural organizations, and preparations were made to bring tens of thousands of African Americans to Washington on July 1, 1941.[35]

President Franklin D. Roosevelt, fearing an African American march on Washington would attract violence, kept informed about the preparations. Roosevelt finally decided to meet with Randolph, Walter White, and other Black leaders to discuss the issue and then agreed to call on the Justice Department to fashion an executive order to ban discrimination in employment in defense industries. Executive Order 8802 prohibited job discrimination on the basis of race, creed, or color by defense contractors and established the Fair Employment Practices Commission (FEPC) to investigate complaints of discrimination and make recommendations to the federal government. Although the executive order was issued, the FEPC was given no enforcement powers.[36]

The launching of the National Defense Mobilization in 1940 led to the phasing out of several New Deal programs, including the National Youth Administration. However, national defense training programs were set up in public and private schools around the country, and the Vocational Education for National Defense (VEND) program was established to train the skilled industrial workers needed in defense industries. Many African American youths completed the VEND training, but they were still unable to find employment in defense industries due to persistent discrimination. In Tulsa, Oklahoma, for example, the NAACP youth council joined the senior branch in picketing at a local defense plant over discriminatory hiring practices. They were eventually successful in gaining employment for Black workers, but primarily in service areas.[37] In Philadelphia, the NAACP youth council organized protests against the discriminatory practices of defense contractors and urged Black youths to enroll in the VEND program. Subsequent investigations revealed that Black youths who completed these courses gained employment due to the wartime labor shortage, but because of continued racial discrimination, few obtained skilled jobs in the local defense industries.[38]

James Robinson organized the NAACP's first annual Student Conference in 1940, and the meetings continued during the war years under his successors, Madison Jones and Ruby Hurley. Their main purposes were to obtain "equal educational opportunity, . . . equal employment opportunity, . . . civil liberties, . . . and antilynching legislation." Madison Jones served as NAACP youth director between November 1940 and February 1943 and was active in expanding the number of college chapters to seventeen and youth councils to eighty-three. Ruby Hurley attended Miner Teachers College and Robert Terrell Law School and had worked to reorganize the NAACP branch in Washington, DC. She was appointed national youth director in November 1943, and when she left the position in 1951 there were 336 active youth councils, and 88 college chapters.[39]

At the end of the war, the Fourth World Youth Congress was held in London in 1946. Gloster Current, formerly a member of Detroit youth council's central committee, represented the NAACP and Esther Jackson represented the SNYC. Over six hundred delegates from sixty-three countries passed resolutions calling for an end to all forms of fascism, self-determination for colonized and oppressed peoples, cultural exchanges and international cooperation among youth, and equal educational and employment opportunities. Throughout the postwar period SNYC branches joined NAACP youth councils in pushing for antilynching legislation. Historian Rebecca de Schweinitz reported that "in the 1940s NAACP youth also desegregated theaters in Indiana, Illinois, and other Midwestern states. They picketed Philadelphia Woolworth stores; demonstrated against segregated schools, . . . and integrated swimming pools and skating rinks in Cleveland as well as bowling alleys, unions, and automobile factories in Detroit and excursion steamers elsewhere in Michigan." NAACP youth councils also engaged in direct action protests for equal educational opportunity, the desegregation of the US Armed Forces, and the elimination of poll taxes and other restrictions on the right to vote.[40]

NAACP YOUTH COUNCIL SCHOOL BOYCOTT

One of the most dramatic and highly publicized school boycotts launched by the students in the NAACP youth council occurred in Lumberton, North Carolina, in 1946. The two Black schools there, Redstone Academy, built in 1904, and the Thompson Institute, built in 1881, had been constructed through the raising of "cultural capital" among Baptists and Presbyterians in the African American community. The unwillingness of white school officials to provide public schools for Black children in the South meant that African Americans themselves had to provide the land, materials, and other resources to build schoolhouses.[41] This was also the case when the Julius Rosenwald Foundation agreed to provide funding for the building of "county training schools" throughout the South between 1912 and 1932. To have a Rosenwald School, the local Black community had to agree to provide land or other resources that were more valuable than the financial contributions coming from the state or the foundation.[42] While there were fifteen Rosenwald schools in North Carolina, there were none in Lumberton. Moreover, once the county training schools were built, the only funding provided by local or state educational officials was for the salaries of Black teachers, who were paid less than comparably trained and experienced white teachers. This practice led to numerous "salary equalization lawsuits" filed by the NAACP against southern school districts in the 1930s and 1940s.[43]

In the 1930s in Lumberton, rather than build schools for Black children, public school officials decided to take over Redstone Academy and Thompson Institute, but by 1946, both schools were in terrible shape. Faulty electrical wiring made Redstone a firetrap; there was no running water, and the wooden boards in the walls were rotten. Thompson was a brick construction, but was considered in worse shape and had no running water and no electricity. The NAACP youth council in Lumberton had been organized in 1943, and Lillian Bullock and other leaders called a meeting for Tuesday, October 1, 1946. Over three hundred children and teenagers from both schools showed up and agreed to organize a march through downtown Lumberton. They carried signs declaring, "How Can

I Learn When I'm Cold?" and "Down with Our School." Youth council advisor Gus Bullock sent a letter to Governor R. Gregg Cherry outlining the schools' problems, but Cherry promised nothing in his response. So, on Monday, October 7, 1946, over four hundred children and teenagers left their classes and marched into the streets, carrying signs that declared this was "D-Day" and "V for Victory."[44]

The students' strike was opposed by the principals of both schools and some parents. Lillian Bullock McQueen remembered, "There were a lot of people—black people—that said we shouldn't have done that, but what [are] you going to do?" Thompson Institute's principal, G. H. Young, chastised the children for the decision "to resort to radicalism." "Some of the children are striking for the novelty of it," he claimed, "and don't understand what it is. . . . Radicals are not in [a] position to remedy this." But Lillian Bullock McQueen declared the students had "no intention at any time to stir up race strife, but only to insist on fair distribution of educational opportunity." During the nine-day strike, shots were fired into the home of the Bullock family, but no one was injured.[45]

Most reports on the strike that appeared in Black and white newspapers agreed with the students, concluding that these schools were "a disgrace to the state." NAACP youth director Ruby Hurley wrote to Lillian Bullock, "I want you to know that the National Office of the Association stands back of you in your efforts and that we will give you all of the help that we can." Finally, on Tuesday, October 16, 1946, after school officials promised to make "immediate improvements" and to construct new buildings "as soon as conditions permit," the boycotting students returned to school. NAACP special counsel Thurgood Marshall declared, "The strike called by the Youth Council [in Lumberton] was one of the finest things ever pulled by the NAACP."[46]

THE ROAD TO *BROWN* THROUGH PRINCE EDWARD COUNTY, VIRGINIA

In the five lawsuits and court cases that made up the US Supreme Court's ruling in *Brown v. Board of Education*, four were brought by African American parents on behalf of their children—*Brown v. Topeka Board of Education*

(Kansas); *Briggs v. Elliott* (South Carolina); *Gebhardt v. Belton* (Delaware); *Bolling v. Sharpe* (Washington, DC). In the case of *Davis v. Prince Edward County School Board* (Virginia), however, the lawsuit was filed on behalf of the high school students who launched a school boycott to demand improvements in their educational conditions.[47] When the NAACP legal team decided to challenge the "separate but equal" doctrine upheld in the 1896 *Plessy v. Ferguson* ruling and filed lawsuits in the late 1940s and early 1950s, they began as attempts to obtain equal educational facilities for African American students, but ended up challenging segregation in all public educational facilities.

In Prince Edward County, Virginia, like other places throughout the Jim Crow South, public schools and public accommodations were separate, but rarely equal. The all-Black Moton High School was underfunded, overcrowded, and in poor condition. The school had no gymnasium or cafeteria, and the students lacked books and other educational resources. Even the school buses had to be used as makeshift classrooms due to overcrowding. Classrooms were heated with coal stoves, and when teachers tended the fires, students at desks nearby tried to avoid the showers of sparks.[48] In contrast, the all-white Farmville High School faced none of these problems. In fact, for the 1949–50 school year, the monetary value of Farmville High's buildings, equipment, and land was estimated to be four times that of Moton's. When this difference is adjusted for number of students, the disparity is even more glaring. If each school's property value was divided among its students, a Farmville student's share would be six times greater than a Moton student.[49]

Sixteen-year-old Barbara Johns was fed up and she "didn't like the conditions in the school" and decided to do something. She organized an assembly meeting on April 23, 1951, where she urged the students to walk out and boycott the school. "We came up with ten demands. Most were for improvements in the school. . . . We wanted simple things like new books and new desks."[50] The objective was not to enroll in Farmville High; rather, they wanted a new school building with equal facilities and resources.[51] At the same time, the high school students did not seek the approval of the adults for their protest. Barbara Johns recalled, "We knew we had to do it ourselves and that if we had asked for adult help before taking the first step, we would have been turned down."[52]

The Prince Edward County school board tried to ignore the student protesters, but NAACP lawyers Oliver Hill and Spottswood Robinson arrived on April 25, 1951, and met with Johns and the boycotting students at Rev. Francis Griffin's First Baptist Church. When Robinson asked the students what they would do if the school board refused to construct a new building, they declared unanimously that they would stay out, even if they had to go to jail for truancy. Hill and Robinson said that if they filed a lawsuit against the Prince Edward County School District, it would demand not only improvements in the Black schools but also the desegregation of all public schools in the county. The students agreed. "It seemed like reaching for the stars," Johns recalled. "But we had great faith in Mr. Robinson and Mr. Hill."[53] During the boycott Barbara Johns received anonymous threats on her life, and her father decided to send her to stay with her uncle, Rev. Vernon Johns, in Montgomery, Alabama. While she was away, the Ku Klux Klan found out where her family lived and burned a cross on their lawn. The boycott lasted two weeks, and historian Richard Kluger reported that on May 23, 1951, "Spottswood Robinson filed a suit at the federal courthouse in Richmond on behalf of 117 Moton students who asked that the state law requiring segregated schools in Virginia be struck down."[54]

The civil rights activism of the young crusaders in the 1930s, 1940s, and early 1950s demonstrated that children and teenagers were well aware of the disadvantages and discrimination they faced and would face in American society. It also showed that they were not willing to accept these disadvantages because they were contrary to their religious beliefs and the civics lessons they were being taught in their elementary and secondary school classes. With the *Brown* decision and subsequent civil rights legislation, children and teenagers would move to the forefront of organized activities to end legal racial segregation in American society.

Chapter 2

Grace Under Pressure

Children, Teenagers, and School Desegregation

So many people today talk about young kids going to the dogs and I think our example has shown many folk, and ourselves, just what this coming Negro kid is made of and what he [or she] can do under pressure. Sure, we got more than we bargained for, but we held out, and we tried to do it gracefully.

Ernest Green (1958)[1]

"I WAS A SIXTH GRADER at Stephens [Elementary School] in May 1954 when the news about the historic *Brown v. Board of Education* broke," Carlotta Walls LaNier recalled. "My teacher, Mrs. King, explained that the highest court in the land decided it was unfair and against the law for black and white children to attend separate schools. Black children would finally have access to the same opportunities that white students had, she told us." But Carlotta Walls was disappointed when nothing seemed to change in Little Rock, Arkansas, over the next two years.[2] But things did change for some African American children and teenagers, beginning in the fall of 1954. In the District of Columbia, African American students were enrolled in previously all-white schools without serious incidents. In a race relations survey conducted by the *New York Times* in May 1955, it was reported that "marked progress is being made in the elimination of racial discrimination."

Legislators in eight states in the far West—Washington, California, Arizona, New Mexico, North Dakota, Montana, Colorado, and Wyoming—passed measures to combat discriminatory practices in the public schools, although attempts to end prohibitions on interracial marriage failed in Colorado and Idaho; and bills guaranteeing nondiscrimination in public accommodations failed in Nevada and Arizona.[3]

In the southern states, vehement opposition to the US Supreme Court's ruling was expressed by white citizens, parents, and political leaders who declared "Never!" and proceeded to organize a campaign of "massive resistance."[4] In July 1954 in Indianola, Mississippi, just two months after the ruling, the White Citizens' Council (WCC) was organized, signaling the establishment of formal opposition to public school desegregation. The leaders' goals were to thwart the implementation of court-ordered school desegregation and overthrow the Supreme Court's decision through legislative actions and other measures. Robert Patterson, the founder, claimed that by the end of that year there were over one hundred thousand WCC members in Alabama, Louisiana, Virginia, Texas, Georgia, and Mississippi.[5]

THE MILFORD TEN: A PORTENT OF THINGS TO COME

In the fall of 1954, the most widely publicized anti-desegregation protests took place, not in the Deep South, but in a so-called border state. Massive protests and boycotts erupted in September 1954 when eleven African American students were enrolled in the all-white high school in the small town of Milford, Delaware. A slave state that remained in the Union during the Civil War, Delaware's constitution of 1897 "prohibited discrimination on account of race or color," but also declared that "separate schools for white and colored students shall be maintained." Black public schools were separate but unequal in Delaware, and African American parents and NAACP attorney Louis Redding filed lawsuits against Delaware school officials beginning in 1950. Their attempts to improve the conditions in the "colored schools" and provide equal educational resources for African American students were unsuccessful. In 1952, the state supreme court examined the NAACP's evidence of educational inequality and ordered the admission of African American students to the public elementary schools in Hockessin and Arden and the all-white high school in Claymont, Delaware. Because there was no organized opposition from white parents and school officials, state educational officials allowed the African American students to remain in those schools, but decided that no other schools would be desegregated until the US Supreme Court ruled on *Gebhardt v. Belton*, brought earlier by the NAACP and Black parents in Claymont, Delaware, and one of the five cases included in the 1954 *Brown* decision.[6]

In September 1954, following the Supreme Court's ruling, school officials throughout Delaware began to enroll African American students in previously all-white elementary and secondary schools. In Milford, the all-Black public school, Benjamin Banneker, only went through the junior high school grades. To attend high school, African American teenagers had to travel over twenty miles to Dover, Delaware, or seventeen miles to Georgetown, Delaware. Thus, at the opening of the 1954–55 school year, school officials allowed eleven Black students, six boys and five girls, to enroll at Lakeview High School, the only high school in Milford.[7]

White parents soon began to protest to school board members about the enrollment of the African American students. Some white residents claimed that the Black students were admitted without the approval of the state department of education. School board members began to receive threatening phone calls from anonymous callers, while segregationists set up picket lines outside Lakeview High and urged white parents to boycott the school. As a result, each day fewer and fewer white students showed up and the protest began to receive more and more national and international attention. After anonymous death threats were made against the Black students and all four school board members (who later resigned), Milford school administrators decided to close both the elementary and the high school on September 15, 1954.[8]

The protests in Milford also attracted the attention of white supremacist Bryant Bowles, a former marine from Florida who founded in December 1953 the short-lived group National Association for the Advancement of White People (NAAWP). Bowles showed up in Milford and began holding rallies and recruiting members. At a rally held at the Harrington Air Field on September 26, 1954, it was estimated that up to three thousand people attended. "The integration movement was backed by organized agitating groups which if not communist-supported," declared Bowles, "were playing into the hands of the communists." He told Milford's white parents, "You certainly have the right to protect your child by keeping it at home." And he pledged, "I would not permit my daughter, who is 3, to attend school with Negroes while I have breath in my body and gunpowder to burn."[9]

When officials from the state department of education took over the Milford schools and reopened them on September 27, 1954, ten of the original eleven Black students were in attendance, but 70 percent of white students refused to return. And on that same day, white students launched boycotts of public schools throughout the state of Delaware. In Millsboro, for example, only 38 of the 644 elementary and high school students showed up; in Gumboro, 3 out of 116; in Ellendale 18 out of 131; and in Lincoln only 12 out of 140. At this point, state educational officials accused the Milford school board of admitting the Black students without receiving the proper approvals, and they decided to remove the ten Black students from Lakeview High and transferred them to the all-Black high school in Georgetown, Delaware.[10]

The Milford Ten had applied and were admitted to the public high school in their hometown, but became the targets of organized protests by white parents, residents, and outside agitators, only to be removed and sent to what had been demonstrated as an under-resourced facility in another town. *New York Times* reporter Milton Bracker, who covered the protests in Milford, reported that "the ten teen-agers have been transferred to the all-Negro school in Georgetown, seventeen miles below Milford," while the NAACP contested the state officials' decision. "But thousands of men and women are getting used to weekly outdoor meetings at which a glib and folksy Floridian tells them about the 'rights of the white man,' saying that the Negroes will not return to classes—or that if they do, there will in effect be no classes."[11] Although Bryant Bowles was jailed in Beaumont, Texas, in 1958 for killing his brother-in-law, the NAAWP continued. White supremacists learned early that through organized protests and "massive resistance" they could thwart public school desegregation in the face of the Supreme Court rulings and federal or state court orders.[12] However, there was a new generation of African Americans who had learned about their constitutional rights in school, and when they were confronted by white racism, they became angry, rebelled, and stood up for themselves and opposed what they believed was wrong.

TEENAGERS ON THE FRONT LINES

"At that time, teenagers didn't like to ride the special school bus too much," Claudette Colvin recalled. "If you had to stay after school for band practice or rehearsal, or hang around for after school activities, . . . you could still ride on your school pass, but on the regular bus." On March 2, 1955, in Montgomery, Alabama, 15-year-old Colvin was on her way home on the city bus. When she got on the bus there were few riders, but it soon began to fill up with white passengers. Then, the bus driver spied Colvin and shouted, "Hey get up," so a white person could sit down. When Colvin didn't move, "he said before he'd drive on, I'd have to get up." The other people on the bus were getting upset and started telling her, "Why don't you get up?" But Colvin wouldn't move. "This can't go on," the driver shouted, "I'm going to call the cops." He first brought in a traffic patrolman who asked, "Aren't you going to get up?" "No," Colvin announced. "I paid my fare, so I do not have to get up. It's my constitutional right to sit here just as much as that [white] lady. It's my constitutional right."[13]

The driver left the bus and came back with two policemen, who grabbed Colvin, knocked her books to the floor, handcuffed her, dragged her off the bus, put her in the police car, and took her to the police station, where she was placed under arrest. The other students on the bus soon told Colvin's mother what had happened. She went the police station, paid the fine, and Claudette was released. Her mother asked why she did this. "I was just angry," she responded. "Like any teenager might be. I was downright angry."[14]

Much has been written about the bus boycott sparked by the arrest of seamstress Rosa Parks on December 1, 1955, leading to the formation of the Montgomery Improvement Association (MIA) under the leadership of Rev. Martin Luther King Jr. The 26-year-old minister had recently arrived in the capital city and was serving as the pastor of Dexter Avenue Baptist Church. In some accounts of the campaign and the lawsuit filed, the historians note that Claudette Colvin was one of the plaintiffs and, along with Rosa Parks, testified in court against the bus company about her arrest and mistreatment by the police. But little attention has been paid to the reasons for the teenagers' anger over their treatment. In the case of Claudette Colvin, her anger was fueled by the unjustified arrest of 16-year-old Jeremiah Reeves for the alleged rape of a white woman. "He was from Booker T. Washington High School, my school," Colvin recalled. "He was a drummer in the school band." Reeves was a delivery boy and had been seduced into a consensual sexual relationship with a white woman who claimed rape when it was discovered. "The authorities kept him in jail until he came of age, and then they electrocuted him."[15]

Reeves's arrest in 1952 led to Claudette Colvin's politicization. At the time she was in the ninth grade and "that was the first time I heard talk of the NAACP." Her teachers launched a campaign to raise money for Reeves's defense attorneys. "Some people said that the reason they convicted Jeremiah was to prove to the NAACP that they couldn't take over the South." But Colvin was angry over Reeves's unjust arrest, and her mother knew it. "She always knew how hurt I was about Jeremiah Reeves. . . . Our rebellion and anger came with Jeremiah Reeves."[16]

It was the young people's anger over their mistreatment and the well-publicized injustices that took place all the time that raised their political consciousness. For many northern and southern teenagers, it was the obscene torture and murder of 14-year-old Emmett Till in Money, Mississippi, in August 1955 that fueled their anger and spurred their activism. Numerous books and articles have been published on Till's murder for allegedly whistling at a white women, and historian Rebecca de Schweinitz concluded that Till's torture and death "was branded indelibly into the memory of many young people across the South, both horrifying and galvanizing a generation."[17] Civil rights worker Anne Moody was 14 years old at the time and recalled, "Before Emmett Till's murder, I had known fear of hunger, hell, and the devil. But now there was a new fear known to me—the fear of being killed just because I was black. This was the worst of my fears."[18] SNCC activist Julian Bond declared that "like a whole generation of young blacks, I was given unforgettable insight into the cruelties of Southern style racism and moved along the path to later activism by the graphic pictures that appeared in *Jet* magazine of Emmett Till's swollen and misshapen body."[19]

There was the anger over the inadequacies they witnessed in their separate and unequal schooling and the desire for improved educational opportunities that inspired their willingness to engage in the desegregation of all-white public schools. But the question was how much were these young people willing to take from abusive white teenagers and adults to obtain this opportunity? In Clinton, Tennessee, as was the case in Milford, Delaware, outside agitators came into a small town and stirred up opposition to the enrollment of African American teenagers in a high school that was under court order to desegregate. In January 1956 federal judge Robert Taylor rejected the objections coming from white school officials, parents, and other opponents in Clinton, and by July of that year they were mobilizing to thwart desegregation.[20]

THE CLINTON TWELVE

Twelve Black students had volunteered to enroll in Clinton High School, and they arrived on August 27, 1956, at the beginning of the school year. The head of the local branch of the White Citizens' Council, W. H. Till, called in John Kasper, founder of the Seaboard citizens' council, who arrived in Clinton on September 1, 1956. Over the Labor Day weekend when he began fomenting violence and inciting rioting over the desegregation of the high school, US marshals moved in and arrested fifteen people, including Kasper. The violent actions that took place seemed to encourage white students to attack the newly arrived Black teenagers. It was reported that they were subject to "insults, name-calling, jousting in corridors, and pouring ink over Negro girls' books," despite the warning from Principal D. J. Brittain that such actions could lead to expulsion.[21]

After several weeks of harassment, the African American students decided that they had had enough and launched their own boycott on November 28, 1956. This was shocking to many in the Black and white communities, but following the advice of Paul W. Turner, a local Baptist minister (who was white), six of the Black students agreed to return to Clinton High with him on December 4, 1956. As Rev. Turner led the students into the building, he was attacked by a mob of white bystanders, his face was bloodied by the pummeling he received. Inside the school, several students began running through the corridors screaming and shouting racial epithets about the return of the African American students and threatening more violence should they be allowed to remain. At that point, Principal Brittain contacted school district officials, informed them about what had occurred, and received permission to close Clinton High.[22]

Sporadic violence continued, and Tennessee units of the National Guard were called out. Soon peace was restored in the town, but the Black students continued to face abuse and harassment in school. Seventeen-year-old Bobby Cain, one of the Clinton Twelve, reported that it was not unusual to find "ink spilled in his locker, his books tossed out in the rain and stones thrown at him." He was jeered and taunted and "found stickers with Ku Klux Klan emblems pasted on his desk." After about six months, however, things had calmed down. "I made many friends at Clinton and the teachers were nice to me," but he was glad when the school year was over in June 1957, when Cain became the first African American to graduate from Clinton High School.[23]

SALUTE TO THE YOUNG FREEDOM FIGHTERS

On May 17, 1957, on the third anniversary of the *Brown v. Board of Education* decision, leaders of the NAACP, the National Urban League, and civil rights groups from thirty states participated in a "prayer pilgrimage" to Washington, DC, to pursue two objectives: "To call for a more speedy implementation" of the Supreme Court's *Brown* decision and "more action by the Congress in the field of civil rights." The estimated twenty-five thousand men, women, and children who marched to the Lincoln Memorial that day were considered "orderly and thoughtful" as they listened to addresses by the NAACP's Roy Wilkins, Rev. C. K. Steele from Tallahassee, Birmingham's Rev. Fred Shuttlesworth, and Harlem congressman Adam Clayton Powell Jr., who, according to the *New York Times*, urged "the use of boycotts, work stoppages and slowdowns to make their point."[24] The prayer pilgrimage is often remembered for the speech delivered by the young Martin Luther King Jr., who had come into prominence following the successful Montgomery bus boycott. Dr. King declared, "Give us the ballot," and African Americans in the South would use it to elect officials who would carry out the Supreme Court's *Brown* decision and other measures to guarantee equal rights to all US citizens.[25]

In Durham, North Carolina, that year the NAACP youth council came under the leadership of attorney Floyd McKissick. Historian Christina Greene documented the "demonstrations at local bus stations, waiting rooms, parks, hotels, and other places" that the teenagers organized there in the late 1950s.[26] In New York City on May 25, 1957, the NAACP youth division organized the "Salute to the Young Freedom Fighters," attended by over eight hundred young people, to celebrate those courageous children and teenagers who integrated previously all-white schools or worked to bring about public school desegregation in their home towns. Bobby Cain, the first African American to graduate from Clinton High School, was honored, along with Robert Felder, the 9-year-old who brought a lawsuit against Philadelphia's Girard College, a secondary school for orphaned boys that refused to allow African Americans to enroll.[27] Several college students were also honored, including Jolie Fritz (white), who supported the NAACP school desegregation efforts in North Carolina; Fred Moore, who was expelled from South Carolina State University for leading a student boycott against the White Citizens' Council in Orangeburg; and Ernest McEwen, expelled from Alcorn College in Mississippi for leading the opposition to the anti-NAACP articles written by Professor Clennon King (Black).[28]

But the year 1957 is most remembered for the explosive events in Little Rock, Arkansas, involving the nine African American teenagers who were enrolled at Central High School only after the intervention of President Dwight D. Eisenhower and the US Infantry's 101st Airborne Division.

"CLEAN-CUT COLORED KIDS" IN THE VANGUARD: THE LITTLE ROCK NINE

Sixteen-year-old Ernest Green recalled that in the spring of 1957, the teachers at Horace Mann High School (all-Black) circulated a sheet asking the students to sign up if they would be interested in transferring to Central High School (all-white) in the fall. Green would be entering his senior year, and he knew about Central High since "the course books that we used were hand-me-downs from Central. You could tell because they had Central students' names in them." Desegregation had occurred at the public libraries in the city and African Americans had enrolled at the University of Arkansas, and "while it was difficult," the Black college students "were surviving and doing their course work." When Green discussed the possibility of the transfer with his relatives, they all said they would support him. "My mother and aunt were part of a lawsuit in the 1940s that brought equal pay for black and white teachers."[29]

When the teachers at Horace Mann circulated the transfer sheet, Carlotta Walls also signed up, not thinking about the potential problems. The year before she had seen the pictures of Emmett Till's abused body in *Jet* magazine and was horrified and angered, "yet in my mind, my hometown was not as bad as Mississippi. Till's murder had set the bar for racial evil in my mind, and compared with that, Little Rock was somewhere on the other end of the spectrum—or so I thought."[30] And then there was the support that came from not just her parents but also Daisy Bates, the president of the Arkansas State Conference of the NAACP, and her husband L. C. Bates, the co-owners of the *Arkansas State Press*, the local Black newspaper. "Mrs. Bates . . . was tough to the core, with razor sharp edges," Walls remembered. When questioned by reporters or "speaking in front of the camera, she was naturally at ease under the glow of the television lights and quick to fire off the perfect quote."[31]

Carlotta Walls was 14 in September 1957 and the youngest of the Little Rock Nine. In her memoir, *A Mighty Long Road*, she describes the reasons she wanted to attend Central High. "That grand building looming in the distance as I walked to school practically every day. . . . Central High was my neighborhood school." And besides, Ernest Green had signed up. "Ernie was two years older and about to enter his senior year at Horace Mann." They were proud about what they had done and agreed, "we need to contact a few people and see if they want to go with us."[32]

In addition to Green and Walls, the Little Rock Nine included Minnijean Brown, Elizabeth Eckford, Thelma Mothershead, Melba Pattillo, Gloria Ray, Terrence Roberts, and Jefferson Thomas. The grace under pressure that these teenagers demonstrated was transmitted all over the world after white mobs attempted to prevent their enrollment and Arkansas governor Orval Faubus called out the state National Guard to prevent the carrying out of the federal desegregation order. President Eisenhower was forced to intervene and sent the 101st Airborne to escort the students into Central High on September 25, 1957. However, the soldiers remained in the school, serving as the Black students' personal guards, but for only a month, when they were replaced by the Arkansas National Guardsmen. Yet despite the soldiers' presence, these courageous "clean-cut colored kids" were subject to ongoing verbal and physical abuse that only got worse as the school year moved forward.[33]

All nine were harassed and physically attacked on a daily basis, and 16-year-old Minnijean Brown was eventually expelled in January 1958 after she responded verbally to the ongoing attacks coming from white girls and boys. After her expulsion, Brown was invited to attend a private high school in New York City. While there, Brown wrote an article on her experiences, published in *Look* magazine in June 1958, entitled "What They Did to Me in Little Rock." Brown described in detail the abuse she was subjected to in her classes, at her locker, and in the halls. The incident that led to her suspension in December 1957 occurred in the cafeteria. "I tried to walk in the narrow aisles between the tables, holding my tray high as we always had to do. Five boys in a row pushed their chairs back to block me. I stepped back. They moved their chairs in. Then one boy pushed his chair out again. I spilled my bowl of chili over two of the boys." Nothing happened to the boys, but Brown was suspended for ten days. When she returned in January 1958, the incident that led to her expulsion involved a white girl, Frankie Gregg, who stepped on Brown's heels and ran into her screaming "Nigger, Nigger, Nigger." This time Brown responded, "Don't say anything more to me white trash." The students watching what happened started shouting that Brown called Gregg "white trash," and later "at lunch, a boy threw hot soup on me." Crying, she left school immediately, but found out later that evening that the school superintendent had expelled her.[34]

Despite ongoing attacks on the students and their families' livelihoods, it was their religious background and practices that helped to sustain these young crusaders. Carlotta Walls's father was a contractor in the construction business and soon lost much of his work. But from the beginning the young people prayed for themselves and their family members. Walls recalled that when the students prepared to go to Central the first time on September 4, they were escorted by several Black and white ministers, and before setting forth, they agreed that they "needed to pray." Walls explained, "We formed a tight circle and bowed our heads as the reverend asked God to walk with us, strengthen and protect us." After they were turned away and the 101st Airborne had arrived to escort them to Central on September 25, the students and the ministers gathered again, this time in a room in the Bates's home. "One of the ministers in the room led us all in prayer. Heads were bowed, and tears rolled down many cheeks as the minister asked God to protect and guide us on this historic day." However, throughout the school year, Walls recalled experiencing the kicking, tripping, and spitting and the verbal attacks: "Practically everywhere I walked, I felt like one big bull's eye." But there was one place where she could go and not feel like a target: the large classroom that served as the chapel. It was a "place of meditation and prayer. . . . I started each school day there. . . . This became my haven, the place where I found the spiritual fuel I needed to get through each day."[35]

Melba Pattillo Beals's award-winning memoir about that horrendous school year, *Warriors Don't Cry*, is based on the diaries she kept at the time and provides a day by day, week by week account of the physical abuse, the constant spitting and taunting, the fireballs and acid-throwing attacks that sometimes led to painful injuries that she and the others sustained over the school year. The segregationists found out where Pattillo lived, and threatening phone calls started coming regularly. Then, one evening in October 1957, "suddenly I heard a loud popping sound, like firecrackers on the Fourth of July. Then glass breaking." Her grandmother, India Anette Peyton, yelled, "Get down, now!" The green vase on top of the television was shattered, "spraying slivers all over the walls, the floor, and us." Her mother, Lois Peyton Pattillo, shouted, "We gotta get the lights out," and each moved to shut off the nearest lights. "Oh my God," Melba thought, "they're gonna come in and shoot all of us, Grandma and Mama and Conrad," her younger brother, "and me."[36]

India Peyton moved over to her closet, pulled out her rifle, "opened the window, and rested the gun barrel on the sill. She then squeezed off a shot. 'Bingo! I hit it!'" There was a loud explosion; it was a metal oil can. She fired again; then, Pattillo recalled, "we heard people whispering and run-ning along the side of our house, and finally the slamming of car doors." After that incident India Peyton sat on her porch each night with her rifle in her lap. But Melba Pattillo's mother and grandmother could not protect her from the attacks in the halls and classrooms, which picked up once the soldiers from the 101st Airborne were replaced by the Arkansas guardsmen, who were "visibly hostile to us." The students labeled them "Arkansas Na-tional slobs." Whenever a favorable newspaper or magazine or television report on the nine crusaders appeared, "the next day the harassment inside Central would increase."[37]

Then, in February 1958, it was announced by the authorities that even the Arkansas guardsmen were to be removed from the school. "That an-nouncement granted segregationists more permission to have a field day with us." Pattillo noted in her diary that the next day, "as I came around a corner, a red-headed, freckle-faced girl tripped me so that I fell down a flight of stairs. I picked myself up to face a group of boys who then chased me up the stairs." That same week, Melba "got hit across the back with a tennis racquet. . . . I spit up blood in the rest room." Her locker was reg-ularly vandalized, and her books and school materials were doused with water. "The boys [were] throwing lighted paper at me in study hall." She feared her "grades would suffer horribly because [she] couldn't concentrate. Every moment of every day was filled with awful surprises that began early each morning." In early May 1958, the nine were given bodyguards to fol-low them around because "the segregationists were heating up their cam-paign to prevent [Ernest Green] from graduating." Pattillo pointed out that they even started "a rumor that Ernie had a roving eye and was flirt-ing with a particular white girl. . . . Even when the girl in question forced herself on him, sitting too close to him in the cafeteria, and flirting with her eyelashes. . . . Ernie ignored her and went about his business. I admired how he handled himself in the face of enormous pressure."[38]

In spite of the verbal and physical abuse leveled against him, in June 1958 Ernest Green became the first African American to graduate from Little Rock's Central High. He reflected on what he and the other teenag-ers experienced in an article he wrote for *Jet* magazine. He mentioned that "as a senior, I was spared a lot of the violence. Most of my classmates were friendly and didn't want to get 'into the mess.' All seemed more content to 'get out' or graduate." But Green believed that the majority of the white students were not interested in harassing their Black classmates. "Sure, there were the hecklers and the racists. I'd say about 50 or 60. . . . But in a student body of 2000, this is a small percentage." Green mentioned that "the only time I got socked happened in January [1958] when a red-headed youth hit me when I refused to recognize his name calling. The blow took me off my feet. I was angry, but I was determined to go on." Ultimately, Green made many friends. "Somehow, throughout the eight months of harassment and humiliation . . . examples of friendship helped to inspire me." These acts "helped to prove that the Negro students had many friends and supporters."[39]

Carlotta Walls also concluded that the majority of white students at Central High did not participate in the harassment of the Little Rock Nine. Governor Orval Faubus, however, took political advantage of the situation and decided to seek a third term in office. In July 1958 he won the Democratic primary, which virtually guaranteed his reelection in November. Faubus claimed that his landslide primary victory was due to opposition to the desegregation of Central High School, and he decided to file a lawsuit, *Cooper v. Aaron*, to end the process. The suit was upheld in the Arkansas court. Despite the ongoing campaign to secure its Arkansas membership lists and to ban the NAACP from operating in the state, the organization took the issue to the US Supreme Court, and on September 12, 1958, the Arkansas court's ruling was overturned. The next day Governor Faubus ordered the closing of Little Rock public schools and called for a referendum on public school desegregation. It was held on September 27, 1958, and Arkansas voters overwhelmingly endorsed the governor's decision. Within a month, public school officials allowed white groups to open private schools in empty buildings and enrolled over nine hundred white students, while the majority of African American students were left without schooling.[40]

At the same time that the Little Rock Nine were admitted to Central High School, other African American students who were enrolled in all-white public schools also were subjected to verbal and physical abuse. The novelist James Baldwin had recently returned to the United States from Paris and was commissioned by *Harper's Magazine* to travel to the South and interview Martin Luther King Jr. and others involved in the civil rights campaigns. In Charlotte, North Carolina, Baldwin talked with 15-year-old Gus Roberts, who in September 1957 enrolled at the city's Central High School. When Roberts entered the school on his first day, some white students tried to stop him. Baldwin asked, "What did you feel when they blocked your way?" "Nothing, sir," Gus responded. Shortly afterward the principal came out and escorted Roberts into the building. In the halls and in his classes, however, they called him names. "It's hard enough to keep quiet and keep walking when they called you 'nigger,'" he admitted. "But if anybody ever spits on me, I know I'll have to fight." His mother had noted that Gus was mostly silent and developed a "nearly fanatical concentration on his schoolwork." "Pride and silence were his weapons," Baldwin surmised. "Pride comes naturally, and soon to a Negro, but even his mother, I felt, was worried about [Gus's] silence, though she was too wise to break it."[41]

Delois Huntley enrolled at all-white Alexander Graham Junior High and Givaud Roberts at all-white Piedmont Junior High in Charlotte in September 1957 and were subjected to verbal attacks. However, when 16-year-old Dorothy Counts entered all-white Harding High School in Charlotte, she faced huge mobs of jeering whites. Within the school and classrooms Counts was alone and was subjected to ongoing harassment from white students and teachers, so her parents decided to remove her from Harding High.[42] In Winston-Salem, North Carolina, Gwendolyn Bailey entered all-white Reynolds High School, while Russell Haring, Elijah Herring, Harold Davis, Brenda Florence, and Jimmy Florence were admitted to Gillespie Park Elementary School in Greensboro.[43] But when 17-year-old Josephine Boyd came to enroll at all-white Greensboro High School at the same time, she faced screaming students and white men and women chanting, "We don't want you here! Go back to where you come from!" Despite attacks on her father's store, the slashing of the tires on the family car, and ongoing threats and violence from white students, Boyd persevered over the next nine months, and in June 1958 became the first African American to graduate from Greensboro High.[44]

THE YOUTH MARCHES ON WASHINGTON

In many ways, however, Josephine Boyd's educational success was the exception due to ongoing opposition to school desegregation mounted by the massive resistance movement. Historian Rachel Devlin found that

> between 1955 and 1958, southern legislatures passed nearly five hundred laws to impede the implementation of *Brown*. By 1958, Arkansas, Florida, Georgia, Louisiana, Mississippi, North Carolina, and South Carolina all had legislation in place that could be used to close schools if desegregation appeared imminent. The [white] Citizen's Council—that aspired to be more respectable than the Ku Klux Klan but had the same objectives—sprouted in every county and city where black parents and students made any move to desegregate the schools.[45]

And even more frightening was the increasing number of arson attacks and bombings of African American homes, churches, and schools, as well as Jewish community centers. Historians have designated 1958 "The Year of the Bombings." In February 1958, anonymous white supremacists claimed credit for the fire that destroyed the gymnasium at Arkansas Baptist College (Black) in Little Rock. In March, Jewish community centers in Nashville and Miami were blasted by dynamite, as was the home of a Black family that moved into a white neighborhood in Atlanta. Rev. Charles H. Mason Jr.'s home and the edifice for the Church of God in Christ he pastored in Memphis were destroyed by dynamite. In Jacksonville, Florida, in April, a Jewish community center and the all-Black James Weldon Johnson Elementary School were bombed. The Jewish community center and the homes of local civil rights activists Ernest Coppins and Dora Maudlin were bombed in Bessemer, Georgia, as was the newly purchased home of Essie Mae Ellison in nearby Columbus. Clinton High School in Tennessee, the scene of racial violence in 1956, was bombed in October 1958, destroying sixteen classrooms and causing over $300,000 in damage; and in November, there was a dynamite explosion in the recently desegregated Osage Junior High School in West Virginia. New York congressmen Emmanuel Celler and Kenneth Keating introduced a bill into the US Congress to give the FBI the authority to intervene in school and church bombings and to make it a federal crime to possess or transport dynamite used in attacks on religious, educational, or charitable institutions. Unfortunately, opposition from southern Democrats prevented the measure from leaving the congressional committee.[46]

Given these circumstances, civil rights leaders recognized the need to demonstrate that these incidents had not dampened the spirits of Black and white youths committed to public school desegregation. Originally conceived by labor leader A. Philip Randolph nearly twenty years earlier, a march on Washington was organized by NAACP youth director Herbert Wright to take place in 1958. He worked with the youth councils and college chapters in New York, Pennsylvania, New Jersey, and several other states. In his letter to the young people, Wright emphasized that "the purpose of the march [was] to enable American youth, both Negro and white, and from the South as well as the North, to express their firm support for efforts aimed at securing compliance with the Supreme Court's rulings on desegregation in the public schools."[47]

The first "Youth March for Integrated Schools" was held in Washington, DC, on Saturday, October 25, 1958. Youth councils brought young people by the busload from New York City, Philadelphia, Baltimore, and other cities and towns. The American State and Municipal Employees Union chartered buses that brought 550 of the over 1,000 young people who came from New York City. Governor W. Averell Harriman declared Saturday, October 25, Youth March Day throughout New York State. The protest brought an estimated ten thousand people to the nation's capital, including baseball great Jackie Robinson, A. Philip Randolph, and Coretta Scott King, to protest the continuation of racial segregation in US public education.[48]

The one unfortunate incident that occurred that day involved the delegation from the march—including entertainer Harry Belafonte, Fred Moore from Orangeburg, South Carolina, and Minnijean Brown—being turned away from the White House by security guards and presidential assistants who would not allow them to speak to President Eisenhower or even deliver their petition. Sixteen-year-old Michelle Doswell from Camp Minisink, New York, complained, "I don't think that is a good example for democracy. His refusal to speak to us on the matter of integration has made us all the more militant." Seventeen-year-old Joseph Stewart from New York City agreed: "I see no reason whatsoever why President Eisenhower would not have talked with our delegation this afternoon if he could play golf this morning." Edyth Alexander, a 15-year-old student at the Bronx High School for Science, revealed, "I always felt that once given the opportunity young people could do more to solve our own problems than people generally think we can." Another member of the group from Camp Minisink, 17-year-old William Cooper, believed that "this march for integrated schools is significant because it shows how willing we are to fight for what we believe is ours."[49]

Unfortunately, there was little movement toward school desegregation over the next six months. Three Black girls who were admitted to all-white Ozark High School in Arkansas in September 1958 came under attack from the white students, so they decided to leave at the end of October 1958. They preferred to return to the all-Black high school in Clarksdale, Arkansas, twenty-five miles away, and pay $150 in tuition, rather than be subjected to the ongoing mistreatment at Ozark High.[50] In Virginia in September 1958, rather than submit to court-ordered school desegregation, Governor J. Lindsey Almond closed the public schools in Charlottesville, Fort Royal, and Norfolk and turned the school buildings over to the founders of "private academies," who then hired the furloughed public school teachers. However, federal district judge John Paul forbade the assignment of these public school teachers to private white academies, and white parents in those cities sued Governor Almond over his actions. The federal courts ordered the reopening of public schools in those districts by February 1959.[51]

While African American students prepared to enter newly desegregated public schools in Virginia, there was little progress in other parts of the South. In Nashville, Tennessee, court-ordered public school desegregation began in September 1957 with the admission of nineteen African American 6-year-olds into previously all-white elementary schools. However, white protests and threats of violence, as well as the bombing of the Hattie Cotton Elementary School, meant that a large number of Black parents withdrew their children from the newly desegregated schools. Continued threats of violence meant that by December 1958 there were only ten Black students enrolled in previously all-white public schools in Nashville.[52]

The slow movement on school desegregation led to the organizing of a second Youth March for Integrated Schools in Washington, DC, which took place on Saturday, April 18, 1959. Larger than the first march, it was estimated that over twenty thousand young people and adults participated, and the speakers at the event included Jackie Robinson, the NAACP leader Roy Wilkins, and Martin Luther King Jr. Carrying signs and banners proclaiming "It's Time for Each State to Integrate" and "Equality Is the Thing That Makes Freedom Ring," the young marchers chanted, "Two, four, six, eight, the United States must integrate." As in the first march, a petition was drawn up to be presented to President Eisenhower, calling on him to do more to bring about public school desegregation. Eighteen-year-old Josephine Boyd from Greensboro and 17-year-old Sally Phillips from Hartshorne, Oklahoma, were in the White House delegation. This time they were met by Gerald D. Morgan, a deputy assistant to the president, who conveyed "Eisenhower's best wishes to the group" and assured them that he and his administration "will never be satisfied until the last vestige of discrimination has disappeared."[53]

In August 1959, several months after the march, the NAACP youth council in Nashville organized a two-day workshop, "School Integration: Our Responsibility," attended by young people from Knoxville and Memphis as well as Nashville. The purpose was to inform the participants about what to expect should they agree to seek admission to all-white public schools or decide to engage in nonviolent direct-action protests against legal segregation in public accommodations. Within months, many of the children and teenagers who participated in the workshop would become the young crusaders in the famed Nashville Movement and other civil rights campaigns in Tennessee.[54]

Chapter 3

High School Students and Nonviolent Direct-Action Protests

*Brenda Travis is a 16-year-old Negro girl who is
now in a reformatory because she took part in a sit-in
demonstration and then was arrested during a prayer
meeting on the steps of City Hall in a Southern Town. . . .
She is not in high school anymore; she was suspended.
She is in a Colored Girls Industrial School for one year.
Where? In Raymond, Mississippi.*

Joanne Grant, *Freedomways* (1962)[1]

"SOCIAL AND ECONOMIC progress in those years [was] exceedingly difficult for Wichita's small, closely knit black community," Ronald W. Walters recalled. "Even though the signs 'black' and 'white' were not publicly visible as in the South, we lived in separate worlds, just as blacks and whites did in the southern states." Wichita, Kansas, is in the Midwest, but before the mid-1960s, "Blacks . . . attended separate schools up to high school and were excluded from mixing with whites at movie theaters, restaurants, nightclubs, and other places of public accommodation."[2] The nonviolent direct-action protests against Jim Crow practices in Wichita and Oklahoma City in 1958 and in Greensboro in 1960 reveal that it was teenagers who launched the new phase of the emerging Civil Rights Movement that would soon engulf not just the South but the entire nation.

TEENAGERS AND THE LAUNCHING
OF THE 1960s SIT-IN MOVEMENT

Renowned political scientist Ronald W. Walters graduated from Wichita High School East in June 1955 and soon after enrolled at Fisk University in Nashville. At 19 years old in the summer of 1958, Walters was elected president of the Wichita NAACP youth council. Inspired by the Montgomery bus boycott and disturbed by the insulting treatment of African Americans at lunch counters in Wichita's drug and variety stores, Walters contacted Herbert Wright, NAACP national youth director, and informed him of the local council's plans to carry out direct action protests at these lunch counters. But Wright told Walters "the contemplated sit-in was not regarded as an NAACP tactic and that therefore [they] would not receive the benefit of legal coverage from the national office in the event of lawsuits." Walters was equally disappointed by the response of those in the local NAACP chapter: "the adults appeared as intimidated as our brothers and sisters in the South."[3]

Despite this lack of support, on Saturday, July 19, 1958, Walters led ten members of the youth council down to the Dockum Drug Store, where they occupied the seats and asked for service, but were refused. They left only when the store closed, but returned on Saturday, August 2, sat down, and were refused service, so they remained on the lunch counter stools until closing time at 10:00 p.m. When the young activists returned on Thursday, August 7, and began their protest, a group of fifteen to twenty white men entered the store and seemed bent on causing trouble. Fearing violence, Walters telephoned the police, but when they showed up, one officer declared, "I don't see any disturbance. . . . I have been told to keep hands off of this." The police left, but the white men were still there and threatening. Walters then decided to telephone his Black friends in the community, explained the situation, and within minutes carloads of Black men pulled up in front of the store and the white men left the premises.[4]

On Sunday, August 10, 1958, the youth council organized a public meeting that attracted Black and white students from Wichita State University. Walters explained what was happening, and in the following two weeks the college students joined the NAACP teenagers at the drug store. Then in the fourth week, Walters recalled, "a man in his 30s came into the store, stopped, looked back at the manager in the rear, and said, 'Serve them. I'm losing too much money.' This was the conclusion of the sit-in—climactic and anticlimactic." Within weeks, all the other drug stores in downtown Wichita began serving Black customers at the lunch counters.[5]

NAACP leaders and members of the youth council in Oklahoma City were aware of the protests taking place in Wichita in July and August 1958. In *The Origins of the Civil Rights Movement: Black Communities Organizing for Change*, sociologist Aldon D. Morris noted that many activists in Oklahoma City were "personal friends" of Ronald Walters and "following the initial sit-ins in Wichita, members of the two groups made numerous phone calls, exchanged information, and discussed mutual support."[6] In Oklahoma City, public school teacher Clara Luper served as the advisor for the NAACP youth council and fully supported the young people's decision to begin their social activism on Thursday, August 21, 1958, at the Katz drug store. Thirty-five young people staged the initial sit-in, and the manager, J. M. Masoner, told them "they can sit at our lunch counter as long as they wish, but they won't be served."[7] Under the leadership of youth council president, 15-year-old Barbara Posey, it was estimated that sixty-six young people, 6 to 17 years old, and six adults returned to Katz's drug store, while others went to the luncheonette at the Kress department store and stayed until they were served at both lunch counters.[8]

Then on Sunday, August 24, NAACP youth council members decided to fan out across the city to attend services at seventeen all-white churches where they were welcomed. At only one church were the two Black youths asked to leave. The pastor told them, "God did not intend for Negroes and whites to worship together." They decided to leave.[9] Clara Luper revealed that when her 10-year-old daughter, Marilyn, and two other Black children entered Capitol Hill Baptist Church, they were told to wait in the back and then they were taken to a separate room. Soon an unidentified man came in and told them, "God doesn't want all races to mix." The girls asked him "Where that was in the Bible?" The man responded, "I don't know." At that point the young people left the church.[10] Then on Monday, August 25, at least eighty-five young protesters and five adults showed up to sit in at Brown department store, but they were refused service, so they returned every day that week and sat in.[11]

A few days later, on Saturday, August 29, NAACP youth director Herbert Wright was asked what he thought about the teenagers' protests in Oklahoma City. By then it was clear that he had had a change of heart, and he responded, "We are proud of the young people of Oklahoma City. There is nothing more humiliating and embarrassing for Negroes than to be refused service at a lunch counter where whites are served."[12] It was also reported that the young crusaders met regularly at churches on the east side of Oklahoma City for brief prayer meetings before walking together to Brown department store.[13] The protests continued for a few more days until Monday, September 1, 1958, when Clara Luper announced that they would end because the young people had to return to school the next day. She indicated that several "civic, church, and inter-racial groups . . . offered to help negotiate a settlement."[14] While the young people were successful in ending racist practices at lunch counters in Oklahoma City, Brown department store still refused to serve African American customers. Historian Thomas Bynum found that "by the time the Brown department store desegregated in 1961, 117 stores had discontinued their segregation practices" in Oklahoma City.[15]

Historians and other scholars agree that a new phase in the Civil Rights Movement began with the sit-in at the Woolworth's lunch counter in Greensboro, North Carolina, on Monday, February 1, 1960, by Ezell Blair, Joseph McNeil, Franklin McCain, and David Richmond, students at North Carolina Agriculture and Technical (A&T) College. The decision of hundreds of Black and white students throughout the region to engage in sit-in protests at lunch counters in stores and restaurants not only brought in many new recruits to social activism but also grabbed the attention of the press and other media, expanding the debate about legalized racial discrimination in American society. Initial accounts of the Greensboro sit-in suggested that it was an "impulsive act" undertaken after an evening of "bull sessions" in college dormitory rooms. Historian Clayborne Carson, for example, in his history of the Student Nonviolent Coordinating Committee (SNCC), first published in 1981, suggested that "the initial spark for the movement was a simple, impulsive act of defiance, one that required no special skills or resources. Planned the previous night, the sit-in . . . was not the product of radical intellectual ferment. Rather it grew out of 'bull sessions' . . . typical of southern black students of the time, politically unso-phisticated and socially conventional."[16]

Interviews with Ezell Blair, however, revealed that the four had been planning the protest for two days beforehand, and historian Thomas By-num reported that "Blair had revealed his plans to his father (chairman of the Greensboro NAACP branch executive board). His father assured him that he would support his actions." And Joseph McNeil had discussed the matter with Ralph Johns, also on the local NAACP executive board, and Johns "assured McNeil that he would have his full support." But the Greensboro NAACP leaders did not want to be involved and preferred the students to take the lead in the protest because they did not want it to ap-pear that they had put the students up to it. The local leaders would raise bail money if the students were arrested, Bynum noted, but they did not want it to be a protest "instigated by the NAACP."[17]

But what is stressed in Bynum's account, and not emphasized in ear-lier studies of the sit-ins that began in Wichita, Kansas; Oklahoma City; and Greensboro, North Carolina, as well as social activism organized by the NAACP youth councils between 1933 and 1958, is that these were all carried out by teenagers; and many of the "college students," such as the Greensboro Four, had engaged in nonviolent direct-action protests while still in high school. This was also the case with the women at Bennett Col-lege in Greensboro. Many first and second year students who participated in the 1960 sit-ins had been members of the NAACP youth councils and were still teenagers when they joined the picket lines and other demonstra-tions in Greensboro.[18] Ronald Walters pointed out, "Ezell Blair and Joseph McNeil, two of the originators of the Greensboro protest, were officers in the Greensboro NAACP Youth Council. It is highly unlikely they were unfamiliar with the sit-ins elsewhere . . . led by their organizational peers. Indeed, in the 51st annual conference of the NAACP held in 1960, the na-tional office recognized its youth councils for the work they were doing in breaking down lunch counter segregation."[19]

Within a month, the sit-in protests that began in Greensboro spread throughout the South; sociologist Aldon Morris documented at least fifty-eight locations where Black and white students were active.[20] Bynum found that "twenty-nine of the protests were staged by NAACP youth councils."

He also reported that in 1960 throughout the South, "protest demonstrations continued, slowing down only during examination periods and semester break; however, many high school students (belonging to the youth councils) continued the demonstrations during their summer vacations."[21]

What has not been emphasized in earlier studies is the participation of high school students in the sit-ins and civil rights marches *from the beginning* of the protests. The high school students literally "continued the demonstrations" in which they were already involved. In 1960, in Greensboro, for example, the students at Dudley High School were engaged in sit-ins along with the students from North Carolina A&T and women from Bennett College and Women's College of Greensboro. While a student at Dudley High in the late 1950s, William Thomas served as president of the NAACP youth council in Greensboro. Historian William Chafe points out, "As a high school student, Thomas had led the picket line during the summer of 1960 when the college students left Greensboro, ensuring that the momentum of the sit-ins would not be lost. There he learned the skills of organizing, passing out leaflets, going door to door to support the economic boycott, and providing much of the impetus for continued pressure on downtown merchants." Thomas eventually became one of the organizers in North Carolina for the Congress of Racial Equality (CORE). "We had something going at that time," Thomas recalled. "We started with economic action, we started political action, [and] our demands broadened."[22]

In Chattanooga, Tennessee, it was thirty students from all-Black Howard High School who launched the sit-ins after they learned of the protests organized by college students in Nashville. In the fall of 1959, Rev. James M. Lawson organized workshops on Gandhian approaches to nonviolent direct-action protest. The participants included students from American Baptist Seminary, Fisk University, Meharry Medical School, and Tennessee Agricultural and Industrial University. Fisk student Diane Nash recalled, "When the students in Greensboro sat in on February 1 [1960], we simply made plans to join their effort by sitting in at the same chains. . . . We were surprised and delighted to hear reports of other cities joining in the sit-ins."[23] On February 19, 1960, Howard High School students headed for downtown Chattanooga and staged a sit-in at the lunch counter at McLellan's store. They were refused service, so they remained about thirty minutes, prayed, sang freedom songs, and then left. When the students returned on February 22, they were attacked on the streets by six white men, who were later arrested. The high school students' next target was Warner Park, the all-white recreational facility. When the managers saw the teenagers coming, they closed the rides and concessions and called the police, who then told the teenagers to leave.[24]

The high school students' activism led adults to mobilize for civil rights. Some local ministers formed picket lines in front of several downtown Chattanooga businesses. But the Howard High students renewed their own protests in April 1960 outside the Kress and Company store and at the lunch counters at W. T. Grant, and Woolworth's. The store owners eventually summoned the police, and on May 13 fifty teenagers were arrested and taken to the police station, where six refused to post bond. Upon learning of the arrests, the local NAACP leaders organized a picket line around the police station. The teenagers were finally released after the store managers decided not to press charges. The student protests continued into February 1961 when the local Interdenominational Ministerial Alliance called for a boycott of downtown merchants. Picketing and other protests by teenagers and adults continued in Chattanooga into 1962.[25]

In Baton Rouge, Louisiana, the student sit-ins began on Monday afternoon, March 28, 1960, when seven students from Southern University filed into the S. H. Kress variety store and sat down at the lunch counter. The store manager, R. R. Mathews, telephoned the police chief Shirley Arrighi, and Mathews told him, "They're all yours." The chief soon arrived with four uniformed officers, Captain Robert Weiner in plain clothes, and the patrol wagon. The student activists were arrested and taken to the basement of the courthouse, booked for "disturbing the peace," and held on $10,500 bond. They remained in jail for over three hours before being released on bond. News of the arrests spread throughout the campus. Student leaders organized a rally that evening and up to three thousand students were urged to boycott classes if the seven were expelled.

"All I wanted was a glass of tea," one protesting student told the police chief as he was being loaded into the patrol wagon. When asked why they were doing this, Donald T. Moss responded, "I think being a human being gave me the right to do this." It was later revealed that two weeks earlier, meetings were held at Mount Zion Baptist Church to discuss what would be done should the students launch sit-ins in Baton Rouge. Also, earlier that month, the Louisiana Board of Education had commanded university presidents "to take strict disciplinary action for any unruly behavior" by the students. Southern University president Felton Clark was out of town attending a conference in Washington, DC, but was informed of the students' arrest.[26]

On Tuesday, March 29, 1960, the university students held a rally on campus and then marched on the capitol downtown. This time nine staged a sit-in at the Kress store and were arrested. Rev. J. T. Jemison, pastor of Mount Zion, made arrangements with attorney Johnnie Jones to bail the students out. At the rally later that same day, Rev. Jemison called for a boycott of the downtown stores until the merchants changed their practices. "Let them feel a little pressure during their biggest season—Easter," declared Rev. Jemison. He urged the protesters to "just clean up the clothes you bought last year."[27]

But it was not just university students who were engaged in the rallies and marches. Students in the university's high school also participated. Joseph P. McKelpin, principal of the Southern University Laboratory School, suspended forty-three high school students for attending the rallies at the university and the march downtown. The teenagers were banned from classes for two days for having left school at the lunch hour, thus violating the rule that no student was to leave the campus without specific permission. These high school students had marched on the state capitol to protest the arrests of the African American customers seeking service at department store lunch counters.[28]

President Felton Clark returned to the Southern University campus on March 30 and expelled eighteen students for their arrests and participation in the protests, but this action only added to the students' anger. They not only organized more rallies, but thousands of students also began to file applications to withdraw from the university altogether. President Clark told his staff not to accept the withdrawal applications, and if the students are not attending classes, they would be subject to suspension. Among those arrested for the sit-ins was 19-year-old Marvin Robinson, the president of the student government. After being bailed out, he spoke at all the rallies, and when he and the others were expelled by President Clark, he urged the students to withdraw from the university.[29]

Faced with thousands of requests to leave, Felton Clark decided to enter into negotiations with the student leaders. Over the next few days the students agreed to return to their classes if none were penalized for their arrests or the protests. Many of the students agreed to return to their classes upon learning of the untimely death of one of their favorite professors, J.W. Lee, who taught biology. Evidently, during the week of protests, Dr. Lee suffered a heart attack in his office, was taken to the hospital, and later died. He had taught at Southern for over twenty years. In early April 1960, the student activists returned to their classes and participated in the funeral services for Dr. Lee.[30]

Later that month Ella Baker, the executive secretary for the Southern Christian Leadership Conference (SCLC), arranged for the students involved in sit-ins throughout the country to come together at her alma mater, Shaw University. SCLC had been founded in 1958 by Martin Luther King Jr. and other Black leaders who were engaged in boycotts and other nonviolent direct-action protests. SCLC had not only launched the Crusade for Justice, an attempt to register hundreds of thousands of Black southerners to vote, but also assisted local leaders and communities in organizing nonviolent protest campaigns. On April 25–27, 1960, when the young people met in Raleigh, North Carolina, Baker advised them that, rather than becoming the "youth council" or "youth branch" of SCLC, they should establish their own independent organization. Dr. King attended the meeting and agreed that the young activists should form their own group.[31]

Over 140 student activists from cities and towns throughout the nation, many still in their teens, attended the organizational meeting, and the largest contingent came from Nashville, where hundreds of students from the four Black colleges and universities as well as Vanderbilt and other predominantly white colleges had engaged in sit-ins at downtown stores and lunch counters. The Student Nonviolent Coordinating Committee (SNCC) was created at that time, and Marion Barry, a Nashville student activist, was chosen as the first chairperson. The student activists committed themselves to using nonviolent direct-action tactics to bring about an end to the legal apartheid that existed in the South and the de facto segregation and racial discrimination in other parts of the United States.[32]

"WEAR OLD CLOTHES AND NEW DIGNITY"

Along with sit-ins, the boycott continued to be a major weapon in the arsenal of nonviolent direct-action protesters in the early 1960s. Its effectiveness had been demonstrated with the bus boycott in Montgomery in 1955 and 1956, and it spread to other southern cities where white merchants discriminated against Black customers or hired African Americans as employees only for menial jobs. When the student sit-ins were launched in Greensboro in February 1960, Woolworth stores throughout the country not only witnessed picketing by local activists but also were boycotted. The boycott eventually received widespread support, and Walter Reuther, president of the United Auto Workers, and George Meany, leader of the AFL-CIO, called on their members to boycott Woolworth stores, arguing that the student sit-ins were similar to the autoworkers' "sit-down" strikes of the 1930s.[33]

In 1960, Easter Sunday fell on April 17. Whereas college students, whether they lived at home or on campus, were not likely to buy new outfits for the holiday, elementary and high school students usually looked forward to sporting new suits or dresses and hats for Easter. Thus when civil rights and student activists began calling for an Easter boycott of stores where African Americans were discriminated against, it impacted children and teenagers the most. But NAACP leader Medgar Evers and other civil rights activists asked children in Mississippi and other southern states to "make the sacrifice for the sake of human dignity."[34]

Rev. J. T. Jemison in Baton Rouge was one of the earliest civil rights activists to call for the Easter boycott in April 1960, asking African Americans to "wear old clothes and new dignity." In Mississippi in these early months of the student sit-ins, there were fewer protests due to public threats coming from white political leaders who promised long prison terms and from Klansmen who predicted widespread violence against protesters. But the students at two private Black schools in Jackson, Tougaloo College and

Campbell Junior College, pushed for a boycott of all the white-owned stores in the city during the Easter holiday.[35] Soon after the students' announcement, white merchants announced that should a boycott take place, there would be immediate reprisals against Black workers.[36] Nonetheless, Black high school students in Jackson took up the cause and organized visits to thousands of homes of Black families, urging them to "wear old clothes on Easter" and to avoid shopping at the stores of white merchants, and most did.[37] Student activists in Florida, Georgia, Tennessee, South Carolina, Virginia, and many other states spread the word, and tens of thousands of Black southerners participated in the 1960 Easter boycott.[38]

In the "Crescent City," the Easter boycott of stores operating in Black neighborhoods was organized by the Consumer League of Greater New Orleans, founded in December 1959. Under the leadership of Dr. Raymond Floyd of Xavier University, the league organized boycotts of white-owned business on Dryades Street in 1959 and 1960. The New Orleans branch of CORE, formed in the summer of 1960, launched its first direct action protest on September 9, 1960: a sit-in at the Woolworth store at Canal and Rampart Streets. The police were called, and seven protesters were arrested and charged with "criminal mischief." The high school and college students who organized the New Orleans CORE chapter—Oretha and Doris Jean Castle, Rudy Lombard, Doratha Smith, Jerome Smith, and Alice, Jean, and Shirley Thompson—first engaged in the boycotts and picketing organized by Dr. Floyd and the Consumer League.[39]

After the arrest of the CORE activists on Friday, September 9, the New Orleans NAACP youth council launched a picket line the next day in front of Woolworth's. Led by Raphael Cassimere, the youth council members carried signs declaring "Jim Crow Must Go" and "They Were Arrested Because They Wanted to Eat" and were often harassed by white youths and the police while on the picket line. In addition to the picketing, the youth council issued a statement urging Black parents to "register your children in the white schools in your vicinity." Teenagers in the youth council maintained the picket lines for weeks and expanded them to include other stores on Canal Street.[40]

New Orleans mayor Chep Morrison announced his directive to the police department to arrest any persons engaged in "peaceful picketing" of businesses in the city on Monday, September 12, the same day four more CORE members were arrested for picketing stores in the Claiborne Shopping Center. The youth council and CORE organized a mass rally that evening and CORE's national field secretary, James McCain, was in attendance. He declared, "Youth are on the move and we can get 2,000 Negroes to walk the pickets in the Claiborne and Canal Street areas, we will see what the police department of New Orleans will do about it."[41]

On Friday, September 16, 1960, six members of the Consumer League were arrested for picketing stores in the Claiborne Shopping Center. Four more were arrested on Monday, September 19, and that evening a protest march calling for "equal employment opportunities" for Black workers took place. The members of the youth council were among the estimated two thousand people who participated. Marching along South Claiborne Avenue and ending at the ILA Auditorium, A. I. Davis, Rev. Alexander Avery, Henry Mitchell, and other speakers "blasted merchants in the area who . . . refused to hire Negroes as cashiers and other supervisory jobs."[42]

In the summer of 1960 in Jacksonville, Florida, it was the NAACP youth council that led the civil rights activism by launching a sit-in at the Woolworth department store lunch counter on Saturday, August 13. Under the leadership of 16-year-old Rodney L. Hurst, over a hundred members assembled at the Laura Street Presbyterian Church, prayed, and then walked to the Woolworth's. The teenagers purchased items in the store "to demonstrate that the store would take our money." Then when they sat down, the waitress announced, "Coloreds are not served at this counter." The manager came over and told them they would not be served. "We still did not move." The manager then closed the lunch counter. Angry whites standing around began hurling racial epithets, and when the protesters decided to leave, the whites stuck them with pins and other sharp objects, and kicked them. Hurst recalled, "One woman blocked my path and stepped on my foot, heel first. . . . A woman's shoe heel makes an impression on the toe of the shoe and on your foot."[43]

Over the next two weeks, lunch counter sit-ins took place, including one by 25-year-old Robert Charles Parker, a white student from Florida State University, who was attacked by whites and had to be rescued by members of the Boomerangs, a Black teenage gang. "They formed a circle around him and walked him out of the Woolworth . . . and away from the store." On Saturday, August 27, 1960, white supremacists were holding a rally in Hemming Park, with a sign announcing "Free Ax Handles." Rather than return to the Woolworth's across from the park, the thirty-four young crusaders decided to sit in at the W. T. Grants store, three blocks away. When they entered and sat at the lunch counter, the manager closed it and then turned out all the lights in the store. As the teenagers were leaving, they "could see in a distance a mob of whites running toward [them]." The manager locked the store behind them, so they had to run. Wielding ax handles and baseball bats, the whites started hitting every Black person on the street. Some were beaten bloody, but Hurst was lucky, and as he was running, Mrs. I. E. "Mama" Williams picked him up in her car and drove him to the Laura Street Church. "I cannot remember her face. . . . I just remember the person asking me if I was hurt and telling me she was a member of the NAACP." Following the "Ax Handle Saturday" attack, youth council members and NAACP officers organized a meeting and called for a boycott of all white-owned businesses in downtown Jacksonville.[44]

SHOWDOWN IN NEW ORLEANS

Throughout 1960 the New Orleans CORE chapter organized marches, boycotts, and picketing, and the civil rights activists could count on the teenagers in the local NAACP youth council to support the protests. Later that year, the Louisiana supreme court and federal courts threw out the arrests and convictions of CORE and NAACP activists for their nonviolent protests in early 1960. The teenagers continued to organize picket lines, marches, and rallies at businesses that refused to hire Black workers as New Orleans was thrust into the national and international spotlight in November 1960 when the first four Black girls were enrolled in two all-white public elementary schools.[45]

As was the case with other Deep South states, after the Supreme Court's *Brown* decision Louisiana legislators passed legislation to punish school districts that moved toward desegregation and fought court orders being handed down by federal judges. When Louisiana and other state courts upheld state laws aimed at preventing the implementation of public school desegregation, J. Skelly Wright of the Fifth Circuit Court of Appeals tossed them out. After many delaying actions, Judge Wright required the Orleans Parish school board to submit a desegregation plan by May 1960. And as was the case in other southern school districts under court-ordered desegregation, Superintendent James Redmond submitted a plan calling for grade-by-grade desegregation beginning with the first grade. Only African Americans entering the first grade would be eligible to enroll in the all-white public schools nearest their homes.[46]

In October 1960, after having undergone a battery of tests and interviews, six Black children, five girls and one boy, were chosen by school officials for admission to all-white public schools. However, when the threats of white violence mounted, the parents of one girl and the only boy withdrew their applications. When school officials announced that the enrollment of the four Black children would take place on Monday, November 14, the local White Citizens' Council sent out a notice telling white parents to keep their children home from the schools where the Black girls were to enroll. Thus when 6-year-old Ruby Bridges was escorted by US marshals through the mobs of angry whites to enter the William Frantz Elementary School, and six-year-olds Leona Tate, Tessie Prevost, and Gail Etienne made their way through the crowds to enroll at the McDonough 19 Elementary School, they became the only students in attendance at both schools.[47]

Many articles, books, and movies have told the story of the four Black girls who desegregated the New Orleans public schools in 1960. While the principals and the teachers for the young pupils were present, they were the only ones in the two schools for the entire 1960–61 school year. The white mobs continued outside the school buildings for several months, but eventually trailed off. And all four girls reported that they liked the white teachers who instructed them. Ruby Bridges remained at the Frantz School all six years and other Black students enrolled, while the number of white students decreased.[48]

At McDonough 19 in the 1961–62 school year, white students returned. Leona Tate, Tessie Prevost, and Gail Etienne became victims of ongoing harassment, so they decided to transfer in the third grade to another newly desegregated school, Semmes Elementary. Historian Rachel Devlin interviewed these pioneering and courageous women for her account of the African American girls and women who desegregated all-white public schools, *A Girl Stands at the Door*. Tate, Prevost, and Etienne reported that at Semmes School they felt they were in "the devil's domain." "The harassment was on a daily basis," Leona Tate recalled, "It was just horrific." Prevost said that they were subjected to not only physical attacks but also ongoing verbal assaults. "The N-word . . . doesn't mean a lot to little children, *Stupid* means more. *Dumb* means more. *Ugly* means more." And most awful, "The teachers were no better than the kids. They encouraged them to fight us; to do whatever it took. . . . Gail got hit with a bat. [Tate] got hit with a bat . . . in the face."[49] Prevost and Tate's parents confronted the teachers and students who harassed their daughters, and after several years of asking their parents to be allowed to leave, Prevost and Tate transferred to all-Black Rivers Frederick School. For Prevost "it was like heaven."[50]

"JAIL, NO BAIL" IN ATLANTA, GEORGIA, AND ROCK HILL, SOUTH CAROLINA

These Crescent City girls were among the youngest crusaders in the civil rights campaigns that took place in the early 1960s; they were also among the most prominent. And despite the young girls' personal challenges, what came to be known as "the Showdown in New Orleans" was a successful outcome after a long, drawn-out legal battle. In other places in 1960, children and teenagers joined adult protesters on the front lines of civil rights struggles and oftentimes ended up in jail, but there were few changes in local Jim Crow practices. This is what occurred in Atlanta. The NAACP filed lawsuits in 1958 and 1959 to end segregation in the public schools, and in the Georgia capital, legislators passed "local-option measures" giving local municipalities the choice of desegregating or abolishing the public school system altogether. Finally, in May 1960, Judge John Hooper gave Atlanta's public school administrators until September 1961 to implement its grade-by-grade desegregation plan, beginning with the eleventh and twelfth grades. NAACP attorney Constance Baker Motley denounced Judge Hooper's ruling, declaring that the Supreme Court never said state judges and legislators "had the right to say when and if a desegregation plan should go into effect."[51]

And there were few advances in other areas, so Atlanta's public accommodations remained segregated in 1960. As in other southern cities with large Black student populations, sit-ins were launched in March and April 1960 and boycotts were initiated in the downtown shopping areas. Students from Morehouse, Spelman, Morris Brown, Atlanta, and other colleges and universities in the city targeted Woolworth's, Kress's, Rich's, and other department stores' lunch counters, but the managers usually closed the restaurants when the protesters arrived. When picketing began in the front of businesses that discriminated against African American customers or workers, the Ku Klux Klan mounted pickets across the street, in effect, protesting the protesters. Then on May 17, 1960, on the sixth anniversary of the *Brown* decision, when Lonnie King of Morehouse and other college students mobilized high school students, their parents, and other adults for a commemorative "March on the State Capital," the over 1,500 protesters were stopped and dispersed by the local police and state troopers.[52]

The mayor of Atlanta, William Hartsfield, tried to serve as an intermediary between the civil rights activists and the merchants and business owners. Negotiations proceeded over several months, and unfortunately, while the national officers of Woolworth, Grant, Kress, and McCrory variety stores claimed that by October 1960 African Americans were being served at lunch counters in over a hundred southern cities, none were being served in Georgia. Thus a new round of sit-ins and picketing was launched on October 19, 1960. Martin Luther King Jr., who had moved to Atlanta from Montgomery in January to become assistant pastor at Ebenezer Baptist Church, was among the fifty-one protesters arrested at Rich's department store. While the majority of activists posted bail, fourteen, including King, refused to post bond. On October 20 a new group of protesters walked the picket lines, and seventy-five were arrested and twenty-two refused to post bond.[53]

Mayor Hartsfield again sought a truce between merchants and the protesters, calling for a sixty- to ninety-day "cooling off period." Both sides eventually agreed to a thirty-day truce, and the merchants agreed not to press charges against those arrested and being held for trial.[54] However, the truce was shattered on December 11, 1960, with the bombing of English Avenue Elementary School, an all-Black public school in northwest

Atlanta. While no one was hurt, the blast damaged classrooms and the auditorium and blew out windows, causing over $5,000 in damages. Subsequent investigations revealed that dynamite had been thrown from a moving car and hit the front of the school. The police reported that there were eighteen explosions in Atlanta over the previous four years; most involved homes and they all, like this latest school bombing, went unsolved. This incident was the first anti-Black violence in Atlanta since the suspension of the sit-ins and picketing in October. Hundreds of elementary and high school students participated in a mass rally at Atlanta University and then marched into downtown Atlanta to protest the school bombing, while the Klan launched picketing at several locations along the route.[55] By the end of 1960 nonviolent direct-action protests were launched in 15 southern states and 156 cities. According to historian Thomas Bynum, "Some 2,089 students had been arrested and fined a total of $128,400" and NAACP officers, members, and friends supplied most of the bail money.[56]

The negotiations between student protesters and Black leaders and merchants led to an impasse, and so a new round of sit-ins began in Atlanta in February 1961 with sit-ins at the cafeteria in the Federal Office Building. Led by Lonnie King, seventeen protesters were arrested on February 7. But this time they refused to post bond and chose to remain in jail. The next day more students participated in the sit-ins, were arrested, and refused to post bond. From her jail cell, 17-year-old Hershelle Sullivan issued a statement on Wednesday, February 8: "We, along with these leaders, appeal to all students from the South to join in the struggle for human dignity. The students in jail have said that they can stand it in there as long as other people can stand it out here."[57]

On that same day, eight teenagers attending Friendship Junior College in Rock Hill, South Carolina, and two adults were arrested for picketing and sitting in at the McCrory's variety store. They were charged with trespassing and sentenced to thirty days in jail or a fine of one hundred dollars. They refused to pay the bond. The next day, February 9, 1961, those arrested were joined by 20-year-old Diane Nash, 18-year-old Ruby Doris Smith, and two 20-something SNCC organizers from Nashville, Charles Sherrod and Charles Jones, who arrived in Rock Hill to support and participate in the sit-ins. They too announced they would not pay the fines or post bond and launched what became known as the "jail, no bail" strategy subsequently adopted by student activists in Atlanta; Montgomery; Lynchburg, Virginia; and Jackson, Mississippi.[58]

In Atlanta, on Thursday, February 9, 1961, more students were arrested so that now a total of thirty-one were imprisoned and were refusing to post bond, the majority still in their teens. By Saturday, February 11, it was reported that there were eighty students in the Fulton County Jail, thirteen in Rock Hill, and six in Lynchburg.[59] In Rock Hill, two teenage activists were released because they were "juveniles," but that left eleven young adults at the York County Prison Farm. Local activists in Rock Hill staged a rally in support of those incarcerated and then several hundred teenagers and adults organized a caravan of sixty cars and headed for the prison farm. Along the way, however, local police and South Carolina state troopers put up barriers to block the protesters and forced the caravan to return to Rock Hill. At the prison farm the following week, eight of the eleven student activists staged a sit-down strike due to the overwork. The strikers were placed in solitary confinement and given only bread and water. Thirty days later the Rock Hill activists were finally released, but there was little change in the discrimination against African Americans in the town. In Atlanta, fifty-two protesters were imprisoned in February 1961, but after fourteen days in jail, Dr. King urged the activists to accept the terms of the agreement worked out with Mayor Hartsfield and the merchants. This brought an end to that round of protests. The store owners conceded that the economic boycott had had a negative impact on their bottom line.[60]

TAKING THE LEAD IN PITTSBURGH

The NAACP youth council in Pittsburgh, Pennsylvania, was reactivated in 1961 by Dorothy Williams, a teacher at the A. Leo Weil Elementary School. Black children and teenagers were not allowed into the West View Danceland, and in September 1961 the youth council filed a complaint against the owner with the Pennsylvania Human Relations Commission. The following month the youth council launched picket lines there and in front of several shoe stores to call attention to the failure to hire African American workers. Their slogan was "If we can buy shoes, we can sell them!" The headline in the *Pittsburgh Courier* declared, "NAACP Youth Picket Fifth Ave. Shoe Stores." Rallies and meetings organized by the teenagers were held at Central Baptist Church and brought support from community leaders and many Black residents.[61]

The picketing and protests resulted in jobs for Black workers in the shoe stores, the five-and-dimes, and department stores. At the annual conference for the Pennsylvania NAACP branches, held in Easton in November 1961, the Pittsburgh youth council was honored "for their fine leadership" and *Courier* columnist Eric Springer observed, "One can only feel a swelling sense of pride in the NAACP youth who have fought successfully against the discrimination which keeps the bread from our families." Through the youth activism, he noted, "we are now more willing to meet discrimination head on."[62]

BRENDA TRAVIS, FREEDOM FIGHTER

One of the most widely publicized protests organized by high school students in 1961 occurred in McComb, Mississippi. SNCC organizers Bob Moses and Travis Britt arrived in the city of fifty thousand in July to start a voter registration campaign. At that time, in Pike County, where McComb is located, African Americans were 44 percent of the 35,789 total population, but only an estimated 225 were registered to vote. Working with several local residents, a voter education project was set up in August. One afternoon Moses was on his way to the voter registration office in Liberty, Amitie County, with two local Black residents, Curtis Dawson and Rev. Alfred Knox. The three encountered three white men, including the cousin of Sheriff J. L. Caston, Billy Jack Caston, who attacked Moses, causing a wound that required eight stitches.[63] When Travis Britt accompanied African Americans seeking to register in Liberty, he was attacked by Bryant Jones. No charges were brought against the attackers. Then, in September 1961, Herbert Lee, who was working with the SNCC workers on the voter registration project, was shot and killed by E. H. Hurst, a state legislator, who claimed self-defense—"He had a tire iron in his hand"—and was later declared not guilty by a coroner's jury.[64]

Later that month, five Black teenagers were arrested for "disturbing the peace" when attempting to obtain service at the restaurant in McComb's

Greyhound Bus Terminal. The youths were finally released on a two-thousand-dollar bond each on Saturday, September 30. But two days later, on Monday, October 2, 16-year-old Brenda Travis was suspended and not allowed to return to Burgland High School for Negroes. The school's administrators claimed she could not return because of the pending disorderly conduct charges against her. When the students at Burgland High learned that Travis had been suspended, over two hundred organized a walkout on Wednesday, October 4. Some made signs calling on Black adults to register to vote and carried them while marching down the main street to city hall, where they held a rally and prayed. The police showed up and began arresting the youngsters as angry whites denounced the teenagers' protest. At least 115 students were arrested, and some were also beaten by the police. SNCC organizer Robert Zellner arrived to observe the student protest and was attacked when the whites saw him trying to help the students, and he too was arrested.[65]

When parents began to show up at the jail, all but eighteen of the teenagers were released because they were considered minors. Nine of the eighteen were charged with contributing to the delinquency of minors and nine were booked for disorderly conduct. Brenda Travis was charged with disorderly conduct and was not allowed to leave. Instead, she was judged to be "a delinquent" and was sent to Oakley Reformatory for Negroes in Raymond. When the Black high school students learned of this, several dozen organized a pilgrimage to Oakley Reformatory on Sunday, October 15, but the police were alerted. When the teenagers arrived, policemen with dogs prevented them from entering the facility and they were forced to return to McComb. At school the next day, at least sixty-five of the students who had been arrested refused to sign loyalty oaths agreeing not to participate in future walkouts. Instead, throughout the week the teenagers turned in their books and attended civil rights workshops led by Bob Moses and Charles McDew at St. Paul Methodist Church and at the Negro Masonic Hall that they dubbed "Nonviolent High School."[66]

That same week of October 15, 1961, police chief George Guy authorized the arrest of Curtis C. Bryant, president of the McComb NAACP. Bryant worked at the rail yards and was a deacon and Sunday school teacher at Society Hill Church. Chief Guy and Mayor C. H. Douglas believed that

Bryant "was mixed up in this thing making speeches," but Bryant was reported to have initially advised the students against organizing the protest march. The mayor, police chief, and the publisher of the *McComb Enterprise Journal*, J. Oliver Emmerich, attributed the protests to "outside reformers"; however, in a speech at the NAACP rally at Society Hill Church on Thursday, October 19, Bob Moses denied the charge and suggested "at best we are catalysts. It wouldn't be possible for local people to do what we've been doing and live here. I view our function as buffers: the white people can take their wrath out on us."[67]

Emmerich penned an editorial in the *Enterprise Journal* labeling Brenda Travis "a delinquent" who belonged in the reformatory. Moses denounced this as a "smear campaign" against Travis. "The issue is not whether Brenda is a delinquent. The issue is: when will the white community begin to allow the Negro community to have its legitimate rights." Medgar Evers, executive secretary for the NAACP in Mississippi, also spoke at the rally at Society Hill Church. "Brenda's in the reformatory because she is sick and tired of discrimination and segregation. She's the symbol of the fight for freedom down here." With regard to teenagers taking the lead in voting rights activism, Evers declared that the students' demonstration "focuses the spotlight on the terrible conditions by dramatizing the situation . . . and forces the parents to take a firm stand." Aaron Henry, state president of the NAACP, told those at the rally that at a recent meeting with Ross Barnett, the governor became angry and started shouting when Henry mentioned that the NAACP would be testing the ICC regulation against segregation in bus terminals that would go into effect November 1, 1961. "There's no need to raise your voice, Governor," Henry told the red-faced politician. "The Negroes who are afraid of you have already gone to Chicago. The rest of us are here to slug it out." Local NAACP leader Curtis Bryant told those assembled, "Where the students lead, we will follow."[68]

"YOU DON'T HAVE TO RIDE JIM CROW"

The Interstate Commerce Commission (ICC) regulation banning racial segregation in interstate bus travel came about as a result of the Freedom Rides organized by CORE beginning in May 1961. James Farmer, CORE chairman, decided that it was important to test the implementation of the US Supreme Court's 1960 decision in *Boynton v. Virginia*, which declared segregation laws and practices in interstate transportation unconstitutional. CORE received support from the NAACP, SNCC, SCLC, and the Nashville Student Movement. Moreover, this example of courage and bravery served as an inspiration for southern children and teenagers who would put their bodies on the line for freedom and equal rights. This was especially the case because many of the Freedom Riders were still in their teens.[69]

Over the course of the Freedom Rides between May and December 1961, 25 percent of the participants were 18 or 19 years old. The youngest Freedom Riders were Hezekiah Watkins (13); Leo V. Blue (14); Gainnel Hayes, Dolores W. Lynch, and Andrew Horne (15); and 16-year-olds Mildred Blue, Samuel Givens, Emma Lee Horne, Alphonso K. Petway, and Paul E. Young.[70] In Birmingham, Jackson, New Orleans, and other cities where the young Freedom Riders arrived and stood up for freedom and equality in the face of white violence and brutality, teenagers witnessed this religiously-inspired, nonviolent civil rights activism and soon took up the banner and in some places took the lead in challenging Jim Crow practices in their communities.[71]

The first Freedom Riders left Washington, DC, on two buses, one Greyhound and the other Trailways, headed to New Orleans. The group of twenty included James Farmer, Genevieve Hughes, Catherine Burks, Ed Blankenstein, and James Peck. The three teenagers included in that first Freedom Ride were Ivor Moore, Hank Thomas (19), and Charles Person (18).[72] The Black and white activists challenged segregation practices on the buses by having the Black activists sit in the front of the buses and whites sit in the back. In the terminals, the Black Freedom Riders went into the whites-only waiting rooms, restaurants, and rest stops. When the Greyhound bus carrying the Freedom Riders arrived in Anniston, Alabama, on May 14, 1961, a white mob was waiting and attacked the buses, setting one on fire, and beat the Freedom Riders as they fled the flames. Several had to be taken to the hospital in Anniston, and some vicious racists followed the cars there to continue their violence, frightening the hospital personnel, who then told the Freedom Riders to leave. "Trapped between the mob's anger and the hospital's nerves, without means of transportation,"

Taylor Branch observed, "the Freedom Riders huddled in one hospital corner after another, being told repeatedly to go somewhere else." Finally, eight carloads of Black men from Rev. Fred Shuttlesworth's church arrived at the hospital and brought the injured men and women back to Birmingham.[73]

When the Trailways bus arrived in Anniston, the white driver got off and eight white men entered the bus and began attacking the Black riders sitting in the front and the white riders in the back. These Klansmen then dragged the white protesters, beaten and bloody, to the front of the bus and dragged the Black riders to the back. The bus driver returned with a police officer, who assured him, "Don't worry about no lawsuits, I ain't seen a thing."[74] The driver got back on board and drove the bus to Birmingham, where a mob of white racists was waiting in the terminal to attack. They began to punch, kick, and pummel the Freedom Riders, dragging some from one end of the depot to the other. After fifteen minutes of brutal mayhem, Birmingham police officers showed up. Among those beaten by the mobs were radio, print, and television journalists who spread the news nationally and internationally of the unprovoked attacks on the nonviolent activists. On May 15, 1961, the eighteen remaining Freedom Riders decided to take a plane from Birmingham to New Orleans, but the white racists learned of that plan and began telephoning bomb threats to the airport, delaying their departure. After several hours and under the cover of darkness, the plane finally took off at midnight carrying the wounded crusaders.[75]

Rudy Lombard and CORE members in New Orleans made arrangements to receive the Freedom Riders. Lombard prevailed upon Dean Norman Francis at Xavier University to allow the Freedom Riders to stay in the dormitory on campus. They remained there for two days before returning to Washington, DC.[76] But rather than calling off the Freedom Rides, Diane Nash and others recruited a contingent of students who had been active in the Nashville Movement in 1960 to continue them. On May 17, 1961, twenty-two young people from Nashville set off for Birmingham; and ten members of this new contingent were either 18 or 19 years old. When the nonviolent activists arrived in the terminal, they also were attacked by a white mob and then arrested by Sheriff Bull Connor's police. Through the intervention of Attorney General Robert Kennedy, working with Alabama governor James Patterson, the Freedom Riders were released and allowed to leave Birmingham. They headed for Montgomery, but when they arrived there, the local police and the FBI allowed them to be attacked by another white mob.[77]

At this point, Martin Luther King Jr. made it known that he was going to Montgomery and would participate in a mass meeting at Rev. Ralph Abernathy's First Baptist Church in support of the Freedom Riders. While the rally was taking place, angry whites gathered outside the church and began firing shots, throwing rocks through church windows, and setting the cars outside the church on fire. Dr. King alerted Attorney General Kennedy, who then dispatched US marshals to the scene to end the violence and to protect those attending the mass meeting. Those in the church had to spend the night, and the next day the bus carrying the Freedom Riders was escorted by the US marshals out of Alabama. However, once they arrived in Jackson, Mississippi, the police were waiting and arrested them.[78]

James Bevel, Bernard Lafayette, and others active in the Nashville Movement agreed to continue the Freedom Rides and arrived in Jackson, Mississippi, in July 1961. There, they faced violent assaults and were arrested immediately, fined up to two hundred dollars, which they refused to pay, and were imprisoned. While still in jail, however, Bevel and Lafayette began civil rights organizing, and once released, they were joined by Diane Nash, Bob Moses, Bob Zellner, and others in the Mississippi voting rights movement. They recruited many young people in Jackson, McComb, and other parts of the Mississippi Delta to work on voter registration projects.[79]

HELPING THE CAUSE OF FREEDOM: ALBANY, GEORGIA

Attorney General Robert Kennedy, in June 1961, had requested the Interstate Commerce Commission to issue regulations banning racial segregation in bus transportation, including the restrooms, restaurants, and waiting rooms in the terminals. The ICC finally voted in September 1961 to ban segregation in all aspects of interstate bus travel. Robert Kennedy called the measure "the most far-reaching administrative action ever taken by the federal government" and he promised full enforcement when it went into effect on November 1, 1961.[80] Unfortunately, when SNCC organizers

Charles Jones, James Forman, and James Bevel tested the new regulation at the Trailways Bus Terminal in Atlanta on November 2, 1961, they were arrested. Georgia legislators claimed that in issuing the desegregation measure the ICC and US Justice Department had overstepped their authority, and they promised a lawsuit.[81] And in McComb, Mississippi, district court judge Sydney Mize issued a restraining order against CORE on December 3, 1961, preventing Freedom Riders from entering the "white sections" of local bus terminals. CORE officials declared that they hoped for the day "when all can travel with dignity, without fanfare" or mobs and angry "crowds all over America."[82]

In early November 1961, after SNCC organizers Charles Jones, Charles Sherrod, and Cordell Reagon arrived in Albany, in southwest Georgia, they organized several meetings and rallies in Black churches to gain local support for a voter registration campaign and against the continued practice of racial segregation in public accommodations in the city. Most of the adults in attendance at the rallies seemed reluctant to participate, but high school students Evelyn Toney, Eddie Wilson, and Julian Carswell, members of the NAACP youth council, along with Albany State College students Bertha Gobel and Blanton Hall, went to the Albany bus depot on Wednesday, November 22, 1961, purchased tickets for Tallahassee, Florida, and then entered the restaurant and tried to obtain service. Local police chief Laurie Pritchett was alerted and decided to drive over to the bus depot. When he entered the restaurant, Pritchett ordered the students to come outside, where he told them if they reentered it, they would be arrested. The five turned around and reentered the restaurant. Chief Pritchett came in after them and placed them under arrest. After loading them into a police van, he took them to the station, where they were charged with disturbing the peace, fingerprinted, and photographed. The young activists said they didn't mind being treated as "hardened criminals if this treatment will help the cause of freedom." After making phone calls to attorneys Thomas Chatmon and E. D. Hamilton and a one-hundred-dollar bond for each was paid, Toney, Wilson, and Carswell were released.[83]

Bertha Gobel and Blanton Hall, however, refused to pay the one-hundred-dollar bond and remained in jail. SNCC organizers Jones, Sherrod, and Reagon visited Gobel and Blanton in jail and reported on the statement made by Bertha Gobel: "I hope my stay in jail presents to the community in Albany and the nation the evil and inconvenience of segregation. We have a legal and moral right to use the facilities at the Bus Station as interstate passengers. Those who should be arrested are those who violently attack us and actually disturb the peace of the city."[84] The following day these arrests sparked a massive protest march downtown by college and high school students. Once the students, singing freedom songs, reached police headquarters, they were surrounded by police and Chief Pritchett told them to disperse. They did, and as they walked back to their schools, the young people continued to sing freedom songs.[85]

After learning of the five students' arrests, nine members of SNCC, who considered themselves Freedom Riders, took the train from Atlanta to Albany on Sunday, December 10, 1961. They were met in the station there by two Albany State students, and all eleven then went into the "white section" of the station and sat down. Police chief Pritchett showed up and, accusing them of "blocking the flow of traffic," placed them under arrest, loaded them in the police van, and took them to the police station. The local magistrate set the bond at two hundred dollars each. They refused to pay the bond and remained in jail.[86]

The next day, despite the pouring rain, between four-hundred and six-hundred high school and college students marched on the police station over the Freedom Riders' arrest. Singing all the time "We want freedom; we are not afraid," the young people were confronted by police officers who arrested many of them, albeit "nonviolently," and took them to city and county jails. Of the 267 arrested on Tuesday, December 12, 96 were high school students.[87] The protest marches continued into a second day, December 13, 1961, and this time it was estimated that up to 700 people participated in the rally; and when the marchers reached the downtown, 202 protesters were arrested, and the majority—118—were "juveniles."[88]

Bernice Johnson Reagon was still a teenager when she joined the protests in Albany. "I ended up being arrested in the second wave of arrests in Albany." When she got to the jail, Slater King, a longtime friend, cried out, "Bernice, is that you?" When she answered yes, he said, "Sing a song." She knew he was not asking her to sing a solo, she recalled, but wanted her "to plant the seed." "The minute you start the song, the song is created by everybody there." Bernice Reagon had experienced the power of the freedom songs at movement meetings.

> I'd had songs . . . in high school and church, but in the movement, all the words sounded different.
> "This Little Light of Mine, I'm going to let it shine," which I'd sung all my life, said something very different. We varied the verses: "All in the street, I'm going to let it shine. All in the jailhouse, I'm going to let it shine." [In jail] they could not stop our sound. They would have to kill us to stop us from singing. Sometimes the police would plead and say, "Please stop singing." And you would just know that your word was being heard, and you felt joy.[89]

The Albany Movement, often referred to as "the Singing Movement," came into being with protests over the arrests of the teenagers. It was led by physician William Anderson, who announced on December 16 that a boycott of all white-owned stores in the downtown area should begin. The adults who were arrested that day were held at the National Guard armory and charged with unlawful assembly, holding an unlicensed parade, and congregating on the street. The teenagers arrested were sent to the juvenile detention center in Camilla, Georgia. When those arrested were unable to pay the bonds, they were transferred to jails in Baker, Lee, Terrell, and other nearby counties. Police chief Pritchett declared, "The arrests will continue if I have to put them in jails all over Georgia." At first the five-man city commission refused to meet with Dr. Anderson or other Black leaders, and Mayor Asa Kelley claimed that there was "no area of possible agreement" between city officials and protesters.[90]

With the arrival of 150 national guardsmen on December 14, 1961, city officials began negotiations with Albany Movement leaders, including Rev. H. S. Boyd, Bennie Cochran, and Solomon Walker, who demanded, in return for an end to the demonstrations, release from jail without bond of those arrested, the end of segregation enforcement at the bus and railroad stations, and plans to end segregation in stores, restaurants, and other public places. Negotiations were suspended, however, when the Black leaders learned that SNCC organizer Charles Sherrod had been "brutally beaten" in a Terrell County jail.[91]

Dr. King and Rev. Abernathy arrived in Albany on Friday, December 15, and spoke at rallies held at Shiloh Baptist and Mount Zion Baptist Churches. Dr. King and Dr. Anderson announced a prayer march to the city jail the next day to call for the release of those arrested earlier in the week. On Saturday afternoon hundreds participated in the silent march led by Dr. King. Police chief Pritchett confronted King and the other leaders and asked if they had a parade permit. They said no, and police and guardsmen moved in and began to escort them to the police station, where they were later booked and placed in jail. Mayor Kelley told reporters that he would make "no concessions" and broke off all negotiations with the Albany Movement and SCLC leaders. Of the 264 protesters arrested at that time, 111 were children under age 16. Juvenile court judge Hudson Malone turned over 69 youths to their parents, but 42, considered "second offenders," though under 16 years of age, remained under arrest.[92]

While Dr. King remained in jail, Rev. Abernathy posted bond and once free announced to reporters that SCLC was now leading the protests in Albany. This announcement disturbed both the Albany Movement leaders and the SNCC organizers and caused a minor split in the protest campaign. Marion Page of the Albany Movement said SCLC had not "taken over" the protest and sought to reopen negotiations with Mayor Kelley. Page also announced that no further demonstrations would be carried out.[93] While the peaceful demonstrations were suspended, the economic boycott continued and carried over into the next year. The protest movement led to the bankruptcy and closing down of the Albany Bus Company in February 1962.[94]

There were no changes in the practice of racial segregation in public accommodations in the city of Albany in January 1962. Each time high school or college students, with or without the support of the leaders of the Albany Movement, organized nonviolent protests, the police responded "nonviolently" and arrested the students and others, who were then held until their bond was paid or they served their sentence.[95] Frustrated with the lack of progress in negotiation with city leaders, Albany Movement leaders asked Dr. King and SCLC organizers to return to participate in another round of protests in July 1962. Dr. King and Rev. Abernathy led a group of over five hundred marchers into downtown Albany on Monday, July 9. Confronted by police chief Pritchett and his men, they were ordered to disperse, and when they refused they were arrested.[96] Eleven teenagers who marched with King and were arrested were sent to the juvenile detention center at Camilla.[97] At the mass meetings held following the arrests, some people hurled bricks and bottles at police cars stationed outside the event. No one was hurt or arrested. The next day, in one of the strangest events in King's and Abernathy's careers as civil rights activists, they were released from jail. When asked why they were being freed, Chief Pritchett indicated that an "unidentified benefactor" had paid their fines. King was quoted as admitting, "This is one time I am out of jail that I am not happy to be out."[98]

King and Albany Movement leaders met with Chief Pritchett the next day and sought the release of the eleven teenagers held at the detention center, the charges dropped against those who were arrested in December 1961, and the return of the cash bond paid upon release. Pritchett agreed only to substitute the "$400 security bonds" for cash bonds paid earlier. Those arrested would have to sign over their property if the cash bond was returned. The police chief also vetoed the demand for the formation of a "biracial committee" to work on "racial grievances" in the city and claimed that racial segregation at the bus and train stations was no longer being enforced in compliance with the ICC regulation. William Anderson, the Albany Movement leader, disagreed and said that African Americans who entered the white sections of the terminals were still being harassed by the police.[99]

Dr. King had to return to Atlanta, but from there he sent a telegram to Mayor Asa Kelley on July 16, signed by leaders of the Albany Movement, calling for a meeting with the city commission to negotiate the release of those arrested and the dropping of charges against more than seven hundred protesters arrested since December 1961. Mayor Kelley acknowledged receiving the telegram, but declared that "it is the decision of the commission not to deal with law violators." King responded that this left them no alternative but to renew nonviolent marches and demonstrations in Albany.[100] The demonstrations continued into August 1962, and King and Abernathy were arrested again along with hundreds of protesters, including many teenagers. While Dr. King was in jail, Attorney General Robert Kennedy intervened and spoke with him and Mayor Kelley in an attempt to end the demonstrations. Given some assurances from the mayor, King allowed himself to be released from jail, but other protesters were not. Indeed, Chief Pritchett continued to harass and arrest Black citizens who attempted to register to vote. As had occurred in July 1961, college and high school students began organizing marches and demonstrations in December 1962 at voter registration offices, and many were arrested.[101] However, after more than a year of marches, demonstrations, and over 1,200 arrests, it was clear that the Albany campaign had failed to achieve its objectives, public facilities remained segregated, and there was no large increase in the number of African Americans registered to vote in the city.

TEENAGE PROTESTERS IN AMERICUS, GEORGIA

Sam Malone was a high school student in Americus, Georgia, who had been active in the Albany Movement. In February 1963, when SNCC workers Ralph Allen, Don Harris, John Perdew, and Zev Aeloney arrived in Americus, they held several rallies and voter registration clinics. At the end of the 1962–63 school year, Malone, Alex Brown, and Robertina Freeman led several hundred high school students in picketing a local movie house that refused to desegregate. The police arrested many of the students at the site, but they were soon released. However, a week later the police arrested the four SNCC organizers, charging them with insurrection and violating Georgia's 1871 Treason Act. Historian Stephen G. N. Tuck documented SNCC's Southwest Georgia Project and pointed out that following the arrest and jailing of the Americus Four, "it was the presence and attitude of local high school students that fueled the movement."[102]

The teenagers published their own monthly newspaper, the *Voice of Americus*, and used its columns to report on civil rights activism in the region and to rally student support. Tuck found that the "students also accompanied [SNCC] staff workers in the less glamorous tasks of rural networking and organizing throughout Sumter County. Typically, five students would join two SNCC members in the shanties along the roads leading out of town." Throughout 1964 and early in 1965, voter registration activities took place, but it was the arrest of Alex Brown and Robertina Freeman in March 1965 and four local women in June 1965 that brought the teenagers and adults back into the streets of Americus. The protesters called for "the release of the women, police protection, . . . Saturday opening for [voter] registration, and a biracial committee to solve the impending racial crisis." Unfortunately, armed Black self-defense groups attending the nighttime rallies and the shooting of a young white marine recruit negatively affected the protest campaign in Americus. Tuck reported, "The demonstrations dissipated in the face of retaliatory violence and the uncompromising stance of the city government." Only with the passage of the Voting Rights Act in 1965 would SNCC's use of teenagers as canvassers in Americus and, in voter registration drives in rural areas, bring about a much-needed shift in the political environment in southwest Georgia.[103]

Chapter 4

The Birmingham Children's Crusade and Southern Student Activism

I remember saying to my Mama,
"Mom, this isn't right!"
Why do these people hate me,
Is it because their skin is white?
I didn't wait for an answer.
I just took to the streets.
And hordes of other children
Joined in with my beliefs.
We were thrown into jails,
But soon dignity came.
And in nineteen sixty-three,
The bell of freedom rang!

Gloria Washington Lewis-Randell (2005)[1]

"I WAS SIXTEEN in 1963, and I expected to be arrested." Larry Russell attended the meetings at Sixteenth Street Baptist Church leading up to the protest marches in Birmingham, Alabama, in May 1963. The meetings were mentioned by radio disk jockeys Shelley Stewart and Paul White, who announced, "There's going to be a party Monday night at six at Sixteenth Street Baptist Church . . . everyone invited." Russell and other teenagers understood there would not be a party at the Baptist church: "You knew it was coded for the protection of their jobs." Russell marched with the children and other teenagers on Thursday, May 2, and was arrested. "Jail was a totally different experience. . . . They took us in to be fingerprinted. Once the gate closed, we were treated like common criminals. We weren't treated like kids. . . . They wanted to make it uncomfortable for us, so they would call our parents to come and bail us out. But our intent was not to be bailed out."[2]

When we think of children and teenagers' contributions to the civil rights campaigns of the 1950s and 1960s, Birmingham's Children's Crusade in May 1963 immediately comes to mind. The photographs and videos of children, as young as 6 years old, marching in the streets and facing lines of policemen carrying billy clubs, who held back snarling dogs and wielded high-powered water hoses to stop the young people, are heart wrenching. The students were gathered up and loaded into police vans and buses and taken to jails, police stations, and makeshift holding locations where they were charged and held until bail was posted. The documentary film *Mighty Times: The Children's March* (2004), produced through the Southern Poverty Law Center's Teaching Tolerance Project, provides the most vivid account of the protest and what the children faced from Sheriff Eugene "Bull" Connor and his police forces.[3]

As has been emphasized in earlier chapters, children and teenagers were on the front lines of civil rights activism before and after the launching of the Montgomery bus boycott in 1955, considered by many historians the beginning of the Black-led *social movement* that brought about the end of apartheid—legal racial segregation—in the United States.[4] And in the history of the Civil Rights Movement, the Birmingham campaign is a turning point, leading to the introduction of a comprehensive civil rights bill into the US Congress by President John F. Kennedy in June 1963; the March on Washington on August 28, 1963, where over 250,000 people demonstrated their support for "jobs and freedom"; and the passage of civil rights legislation in June 1964.[5]

This chapter examines the protests in Birmingham and the impact they had on young people living there and in other parts of the South. After witnessing on television the social activism of young people in Birmingham, children and teenagers in North Carolina, Louisiana, South Carolina, and other states mobilized and mounted demonstrations to challenge racial discrimination in education, employment, and public accommodations.

THE BATTLE OF BIRMINGHAM

On December 17, 1962, Bethel Baptist Church in Birmingham was bombed. At the time of the explosion, twelve children were practicing for the Christmas play. No one was killed, but it was terrifying as debris rained down on the children in the basement, and an 8-year-old boy received minor injuries. The blast shattered windows in nearby homes, injuring a 7-month-old girl. This was the third time in three years that Bethel Baptist had been bombed and the latest in a long series of explosions aimed at terrorizing Black residents, especially those involved in civil rights campaigns in Alabama.[6] Rev. Fred Shuttlesworth had been pastor of Bethel Baptist and served as chair of the Alabama Christian Movement for Human Rights (ACMHR), organized in 1956 by a group of local Black ministers and residents to engage in civil rights activism after the NAACP was banned from operating in the state. The group's objective was to challenge the Jim Crow laws and practices in Birmingham and throughout Alabama and to file lawsuits to desegregate the schools and other public facilities. The ACMHR organized marches and demonstrations to protest not only racial discrimination but also police brutality.[7] This brought Rev. Shuttlesworth and ACMHR into direct conflict with Sheriff Bull Connor, Birmingham's longtime police chief. Thus, when the courts ruled in favor of the Montgomery Improvement Association in June 1956, ending legal racial segregation in public transit in the state, Rev. Shuttlesworth and ACMHR members attempted to desegregate the buses in Birmingham, but were arrested by Sheriff Connor's men. On Christmas Day 1956, Rev. Shuttlesworth's home was bombed, but luckily, he and his family were not injured.[8]

In September 1957 Rev. Shuttlesworth and his wife, Ruby, attempted to enroll two of their three children in all-white Philip High School, but on the way there they were attacked by Klansmen with chains and bats. Rev. Shuttlesworth received a slight concussion and his wife and one daughter received minor injuries. They did not return. Rev. Shuttlesworth became one of the founders of the SCLC in 1958 and subsequently worked on the group's voting rights campaign, the Crusade for Justice. When CORE's Freedom Riders reached Anniston, Alabama, on May 14, 1961, the bus they were traveling in was bombed. Shuttlesworth had them brought to

Birmingham to recuperate; and when the riders were prevented by white mobs from boarding buses to leave the city, Shuttlesworth made arrangements for them to take a plane to New Orleans.[9]

Rev. Shuttlesworth left Birmingham in 1961 to become pastor of Revelation Baptist Church in Cincinnati, Ohio, but as an officer in SCLC, he traveled back and forth to Birmingham throughout the 1960s to work with those engaged in civil rights campaigns in the city. Indeed, it was Shuttlesworth who finally persuaded Dr. King in 1962 that Birmingham should be SCLC's next target. After what he considered was the failure to bring about changes in racial practices in Albany, Georgia, using nonviolent protests—even after mobilizing large segments of the African American community, especially the young people—King was open to Shuttlesworth's recommendation.[10]

SCLC and SNCC organizers James Bevel, Andrew Young, and others began holding meetings in the Black churches in Birmingham in January 1963 to instruct local residents in nonviolent tactics. They also met with students at Miles College, the historically Black liberal arts institution located in Fairfield, Alabama, southwest of the city. The college students were recruited to engage in sit-ins at the department store lunch counters. Labeled Project C (for "confrontation"), the protest was launched on April 3, 1963, when Dr. King issued the "Birmingham Manifesto," which called for desegregation of all downtown department stores, including their lunch counters, restrooms, and drinking fountains; the hiring of Black workers in businesses and industries; and the formation of a biracial committee to develop a schedule for the desegregation of other public accommodations in the city.[11]

That day, the first sit-ins took place at lunch counters in five department stores; sixty-five people, mainly college students, were arrested. This was followed by silent marches down the main streets by several hundred people. To end the marches, Sheriff Connor obtained an injunction against further demonstrations from a state circuit court judge. Then another problem arose for SCLC: there was insufficient bail money for those who would be arrested. Acting on his strong religious faith, Dr. King decided that on Good Friday, April 12, 1963, he would march downtown in violation of the injunction. At a church rally the night before, he was able to convince a few others to join him, including 14-year-old Bernita Roberson.

"It was the Thursday before Good Friday, and my mother and father and I were in church," Roberson recalled. "Dr. King made a call for people to join him, and all these people said they'd go to jail with him." Roberson and her young friends volunteered and met at Sixteenth Street Baptist Church the next morning. "We held hands and just walked. . . . My father stood on the sidelines." With Dr. King in the lead, "the police stopped us about a block from the church." They told the marchers to disperse, "but I knew what I was going to have to do." The group knelt and prayed. Bull Connor and his men grabbed Dr. King and Rev. Ralph Abernathy by their belts and shoved them into paddy wagons and then began grabbing and loading the other protesters, including Roberson, into waiting vans. "They carried us to the county jail. All of us were in the same cell. There may have been about fifty people." The police then came for the children and took them to juvenile detention. "I was in jail for four days."[12]

On the day after the march and arrests, local white ministers published an open letter in the *Birmingham News* condemning the demonstrations as "ill-timed" and Dr. King and the SCLC and SNCC organizers as "outside agitators." From his jail cell, King decided to respond to the ministers' letter and wrote what became one of the most important statements ever written on nonviolent protest, "Letter from a Birmingham Jail." There King argued the oppressors never believe that the protests of the oppressed are "well-timed," and that he and the other civil rights activists came to Birmingham to protest because "injustice is here."[13] The letter was written on scraps of paper smuggled in by visitors, who then put them together into a statement and sent it to New York City. It was published as a pamphlet by the Friends of Negro Freedom, a support group, and used as a fund-raising vehicle for those jailed in Alabama.[14]

The marches continued over the next two weeks, but soon the movement stalled because all the adults who were willing to go to jail had been arrested. Once King was released, James Bevel and his wife, Diane Nash Bevel, who had been working with Bob Moses and Anne Moody for over a year with teenagers in Jackson, Mississippi, recommended using large numbers of children and teenagers in the protests. Rufus Burrow Jr., in *A Child Shall Lead Them: Martin Luther King, Jr., Young People, and the Movement*, describes in detail the arguments back and forth between King and

James Bevel in the hotel room in Birmingham about the advisability of using children, even very young children, in the civil rights protests. At first King would only agree to let high school students participate, but Bevel voiced his objections. Bevel "reminded King and others in the room that the black Baptist Church had never raised a concern over the fact that children join the church and make a faith commitment at five or six, and no adult member contests it." Bevel believed that young children "should be allowed to *live* their faith, even to the point of participating in demonstrations." It was not possible to shield African American children from the effects of white racism. King finally agreed, but only reluctantly. However, Bevel had the strong support of Andrew Young, Dorothy Cotton, Wyatt T. Walker, Hosea Williams, Fred Shuttlesworth, Ike Reynolds, and King's brother, A. D. (Alfred Daniel). Walker and Shuttlesworth agreed that "the children would get a better education in a week in incarceration than five months in school." And they were right.[15]

Annetta Streeter Gary was a junior at Samuel Ullman High School in Birmingham, in which about twelve hundred students were enrolled in the 1962-63 school year. On May 2, 1963, the day of the children's march, "Hosea Williams was the movement person" who came to the school, she recalled. "I think it was about one thousand and something children that came out of Ullman High School on that day. I can remember now the feeling. It was just like, 'It's here! It's about to happen!' And the joy of seeing all these children coming out to participate in the movement. It's a feeling you can't describe." Marching with the others downtown, the corner of Seventeenth Street "was when the water hose met us. . . . If they put the water hose on you, [you were supposed] to sit down and cover your face so that the pressure of the water [wouldn't] hurt your eyes." But that was not enough. "I can remember us balling up, hugging together, and the water just washing us down the street. Forceful. It was like pins maybe, sticking you in your arms and legs and things. The water was very, very forceful." Gary was arrested and her parents had to come and bail her out of jail. As was the case before and after the Birmingham campaign, her parents "began to attend the mass meetings after the first time [she] was arrested."[16]

Mary Gadson also attended Ullman High School and recalled that when the teenagers received word that it was time to go downtown to protest, "eleven hundred of us were over the fence. We were gone!" The young crusaders were talking and singing "a lot of the old spirituals like 'Go Down, Moses.' [They] considered Birmingham was Egypt." Gadson's group didn't make it downtown because the police stopped them. "Bull Connor was right out here on Sixth Avenue. He had dogs out there, and he said if we marched, he was going to turn the dogs on us. They had fire hoses also. That water was strong. It could knock you down. He let it go and sprayed us. I got wet, and I almost got bitten. There were hundreds of us." They ran, and Gadson was one of the lucky ones: "I wasn't arrested that day."[17]

Twelve-year-old Myrna Carter, like Larry Russell, was not so lucky. Her group of children made it all the way downtown. "When the police realized what had happened, some called a paddy wagon. They lined us up and snatched our signs from us." Carter recalled that "in jail we would have prayer meetings in the mornings and at twelve and at night. Prayers from your heart, and freedom songs and Negro hymns. One night when we were in jail, they bombed the Gaston Motel." They heard the explosion, but didn't know what had happened. "The police got on the P.A. system and started singing 'I Wish I Was in Dixie' over and over. But we didn't lose a beat. We just continued to sing our songs."[18]

Sixteen-year-old Willie A. Casey was a student at Carver High School and on May 1, 1963, "D-Day" (Demonstration Day), headed for the demonstrations with his friends. "We were walking for about two on three blocks, singing 'We Shall Overcome.' Then the police stopped us, let the dogs out, and put us in a paddy wagon. . . . They crammed us in there like sardines. It must have been thirty of us in there." The teenagers were first taken to the city jail and then by bus to the juvenile court and held there until two o'clock in the morning, when they were placed on another bus. Casey continued, it "carried us to Bessemer and put us in jail. We stayed down there about two weeks." His sister served as his guardian, but the family was not told where Casey was. "The cops didn't notify them." When Casey finally was released, James Orange, his next-door neighbor and a SNCC organizer, "came over and told [Casey] he was proud of [the teenager]. He said, 'You're a real man now.' It made me feel real good."[19]

Gwen Sanders Gamble was 16 years old and had participated in numerous sit-ins and other protests before D-Day and had been arrested. "My first arrest . . . I had to strictly scrub floors because I put my head down, and the punishment was to scrub floors with a toothbrush. I was arrested because I refused to move after being told by a [police] officer and also parading without a permit" in front of J. J. Newberry's restaurant. Gamble was placed in a paddy wagon with a police dog. "So from Newberry's to the jail, the dog was in the paddy wagon with us . . . to frighten us." Luckily, no one was bitten. Gamble and her two sisters were trained to recruit other students at Ullman High. On D-Day "all we had to do was give them a cue . . . and they followed."[20] Thousands of students were arrested and taken by school buses to the Birmingham fairgrounds where the police locked the children in open hog pens.[21]

The following day, May 2, 1963—Double D-Day—the students met at Sixteenth Street Baptist Church and then headed downtown. Once again Sheriff Connor shouted, "Bring the dogs. . . . Open up the hoses." The police attacked the children and teenagers and hundreds were arrested. Over the two days of marches and demonstrations, 2,500 people were arrested; 2,000 were children and teenagers. Gamble and her sisters were arrested at the demonstrations. She was later told that as an eleventh grader, she would be expelled. Her sister was a senior, and she was told she could not graduate. The expulsion from school of over a thousand elementary and high school students was challenged in court by the NAACP and eventually overturned. Carolyn Maull McKinstry was one of the high school students who participated in the demonstrations and was eventually allowed to return to school. However, she revealed that "for the following forty-six years, the state of Alabama refused to erase from its books the names of the two-thousand arrested children. The children had official criminal records that followed them throughout adulthood." It was not until August 2009 "that the city decided to pardon the children who had participated in the 1963 D-day and Double D-day protest."[22]

President John F. Kennedy watched the film footage on television of the children being assaulted by the police and he said it made him sick. He sent senior advisor Burke Marshall to the city to try to negotiate a settlement. Local businessmen understood the damage that the televised violence would have on the city's reputation. They encouraged the newly elected mayor Albert Boutwell to come to some kind of settlement with the civil rights leaders. They finally came up with the Birmingham Truce Agreement on May 10, which brought an end to the demonstrations and called for the desegregation of public facilities and the hiring of African Americans in downtown stores and other businesses in the city.[23]

While Dr. King was later quoted as saying that the Birmingham struggle was "the most significant victory for justice we've ever seen in the [D]eep South," Rev. Fred Shuttlesworth at the time, and many others later, disagreed, because it was based only on an oral agreement with white public officials and businessmen.[24] And less than a week after the truce was finally signed, the merchants began to backtrack on the terms of the agreement. As historian Rufus Burrow observed, "white resistance and racial violence continued in Birmingham and other Deep South cities long after the agreement."[25] In 1963 and 1964, the violence and discrimination did indeed continue, and the children and teenagers continued to seek out opportunities to become crusaders in the campaigns "to redeem the soul of America."[26]

"LET'S CRUSH SEGREGATION" IN NORTH CAROLINA

According to Lapois Ashford, NAACP national youth director, "The Task Force is a team of NAACP youth members who travel to different areas and who are capable of executing every type of civil rights program, such as fundraising drives, membership drives, direct action, negotiations, strategy conference[s], handl[ing] complaints of discrimination in all areas, and organiz[ing] an NAACP unit." Following the launching of the student sit-ins and the formation of SNCC in April 1960, Ashford prevailed upon the association's executive director, Roy Wilkins, to organize youth task forces that could be dispatched to assist local youth councils and NAACP branches in organizing nonviolent demonstrations, other civil rights activities, and fund-raising. Under the direction of the NAACP's state youth director, the youth task force in Clarksdale, Mississippi, came to be known as "the Bravados"; and in Jackson, Mississippi, they were "the Matadors."[27]

Attorney Floyd McKissick was the NAACP state youth officer in North Carolina, and the members of the task force there called themselves "the Commandos."[28] Historian Thomas Bynum examined the encounter between the Commandos and NAACP members in Monroe, North Carolina, in 1961. Under the leadership of NAACP branch president Robert Williams, local residents engaged in armed self-defense when confronted by violent white supremacists. Thus, in August 1961, following attacks by white racists, Williams led the Black residents in defending Black families in the hamlet of Newton, North Carolina, and several people were injured. Blamed for the violence and sought by the local police and federal authorities, Williams and his family fled to Cuba.[29] When the NAACP Commandos arrived in Monroe in June 1963, they found that the members of the Monroe Action Committee, formerly headed by Williams, were uninterested in nonviolent tactics and preferred armed resistance to white racist violence. Faced with little or no support, the Commandos left Monroe and headed for Fayetteville, North Carolina.[30]

When the student sit-ins erupted in Greensboro on February 1, 1960, they spread quickly to other cities and towns, especially in North Carolina. On February 10, 1960, forty students from Fayetteville State Teachers College conducted a sit-in at the Woolworth's and the McCrory's where they were denied service, and remained in their seats until the managers closed the lunch counters. A group of twelve students renewed the protests at Woolworth's two weeks later, on February 23. Negotiations were conducted with merchants by Mayor Wilbur Clark and led to promises of desegregation of public accommodations and nondiscriminatory hiring by the local government. These concessions affected the momentum of the protests, which then trailed off. However, there was little real change in race relations over the next two years. Bynum reported that by 1962, "although such promises were made, de facto discrimination continued in hiring, and businesses did not end their practices of segregation." However, the civil rights victory in Birmingham inspired the youth in Fayetteville to resume their efforts to bring about social and economic change.[31]

In May 1963, right after the Birmingham Crusade, students at Fayetteville State formed an organizing committee to begin nonviolent demonstrations in downtown Fayetteville. Led by 20-year-old Willis Mcleod, beginning on Saturday, May 18, 1963, the students rallied and, carrying signs declaring "Hire Us Now" and "Let's Crush Segregation," they marched downtown and formed picket lines in front of the major department stores and businesses. Soon local Black residents and NAACP members joined the students in manning the picket lines. Mayor Clark created a committee to meet with the protesters, and on May 27, their report was presented to the city council. The council members said they agreed with the demands for desegregation of public facilities and nondiscriminatory hiring practices, and the students decided to suspend the demonstrations.[32]

On Monday, June 10, 1963, following the arrival of the NAACP's Commandos, fifty students were dispatched to the downtown business district to determine if the promised changes in segregation and discrimination had taken place. The testers found they had not, and the next day, June 11, the students marched on downtown Fayetteville again, but this time the police told them to disperse. When they did not, twenty-six were arrested and one of the female protesters was severely beaten by the police. When news of the arrests and attack spread, teenagers from E. H. Smith High School and Washington Drive Junior High joined the protests downtown. This concerned the leaders of the marches, fearing that the teenagers would react violently to the verbal or physical confrontations. Indeed, 17-year-old Eric Freeman was arrested for allegedly "carrying a concealed weapon."[33]

The protests continued, and on Friday, June 14, more than a hundred teenagers in groups of fifteen picketed the downtown restaurants and stores. Then, over a hundred protesters occupied the lobby of the Hotel Rose while a large crowd of whites hurled insults and epithets. When the policemen arrived, they fired tear gas canisters into the hotel lobby. Twenty-three protesters who refused to leave the hotel were arrested. In the week that followed, over two hundred activists were arrested during the demonstrations.[34] At a mass meeting held on Monday, June 17, the teenagers and other young people pledged to continue the demonstrations until total desegregation was achieved. Mayor Clark summoned local businessmen to the negotiations and found that while some white restaurant owners were willing to desegregate, others were not, claiming they were being "blackmailed into surrender." Mayor Clark responded that the issue was "desegregation or bankruptcy—desegregation or bloodshed."[35]

North Carolina governor Terry Sanford, facing demonstrations in several cities, called for a suspension of the protests during a "cooling off period" while negotiations continued. In a televised address, he indicated that he would call out the National Guard if necessary to restore order. But he also emphasized that "by his demonstrations, the Negro citizen has de-livered his message that he is not content, that he has a burning desire to break down the barriers that prevent normal patronage in places open to the public."[36] Governor Sanford called for the application of the Durham Plan, devised after massive civil rights demonstrations in Durham, North Carolina, in May 1963, where over thirteen hundred protesters had been ar-rested. There the plan called for an end of demonstrations and daily reports to Black leaders and city officials on progress in desegregating public facili-ties. Those arrested in Durham were to be released and a nondiscriminatory employment policy implemented by the state government. Sanford called for a similar program in Fayetteville.[37] After negotiations were conducted by Mayor Clark, the managers of the major hotels and motels agreed to desegregate their facilities.[38]

Mayor Clark appointed a biracial committee to conduct further nego-tiations, but made little progress in convincing some store and restaurant owners to end discriminatory practices. The students and local residents resumed demonstrations on Friday, June 28, 1963. This time, in addition to the college and high school students, Black and white soldiers joined the marches and picket lines. By July 12, at least fifty soldiers were involved, with some carrying signs reading, "First Korea, Now Fayetteville, We Will Win Our Freedom" and "GIs and Students Unite for Civil Rights." Finally, on Friday, July 19, the NAACP negotiating team and Mayor Clark's com-mittee came up with a five-point plan that called for the hiring of Black workers by the government and local businesses and the end of segregation in public facilities including restaurants. The demonstrations ended, and by October 1963 the vast majority of public places in Fayetteville had been desegregated.[39]

CHILDREN AND TEENAGERS
MARCHING FOR JOBS AND FREEDOM

The background and history of the March on Washington on August 28, 1963, have been related in numerous books and articles. Among the 250,000 marchers on the capital's Mall were hundreds of children and teen-agers, some of them veterans of civil rights campaigns in various parts of the country. For others, the march served as a spark for future activism.[40] Eighteen-year-old Jimmie Lee Pruitt from Greenville, Mississippi, entered the Mall wearing a sandwich board. On one side it said "Stop Criminal Prosecution of Vote Workers in Mississippi"; the other side read "We Must Have the Vote in Mississippi by 1964." All signs to be displayed by marchers had to be approved by the march's leaders. As Pruitt entered the Mall, a marshal stopped him. "Has your sign been approved?" "It's mine," he replied. "Come with me." When his companion saw what was happening, he shouted to Pruitt, "Show them your paper."[41]

The paper contained the story of Jimmy Lee Pruitt's participation in civil rights campaigns for almost two years. Indeed, he had been arrested in Greenwood for picketing and was sentenced to fifty-two days in the local jail and then was sent to Parchman Penitentiary, where he was placed in a cell with thirteen other demonstrators. Their clothes were taken away and "their bodies were greased. They were told that the grease was poison and not to get it in their mouths." At one point they were placed in the "sweat box," a six-by-six cell, and after several hours Pruitt blacked out. "Electric fans were turned on the naked men shivering in the cold." After reading the note, the security officer gave it back. "Let Mr. Pruitt march with his signs." The next day, Jimmy Lee Pruitt returned to Mississippi and continued his civil rights activism.[42]

The beautiful singer and actress Lena Horne was not feeling well on the day of the march, so when actor and emcee Ossie Davis ushered her to the podium, she said one word very loudly, "Freee-eee-dommm!" The crowd erupted, and in that crowd was a high school student from Washington, DC, Ericka Jenkins. When everyone in her school started talking about the upcoming event, Jenkins went home and announced, "Mama, I'm going to the march." Her mother responded, "No you're not! Something will happen." Ericka told her mother, "You taught us to respect and support our people." "I didn't mean *you*," she replied. But on the day of the march, Ericka Jenkins took the bus to the Washington Monument and stayed all day. She saw Native Americans and Chinese Americans, as well as whites and African Americans, and was inspired by the speeches. Jenkins made a commitment and accepted a "calling"—that is "when you know down deep in your heart you're meant to do something." At the march Jenkins made a "vow to go to college, do something for children, and fight racism . . . no matter where it took [her]."[43]

Raymond Greene was only 8 years old when the march took place. He lived in the District, and the reflecting pool and Lincoln Memorial were among his favorite places. "I still remember the day of the march how I looked into the [reflecting] pool and saw all the different faces of people. . . . Many carried signs that revealed where they were from: Hawaii, California, Maine, Georgia, Mississippi." And Greene recalled the children in attendance. "I also remember a lot of children there, some younger than me, sitting on the shoulders of their fathers. Babies were cradled in their mothers' arms. I had never seen that many people in my life." Greene did not remember hearing any of the speeches, but he did remember the clapping: "It sounded like thunder."[44]

But one aspect of the march is often overlooked. While Dr. King's speech is well known and the participation of NAACP executive Roy Wilkins and SNCC's John Louis is often discussed, James Farmer, the national chairman of the fourth major civil rights organization, CORE, was not present. Farmer could not attend because he was in jail in Plaquemine, Louisiana, "with children and teenagers."[45] Farmer did send a statement, however, that was read by Floyd McKissick, the NAACP's youth director in North Carolina. Farmer wrote:

> From a south Louisiana parish jail, I salute the march on Washington for jobs and freedom. Two hundred and thirty-two freedom fighters jailed with me in Plaquemine, La., also send you greetings. . . . You have come from all over the nation and in one mighty voice you have spoken to the nation. You have also spoken to the world. You have said to the world . . . violence is outmoded to the solution of problems of men. It is a truth that needs to be shouted loudly. And no one else in the world is saying it as well as the American Negro[es] through their nonviolent direct action. The tear gas and electric cattle prods of Plaquemine, like the fire hoses and dogs of Birmingham, are giving to the world a tired and ugly message of brutality and terror and hate. . . . We will not slow down. . . . We will not stop our marching people until our children have enough to eat and their minds study a wide range without being cramped in Jim Crow schools. . . .[46]

It is important to note that after James Farmer was bailed out and returned to New York City, it was Black elementary and high school students who eventually took over the CORE-initiated protests and demonstrations in Plaquemine. These young crusaders were beaten, teargassed, struck with electric cattle prods, and jailed under circumstances similar to what the children and teenagers experienced in Birmingham.

"THE TEEN-AGERS HAVE TAKEN OVER THE PROTEST DEMONSTRATIONS": LOUISIANA, 1963

CORE had been operating in Louisiana since the summer of 1960, and in May 1961, its members in New Orleans provided resources and housing for Freedom Riders who had been attacked in Anniston, Alabama. Afterward, CORE organizers began working in various towns and cities throughout Louisiana and recruited college students and local adults to participate in civil rights demonstrations and voting rights campaigns.[47] In July 1963, CORE organizer Ronnie Moore arrived in Plaquemine at the request of William Harleaux, principal of Seymourville Elementary School in Iberville Parish. Harleaux was also president of Iberville Independent Voters League, and his school served as headquarters for the voter registration campaign in Iberville and the surrounding parishes. Twenty-year-old Ronnie Moore organized several meetings at Plymouth Rock Baptist Church, led by Rev. Jetson C. Davis. While there were an estimated 9,995 white and 2,700 Black voters registered in Iberville Parish, there were few (if any) African Americans registered to vote in Plaquemine, and the city's mayor, Charles Schnebelen, made it clear that he preferred it that way.[48]

In July 1963, Ronnie Moore, William Harleaux, Rev. Davis, and others organized sit-ins and picket lines in front of stores and restaurants and even at the ferry lines that carried people and goods back and forth across the Mississippi River. CORE chairman James Farmer came to Plaquemine to support the local activists, and on Monday, August 19, 1963, after a rally at Plymouth Rock Baptist Church, he marched along with local adults, teenagers, and children toward Plaquemine's city hall. Along the way the protesters were stopped by police and told by Chief Dennis Songy to disperse. Within minutes, however, the police began hurling tear gas canisters at the marchers, used electric cattle prods on them, and then started making arrests as many ran back to the church. Over two hundred people were taken into police custody, including children between 7 and 14 years old.[49] Farmer recalled, "The town jail did not have space for all of us so the local leaders and I were transferred to the jail in the neighboring town of Donaldsonville."[50]

The next day, August 20, protesters held a rally at Plymouth Rock Church and then marched downtown and launched sit-ins targeting restaurants and department stores. The police arrived and arrested over two hundred people, and the overflow was imprisoned in a warehouse that served as a makeshift jail. Several teenagers were sent to jail in Donaldsonville with Farmer, and many were held in the warehouse-prison in Plaquemine. When city officials obtained an injunction on Thursday, August 22, prohibiting CORE from carrying out further protests, Moore and other leaders called for a halt to the demonstrations. Rudy Lombard, CORE national vice chairman, had come to Plaquemine from New Orleans, and on Saturday night, August 24, he led 150 marchers to the warehouse-prison where the protesters were being held. They sang freedom songs, prayed, and marched back to the church. The police did not stop or arrest them.[51]

On Sunday morning, August 25, several Black activists attempted to attend services at all-white churches in Plaquemine. Teenagers were among those welcomed at St. James Episcopal Church and Northside Baptist Church; and they were among those told to leave by the members of the First Baptist and First Methodist churches.[52] CORE's lawyers were able to get the injunction lifted on August 29, and that day James Farmer and eleven others were arraigned and pled "not guilty" to disturbing the peace and other charges. Farmer and several others were released on three hundred dollars bail and their trials were set for Tuesday, September 3, 1963.[53] The targets of the protests in Plaquemine had been two downtown restaurants, City Café and Colonial House Café, and the sixty-nine people who had made it that far were also arrested. At least fifteen children were injured in the earlier church attack and two had to be taken to the hospital. James Farmer called the attack "an outrage"; it was the first time he had witnessed "horses trample, [and] kick . . . children" who were "later hospitalized."[54]

In light of the attack and given Judge E. Gordon West's injunction, further demonstrations were placed on hold. At his trial on September 3,

Farmer was convicted of disturbing the peace and blocking the sidewalk, but the riot charge was dropped. Fifteen others arrested with Farmer were convicted of a variety of charges. Interestingly, Mayor Charles Schnebelen also presided over the trials by serving as municipal court judge. Ronnie Moore was convicted on two charges, but those against a teenage girl were dropped, and a 16-year-old boy was turned over to juvenile authorities. William Harleaux had four charges against him, and he was convicted on all of them. CORE attorney Murphy Bell announced that he planned to appeal all the defendants' convictions.[55]

Unsurprisingly, Chief Songy managed to obtain another injunction, this time from Judge West banning further demonstrations in Plaquemine. James Farmer attended a rally that evening, September 3, at Plymouth Rock Church. As the protesters made their way toward the downtown, they again came under attack from police deputies and state troopers on horseback. Some people ran back into the church, and the police hurled tear gas inside, burning the activists' eyes and throats. As those trapped scrambled and made their way to the exits or climbed through the church's windows, they were met by the police, who arrested them. White bystanders in the streets joined in the attack, chasing James Farmer, Ronnie Moore, Rev. Jetson Davis, and several hundred others into a nearby funeral hall.[56]

The state troopers soon arrived and began kicking at the door of the funeral hall clamoring for Farmer, claiming they had a warrant for his arrest. The woman funeral director opened the door and asked to see the warrant, and when it was not produced, she refused to allow the troopers to enter.[57] Many of the men inside had guns and were ready to use them. After a few minutes there was a knock on the door. It was Lolis Elie and Robert Collins, two civil rights attorneys from New Orleans, who had learned about the manhunt. They had crawled through the high grass in the graveyard to get there. Then there was another knock at the door. It was "Fred and Bill, ex-marines who carried several guns in their cars at all times." The four men hatched a plan to send out one of the two hearses first, as a decoy to distract the troopers, while Farmer and two others were hidden in the second, driven by Fred and Bill. "Ronnie Moore, Rev. Davis, and I crawled into the back and crouched down. . . . Soon we were off, speeding down the back roads to New Orleans." The following day Farmer called a press conference in New Orleans and announced he was returning to Plaquemine. Attorney Lolis Elie informed FBI agents in New Orleans about the manhunt that occurred. So when Farmer, Moore, and Rev. Davis returned to Plaquemine, "to our relief, five or six FBI agents were on the steps of the courthouse." Farmer learned there was no warrant for his arrest "and no charges were filed against me."[58]

That same month in Hammond, Louisiana, teenagers took the lead in the direct action campaigns there.[59] After attending meetings with Ronnie Moore and other civil rights organizers, the students at all-Black Greenville Park High School left their classes in the middle of the afternoon of September 5, 1963, and headed toward downtown Hammond. As the young people marched, they entered and attempted to gain service at several restaurants and commercial businesses, but were refused. A student leader, 17-year-old senior Herbert Brown Jr., declared that they were "seeking access to all public accommodations and the formation of a biracial committee."[60] When the teenagers arrived at Hammond city hall, Tangipahoa Parish sheriff's deputies and Hammond policemen told them this was an illegal assembly and they had to disperse. There were no arrests, however, and after a few minutes the students made their way back to Greenville Park High. Hammond's mayor, John Morrison, later claimed he had received no demands from the students, but said he would meet with their leaders "after they made an appointment."[61]

When the students arrived back at Greenville Park High, they found out they had been suspended by the principal, Manley Youngblood. The principal had learned that the march was not a spontaneous event, but they had met the night before, on September 4, to plan the protest. Principal Youngblood told the students they could not return for a week. But the next day, rather than staying home, the suspended students set up picket lines in front of the school and announced a boycott. Principal Youngblood offered to let them return if they accepted "school work penalties" for their actions. The students refused, and Herbert Brown, their spokesperson, presented the students' demands: desegregation of public facilities, including public parks, recreation centers, and schools in Hammond, and the formation of a biracial committee to address important racial issues.[62]

Aware of the negative impact of the Birmingham conflagration on the economy in that city, Mayor Morrison decided to meet with Herbert Brown and several adult leaders in late September 1963 to try and end further protests. As a result of these meetings, Morrison established a quasi-official biracial committee in Hammond because, according to historian Adam Fairclough, local "businessmen [had] awakened to the fact that racial violence and racial disorder acted as a powerful brake on economic growth."[63] However, in locations where African Americans were a potential majority of the voting population, state leaders continued to maintain the barriers to African American citizens becoming part of the electorate. Teenagers were recruited by civil rights activists to participate in voter registration drives, but many obstacles remained in place.[64]

The bombing of Sixteenth Street Baptist Church in Birmingham on September 15, 1963, killing four little girls preparing for Sunday school, served as an event, as with the murder of Emmett Till in Money, Mississippi, in 1955, that propelled children and teenagers into greater social activism. It often goes unreported that in Birmingham in the week after the church bombing, 16-year-old Johnny Robinson was killed by a white policeman for allegedly "throwing rocks at cars"; and 13-year-old Virgil Ware was shot and killed while riding his bicycle in a white neighborhood. Governor George Wallace decided to call out the state National Guard to try and prevent further "vigilante violence" in Birmingham.[65] Rallies were held in San Francisco, Chicago, New York, and other cities throughout the United States to protest what was taking place in "Bombingham."[66] In Philadelphia, protesters marched through the streets of Center City, and thousands of young people attended mass meetings at churches and the memorial service at Convention Hall to denounce the "Birmingham massacre."[67] Teenagers would soon join the front lines in the campaign launched by the Philadelphia NAACP to end racial discrimination at Girard College, a state-supported private school that barred African Americans.

Earlier that month, on September 3, 1963, at all-Black Iberville High School in Plaquemine, Louisiana, after learning that a beloved cafeteria worker, Stella Grant, had been fired for participating in the CORE demonstrations downtown, the students organized a "luncheon boycott." Upon leaving the cafeteria, about 150 students held a rally at the football field, and then returned to their classes.[68] A week after the Sixteenth Street Baptist

Church bombing, CORE's Ronnie Moore and Rev. Jetson Davis of Plymouth Rock Baptist Church urged local residents to boycott the downtown businesses in Plaquemine until Black residents were allowed to register to vote. Then on Thursday, October 3, 1963, about five hundred students at Iberville High organized an anti-segregation rally in the auditorium, sang freedom songs, and marched through the halls to the office of home economics teacher Oralee Grant, calling for her firing. They labeled her an "Uncle Tom" and "Aunt Thomasina" because she continued to shop at stores being boycotted by the rest of the Black community. When school district officials arrived at Iberville High to deal with the disturbance, 17-year-old Alandus Faye Williamson charged that school superintendent L. H. Hoffman slapped her. Immediately afterward, her father announced his plan to file assault charges against the white administrator.[69]

The teenagers gathered on Friday, October 4, and announced their plans for another demonstration on the following Monday. But the next day, Saturday, October 5, they learned that between thirty and seventy students who helped to organize the demonstration were placed on "indefinite suspension" by Principal W. O. Williams. That weekend the teenagers gathered to protest the suspensions and put forth additional demands, including equal employment opportunities in the local government, the desegregation of all parish public schools, and the rehiring of cafeteria worker Stella Grant.[70] Then on Monday, October 7, they decided to boycott their classes, gather together four hundred strong, and march on the school district office.

When Plaquemine police chief Songy learned the teenagers were on the move, he called out his police officers to block the streets the students would have to pass to get to the school board's office. When the teenagers reached the barricaded streets, the police began hurling tear gas grenades into their midst. Songy threw the first grenade, later claiming the teenagers "tried to walk over him." The students were routed by the tear gas, and they broke up into small groups and headed in every direction. Sixteen-year-old Kenneth Johnson Jr., one of the leaders of the protest, said that two girls fainted after breathing in the tear gas. Plaquemine Sanitarium reported that many students showed up suffering breathing problems from the tear gas exposure. Seven girls made it to the steps of the Plaquemine High

School—for whites only—where they sat in until the police came along and chased them away.[71]

The teenagers were angered by the police assault, and the next morning, October 8, they came together at Rev. Davis's Plymouth Rock Church and rechristened it "Freedom Rock Baptist Church." From there, several hundred headed toward downtown and Plaquemine High. There, the forces of police chief Songy and parish sheriff C. A. Griffon Jr., acting jointly, confronted the teenagers and again launched tear gas grenades to disperse them. About seventy-five students made it back to the church, and Songy and his men came after them. At the front door Songy announced that this was an illegal gathering and the teenagers had to leave. "If they want to use the church to serve God, that's okay, but they can't use it as a fort." Rather than allowing them time to decide, the police began firing tear gas grenades into the church. The teens, routed by the fumes, began jumping through the church windows, and the police arrested them. Songy said he had warned the students if they gathered in the church, "I was going to break it up." However, 16-year-old Dorasteen Harris declared, "Segregated education is worse than tear gas. If I have to graduate [from] a segregated school, I don't want to graduate." CORE organizer Ronnie Moore said he was contacting the US Justice Department about the ongoing police brutality in Plaquemine, but FBI agents had been present from the first tear gas attack on nonviolent protesters back on August 19 and did nothing.[72]

On Wednesday morning, October 9, nine Black high school students staged a sit-in at a downtown restaurant that refused to serve African Americans. The students sat in the booths and waited. The police entered the restaurant carrying electric cattle prods, and Chief Songy shouted, "All right, let's get out." The young people bolted toward the door, and most made it past the police, but one girl was caught. "Hold her!" Songy shouted, then "he touched her with the cattle prod several times before she was freed." The police chief claimed later that the electricity was not turned on. The children were chased down the street for about a block. Two adult leaders, James Payne and Clarence Oubre, were soon arrested. So Charles M. Hargroder, a reporter for the *New York Times,* declared, "The teen-agers have taken over the protest demonstrations" in Plaquemine, "started by the Congress of Racial Equality in August." Student leader Kenneth Johnson announced that they had formed their own "Committee on Freedom that had no connection with CORE." About forty youngsters then regrouped, locked arms, and marched down the street singing freedom songs. When Chief Songy and his men showed up and started firing tear gas shells and grenades, the teenagers took flight.[73]

The student boycott at Iberville High School was very effective. With a regular daily attendance of 630, in the week of October 7, 1963, only 125 students were present on average. Moreover, the boycott spread to the all-Black Seymourville Elementary School. That semester the school had an enrollment of 945 students, but less than half (416) were present that week. Iberville Parish school officials threatened to bring in truant officers to deal with the boycotting students and claimed that those students who "miss more than five days of school without a legitimate excuse will not be promoted" to the next grade.[74]

Iberville Parish sheriff Griffon managed to obtain a preliminary injunction against CORE from Judge Daniel P. Kimball on October 10 to end further demonstrations by the teenagers and order the closure of the two schools. The restraining order named specific defendants, including William Harleaux, Bertrand Tyson, Ronnie Moore, and four others. Then sheriff's deputies began serving preliminary injunctions on any students they encountered in the streets of Plaquemine.[75] Kenneth Johnson was one of the first students served and was arrested and taken to the State Industrial School for Colored Youth. His father, Kenneth Johnson Sr., immediately filed a writ of habeas corpus to have his son released, but district judge Jess Johnson denied it. However, the judge did grant state attorney Sergeant Pilcher Jr.'s request for the arrest of CORE organizer Ronnie Moore for violation of probation. Moore had been placed on probation after being arrested following protests in Baton Rouge by the Southern University students in 1961. Sheriff Griffon finally agreed to meet with eight Black parents, led by Dave McNair, who sought the sheriff's assistance in obtaining a meeting with district superintendent L. H. Hoffman or members of the school board "before things [led] to bloodshed." However, the parents could reach no agreement with school officials, and Iberville High and Seymourville Elementary remained closed.[76]

During their meeting with Sheriff Griffon, he told the Black parents that any students who were absent from school the following week would be arrested. This threat helped to bring an end to the boycott. On Monday, October 14, Black students began to return to Iberville High and Seymourville Elementary School, and it was reported that 500 of the 630 high school students enrolled were in attendance. The elementary school enrolled 945, and 861 were in attendance. Kenneth Johnson, who had been released from the reform school, did not show up at Iberville High on Monday and was arrested, along with other student leaders, at the order of Sheriff Griffon, who accused them of violating the state's compulsory attendance laws.[77]

The teenagers, including Kenneth Johnson, were released later that day and returned to Iberville High on Tuesday, October 15. However, Ronnie Moore remained in jail for several days, and local Black leaders William Harleaux and Bertrand Tyson were released on bond and were placed on probation. The boycott of the white merchants downtown continued into the winter of 1964.[78] Once released, Moore continued the voter registration drive and put forward a slate of Black candidates to challenge the racist sheriff and other white politicians in the Democratic primary in Iberville Parish in December 1963. None of the Black candidates won, but Sheriff Griffon was ousted, along with other "cattle-prod wielding politicians."[79]

YOUTH ACTIVISM ACROSS THE SOUTH

In the wake of the Children's Crusade and the bombing of Sixteenth Street Baptist Church in Birmingham, there were many other reports in 1963 of instances where children and teenagers participated in and organized their own direct-action protest campaigns. In Clinton, Louisiana, East Feliciana Parish, in the summer of 1963, CORE organizer Herbert E. Vickery (white) had been mobilizing African American young people to participate in a voter registration drive and to protest overt racial discrimination in public accommodations. On Friday, October 11, 1963, teenagers in Clinton launched picketing in front of the downtown businesses. After receiving complaints from white business owners, Sheriff Arch Doughty and district attorney Richard Kilbourne obtained an injunction from Judge John Rarick against CORE to prevent further demonstrations. The police raided the CORE office in Clinton on Saturday, October 12, and arrested Herbert

Vickery. The sheriff and district attorney confronted the teenagers working there, told them to leave the office, and when they refused, they also were arrested. All thirty-one of those arrested were teenagers; eight were under 17 years old.[80]

Once arrested, the teens were charged with criminal mischief and in contempt of the restraining order issued by Judge Rarick. Twenty-four were held for bail, while the eight who were under seventeen were turned over to juvenile authorities. CORE organizer Vickery was held and charged with "contributing to the delinquency of minors." In the raid of the CORE office, sheriff deputies claimed that they found "controversial literature of a Marxist nature." It was also reported that FBI agents were present during the picketing downtown and took photographs but did not intervene.[81] CORE organizers Ronnie Moore and Rudy Lombard contacted the Justice Department about events in Clinton. On October 17, 1963, when Rev. Joseph Carter and forty-two Black farmers went to the courthouse in West Feliciana Parish to register to vote, FBI agents were present. After waiting five hours, Rev. Carter was registered, but all the others were disqualified.[82]

That evening and the following day, white mobs went on the rampage and attacked the homes of Rev. Carter and several of the Black farmers who tried to register. Ronnie Moore alerted the FBI to the attacks, but the racial violence soon ended when the Black farmers armed themselves. "Negroes have vowed to shoot on sight any white face which appears on their property after dark," Moore reported. "Unless Negro citizens are protected and their civil rights guaranteed, blood, both black and white, will be shed."[83] When the voter registration project stalled, CORE organizer Miriam Feingold (white) and Black teenagers attempted to desegregate the Clinton public library in March 1964, but they were arrested. CORE had more success with its call for a national boycott of the Princeville Cannery Company that was accused of discriminating against African American farmers who attempted to register to vote. Fearing economic disaster, company officials decided it would be better to purchase all the Black farmers' crops.[84]

In Memphis, Tennessee, two years earlier, in August 1961, fifty African American children applied for admission to the first grade classes in all-white public schools. The mayor, Henry Loeb, warned school board members that if some Black children were not allowed to enroll in the first grade, they may try and gain admission to the other twelve grades.[85] School officials were able to enroll Black children in four previously all-white public schools in September 1961 before most whites in the city were informed.[86] But there was little movement beyond the first grade in these four schools over the next year, and African Americans parents complained that school desegregation was moving at a snail's pace.[87] By August 1963, overcrowding in the all-Black public schools was severe and most were operating on double shifts. School officials still refused to allow African Americans to transfer to under-enrolled, all-white schools. On August 29, 1963, NAACP leaders organized a protest march of over five hundred teen-agers and adults opposed to the double shifts at all-Black public schools. This was the first mass rally and civil rights march in Memphis in two years, but many followed, culminating with the sanitation workers' strike in 1967.[88]

With the eruption of sit-ins in February 1960, students at all-Black South Carolina State College (SCSC) and Claflin College in Orange-burg launched their nonviolent protests against the downtown department stores and restaurants. Earlier, in 1955 and 1956, SCSC and Claflin students had participated in the economic boycott organized by the local NAACP against white businesses that discriminated against African Americans. During the sit-in protest on February 10, 1960, the police used water hoses and tear gas against the students. Historian Thomas Bynum reported that "during the melee, a seventeen-year-old blind girl from South Carolina State was knocked to the ground by the high pressured water hoses." Many other student protesters were rounded up and jailed by the police. The violence leveled against the students engaging in nonviolent protests dem-onstrated the difficulty in challenging entrenched racial discrimination backed by the police and state officials.[89]

Gloria Blackwell Rackley, a third grade teacher, emerged as the leader in the next phase of civil rights protests and mobilization in Orangeburg. Rackley not only engaged personally in nonviolent direct-action protests, she also encouraged children and teenagers to become involved. In October 1961, Rackley was arrested for sitting in the whites-only hospital where she had taken her daughter who had injured her finger. She eventually filed a lawsuit, *Rackley v. Tri-County Hospital* (1962), against the hospital for her arrest and won. The criminal charges were dropped, and the hospital became the first to be desegregated in South Carolina.[90]

As an NAACP officer in 1963, Gloria Rackley worked with C.H. Thomas, a professor at South Carolina State College, on the development of a ten-point program for the desegregation of public schools and other facilities in Orangeburg. Initially the program was ignored by the city's white leaders.[91] However, the high school and college students became active in what become known as the Orangeburg Movement, participating in sit-ins and picketing at courthouses, restaurants, and other places open to the public. Rackley's religious background undergirded her protest activities, and thus "protesters always prayed before they went out to a demonstration." Rackley and her daughters were among the estimated 1,500 people arrested in the downtown protests in September 1963; the vast majority were teenagers. In an interview Rackley recalled, "I would take a carload of children, . . . my children and others to the protests." One group of young crusaders charged with breach of the peace refused to pay the fine and remained in jail for eight days.[92]

The following month, Rackley was fired from her teaching position for her civil rights activism. In the letter of dismissal, the superintendent claimed that she was "rabid in her zeal for social change and thus was unfit to be a teacher." In response to the firing, Rackley's fellow Black teachers in the public schools went on strike and organized picket lines outside seven public schools.[93] The teachers and students boycotted the schools for over a week until Rackley urged them to return to their classes because she felt it could be detrimental to the students' overall education. The boycott was ended, but the protests continued. Indeed, her teenage daughter Lurma was arrested so often in the protests that she was sentenced to reform school, but Rackley pointed out, "the family was able to have the sentence suspended."[94]

NAACP leaders in Orangeburg then launched the Don't Buy Here boycott campaign and set up picket lines at downtown stores. There was evidence that some white merchants were hurt by the boycott because African Americans were 60 percent of the population in Orangeburg. But some businessmen remained defiant, and when asked about the impact of the boycott, one merchant claimed, "Some of these people could stand 10 years of boycott and not be hurt." However, another store owner reported that when he closed the lunch counter due to the sit-ins, he lost over half his business. NAACP leaders asked Mayor Clyde Sair to convene a biracial committee to address the civil rights demands, but he refused because he was "opposed to integration."[95]

On October 23, 1963, the Orangeburg police arrested fifty-six children and teenagers and two adults for parading without a permit. Gloria Rackley argued, however, that the marchers were on their way to city hall to obtain a permit to mount a demonstration and parade in the streets. The youngsters spent the night in jail before being released.[96] Gloria Rackley filed a lawsuit against the school district for her firing, won, and was reinstated. The Orangeburg NAACP continued to support the civil rights protests mounted by high school and college students and others in the following year, which laid the groundwork for passage of the Civil Rights Act in June 1964.[97]

In October 1963 not only children and teenagers in southern cities and towns were engaged in school boycotts and other civil rights protests but also hundreds of thousands of youngsters in Boston, Chicago, New York, and other northern cities were mobilized and began participating in massive school boycotts as part of the campaigns for quality integrated schooling.

PART II

The Quality Integrated Education Movement

Chapter 5

Freedom Day Boycotts

Chicago, Boston, and New York City

*It's early Tuesday morning and the news is good—only three
children attended school out of 1600 at the Wadsworth School.
Only 200 showed up out of 3800 at Hyde Park High
where there was a powerful lot of teacher pressure.
Only 20 out of Dunbar [High's] 2300 attended school.*

Chicago Daily Defender
October 23, 1963

THE MAJOR ISSUE in Black Chicagoans' increasing demands for educational change in the 1950s and 1960s was the extreme overcrowding in
Chicago public schools (CPS) in Black neighborhoods. The Second Great
Migration brought over 300,000 African Americans to the Windy City
between the end of World War II and 1970. The number of public school
students in Chicago rose from 375,000 in 1953 to 520,000 in 1963, and Black
enrollment skyrocketed. New schools were being opened almost monthly
to accommodate the increasing enrollment, but it was not enough. CPS
officials' response initially was to place overcrowded schools on double
shifts—one group of students would attend from 8:00 a.m. to 12:00 noon,
and a second group from noon to 4:00 p.m. The double-shift burden, however, was not shared equally by all students. In 1960, African Americans
were 40 percent of CPS enrollment but were 90 percent of students on

double shifts. In 1962, at least thirty-five predominantly Black elementary schools in Chicago were on double shifts.[1]

Not only were the students on double shifts receiving less instructional time, but this reduced school schedule also proved to be an obvious burden for working parents. Some parents attempted to enroll their children in nearby all-white public schools that had underutilized facilities and were not on double shifts, but these transfer requests were usually denied by CPS officials. At the beginning of September 1961, the complaints of African American parents about these decisions were publicized regularly in the pages of the *Chicago Defender*, the leading Black newspaper. The issue of overcrowding and the denial of transfers to underutilized, all-white schools was then taken up by the Chicago branch of the NAACP, under the leadership of Rev. Carl Fuqua, and over a hundred parents from the Chatham–Avalon Park neighborhood were recruited to participate in Operation Transfer.[2]

When CPS officials denied the 160 transfer requests, the parents, with NAACP assistance, filed a lawsuit, *Webb v. Board of Education, Chicago*, in which they accused CPS of engaging in de jure and de facto racial segregation. Earlier that year in a ruling on the increasing racial segregation in New Rochelle, New York, public schools, federal judge Irving R. Kaufman ordered that the court-mandated desegregation plans be carried out in this *northern* city where legal racial segregation had been banned for over a century. "It is of no moment whether the segregation is labeled . . . de jure (according to law) or de facto, as long as the [school] board, by its conduct, is responsible for its maintenance," Kaufman ruled. The lawsuit filed by Chicago parents was based on this precedent and made a similar argument: the denial of Black students' requests for transfer to under-enrolled, all-white schools meant that the school administration saw nothing wrong with maintaining racially segregated public schools. The *Webb* case dragged on and was suspended when the school board agreed in 1963 to carry out a comprehensive study of school segregation.[3]

The Woodlawn Organization (TWO) had been formed in 1959 on Chicago's South Side by supporters of Saul Alinsky's Back of the Yards grassroots organizing campaign. Since the 1930s Alinsky had been training community organizers to work in Chicago neighborhoods to improve housing and employment conditions. On October 16, 1961, representatives from TWO showed up at the school board's public meeting, along with NAACP and Urban League leaders who not only charged that the board's policies promoted "segregated education," but also decried the significant disparities between all-white and all-Black public schools in educational resources, physical plant, and relevant curricula. When board members appeared unreceptive to their appeals, TWO, under the leadership of Rev. Arthur Brazier, staged a walkout at the board meeting and launched picket lines outside the CPS building. TWO supported the decision of Black parents to launch a boycott of Cornell Public School in October 1961.[4]

The Cornell School, located on the South Side, was built to accommodate 868 students but had an enrollment of over 1,300 in the fall of 1961. Mrs. Ernest Baker, an untenured teacher at the school, urged parents to keep their children out, and for her efforts she was fired from her teaching position. The campaign to have Mrs. Baker reinstated led to the formation of Teachers for Integrated Schools, which would carry out investigations and support efforts to desegregate public education in Chicago.[5] The Cornell boycott ended after two weeks when parents were given assurances that their requests would be addressed. Superintendent Benjamin Willis and the school board finally issued a multifaceted policy statement in December 1961. Willis announced that an independent survey of the CPS would be conducted by experts chosen to determine the most appropriate strategies to deal with the increasing enrollment. The CPS board said that where feasible, it would allow students in schools with a classroom size of forty or more to transfer to a school averaging fewer than thirty students. And to relieve classroom overcrowding, the board authorized the purchase of mobile classrooms to be installed on the grounds of overcrowded schools. This latter decision would lead to mobilization and organized protests by Black parents, students, and community organizations.[6]

In the early 1960s, the civil rights campaigns in Chicago centered on public education because of white school officials' opposition to, and failure to promote, integrated education. School board members and elected officials' racially based intransigence and refusal to provide African American and other students of color access to "quality integrated education" were the main reasons why public school desegregation failed to come about. Six

or seven years after the US Supreme Court's *Brown* decision, school officials argued that they had no "affirmative duty" to provide a public school
system that was "racially integrated." When confronted by parents, community leaders, and students, school administrators refused to budge from
that position.[7]

When the Chicago Freedom Movement emerged in the early 1960s, it
signaled a break in the civil rights consensus that had been fashioned by
Mayor Richard J. Daley's Democratic political machine in the postwar period. This meant that the public school campaigns pitted Black and white
Chicagoans against each other in an ongoing struggle, and the entrance
of Martin Luther King Jr. and SCLC in Chicago in 1965 only seemed to
aggravate the situation. The *New Republic* and other major publications
complained at the time that "so far King has been pretty much of a failure
at organizing," and his early mentor, social activist Bayard Rustin, called
the Chicago campaign "a fiasco" and "a disaster."[8] However, it was the participation of elementary and secondary school students in the sit-ins and
public school boycotts at the beginning of the 1960s that brought improved
facilities and Black History courses to Chicago public schools by the end
of the decade.

"HOW TO ACHIEVE QUALITY AND
EQUALITY IN CHICAGO PUBLIC SCHOOLS"

The Cornell School boycott was soon followed in January 1962 by the Burnside School boycott and sit-in. Disgruntled parents had made numerous
complaints about the overcrowding there and resorted to nonviolent direct
action when they learned that to relieve the overcrowding at Burnside, students could transfer to the Gillespie School, another overcrowded Black
school, bypassing the all-white Perry public school. Alma Coggs, a parent
who participated in the sit-in declared, "We weren't looking for any notori-
ety or anything like that. . . . We didn't like the fact that [our children] were
going to school on double shifts." The students remained out of school, but
engaged in picketing the CPS building in the Loop downtown, and they
participated in "teach-ins" for over two weeks. After meeting with Superintendent Willis, who upheld the transfer decision, the parents brought

suit against CPS in *Burroughs v. Board of Education, Chicago*. However, the lawsuit was eventually dismissed in November 1962; the judge ruled that the plaintiffs had not yet exhausted the available state remedies.[9]

Elementary and high school students were encouraged to participate in a citywide conference and seminar on Saturday, March 24, 1962, sponsored by the Chicago Urban League (CUL), titled "How to Achieve Quality and Equality in Chicago Public Schools." Representatives from a wide range of community and religious organizations gave talks and participated in workshops that focused on racial segregation in public education as a "northern problem." Edwin C. Berry, the league's executive director, emphasized that the purpose of the meeting was "to educate the people to the magnitude of the problem." Resolutions were adopted urging Mayor Daley to appoint to the school board "people who are committed to providing a policy of integration of the schools."[10]

Several weeks later, representatives from the organizations that participated in the CUL conference came together to form the Coordinating Council of Community Organizations (CCCO) whose purpose was "to serve as a clearinghouse for exchanging information and coordinating individual strategies." The CCCO would provide "a common front when dealing with the mayor."[11] Under the leadership of Rev. Arthur Brazier, Lawrence Landry, and Albert Raby, the CCCO became the most important organization carrying out civil rights campaigns in Chicago over the next three years. The participation of the elementary and secondary students in nonviolent direct-action protests made it possible for civil rights activists to gain some concessions from the school board and Superintendent Willis.

Parents, students, and community activists mounted serious opposition to the installation of mobile classrooms in the school yards of already overcrowded Black public schools. These buildings were constructed ostensibly to relieve classroom overcrowding. However, because they were being built overwhelmingly in all-Black schools, many African Americans in Chicago considered the practice a way to maintain racial segregation and disparagingly referred to the makeshift structures as "Willis wagons." Rather than allowing African American students in overcrowded schools to transfer to underutilized all-white schools, CPS officials built Willis wagons. So to protest this practice, on May 18, 1962, over 90 percent of the students at the Andrew Carnegie School on the South Side staged a boycott of classes. On the West Side, after parents organized a sit-in at the Alexander Herzl School in June 1962, the school board president, Clair Roddewig, decided to meet with them and promised new school buildings were forthcoming. TWO's Rev. Brazier declared that "the whole Negro community is positively opposed to the mobile classrooms because we believe this is a means of maintaining segregation."[12]

The boycotts and sit-ins spurred some action by CPS administrators, and in August 1962 a new transfer plan was announced. It allowed students in schools with class size averaging forty students to transfer to a nearby school where the class size averaged thirty or fewer. This plan was criticized immediately, however, because it guaranteed that average class size in some schools would remain at forty students. Then at school board hearings beginning in October 1962, it was made clear to TWO leaders, parents, and others that CPS officials were committed to the "neighborhood school concept" and transfers would be permitted only within the overcrowded schools' immediate neighborhood.[13]

Members of CORE had assisted parents in organizing school boycotts and sit-ins on the South and West Sides. Formed by organizers James Mc-Cain and James Carey in January 1960 with about a dozen members, the Chicago CORE chapter launched picket lines in front of stores located in predominantly Black neighborhoods that had no African American employees. The CORE-sponsored Chicago Emergency Relief Committee for Fayette County in Tennessee gathered and delivered food, medicine, clothes, and other supplies to Black residents who organized voter registration drives in Fayette and Haywood Counties, but were being "starved out" by white merchants. By the fall of 1962, CORE's membership increased to over a hundred and Black and white activists appeared regularly at school board meetings to register parents' complaints about the glaring deficiencies in the all-Black "neighborhood schools."[14]

The release of an investigative report, funded by the US Commission on Civil Rights and carried out by Northwestern University's John R. Coons, substantiated the claims and complaints of Black parents and community leaders. After a thorough analysis of school data, Coons concluded that the CPS administrators' verbal commitment to the neighborhood school concept did not match their practices.

> From the point of view of racial discrimination or merely that of non-racial equal protection, the confinement of pupils in crowded classes when other facilities were underutilized cannot be justified. The effect of this action was not merely the injury to the children retained in crowded schools. Perhaps the most serious injury was suffered by the school administration itself through the loss of public confidence in its impartiality.[15]

TWO and CCCO leaders and parents felt vindicated by the findings in the Coons report, and in February 1963, the Illinois legislature passed the Armstrong Act, which was considered a first of its kind because the law required "affirmative action from school boards to prevent segregation in the planning of new schools and to rectify de facto segregation in the creation and revision of attendance zones." To fulfill its mandate, the law required school districts to conduct surveys and provide to the Illinois department of education a racial headcount of their student population. In Chicago, this racial survey revealed that in 1963 no African American students were enrolled at Washburne Trade School. Black leaders, parents, and students had been complaining to school officials for over twenty years about this racial discrimination, even after the opening of Dunbar Vocational High School, which soon became virtually all Black. Graduation from Washburne guaranteed admission to a labor union's apprenticeship program, but graduation from Dunbar did not, mainly because of the racist practices of many Chicago labor unions.[16]

In the wake of the Children's Crusade in Birmingham in May 1963, there was added urgency to demands for an end to racially discriminatory policies and practices throughout the country. In June 1963, in Chicago, the Birmingham marches inspired renewed demonstrations at the CPS building over the racially discriminatory practices at Washburne School. At the graduation ceremonies at Dunbar High School that same month, members of the NAACP youth council were joined by representatives of CORE, SNCC, Negro American Labor Council, and Teachers for Integrated

Schools in protesting the commencement speech given by school board member Edith Green, an outspoken supporter of Superintendent Willis. The NAACP youth council declared, "We cannot, in justice to American democracy, stand idly by while a Negro member of the Board of Education betrays the colored school children of Chicago."[17] It was estimated that six hundred high school students, their parents, and local community leaders surrounded Dunbar High, carrying signs declaring "Willis and Green Must Leave the Scene."[18] The *Chicago Defender* reported that "the demonstrators were joined by approximately 100 teen-agers who marched from 35th and State to the Dunbar site and chanted '2, 4, 6, 8, we don't want to segregate.'"[19]

In July 1963, the NAACP's fifty-fourth annual convention was held in Chicago, and many of the delegates were making plans to attend the March on Washington the next month. Convention delegates organized a march through the Loop on July 3 and then rallied in Grant Park in support of President John Kennedy's recently introduced civil rights bill. Thousands of children and adults participated in the demonstration, including Mayor Daley, who at the last minute was not allowed to address the crowd. The rally was considered a success, but the *Chicago Sun-Times* proclaimed a little too soon that "Chicago has made great strides in race relations in the past twenty years," because on Tuesday, July 10, Chicago's CORE chapter, under the leadership of Samuel Riley, launched a sit-in at the board of education building that would last eight days.[20]

While divisions sometimes surfaced over the best strategies and appropriate goals, CORE members remained in the CPS building until they were carried out bodily by the police on Wednesday, July 18. Talks between Rev. Elton Cox, Sam Riley, and school board president Roddewig took place after the sit-in, and future meetings were planned. For their meeting with Roddewig and other administrators on July 30, CORE submitted a twelve-point agenda covering school boundaries, redistricting, and other measures that would advance integrated education.[21] They met, but at that same time portable classrooms were being installed at a school site on the South Side. So on August 2 CORE members joined Black parents and children on the picket line at Seventy-Third and Lowe Streets where the temporary buildings were under construction. The demonstrators blocked the movement of construction equipment, trucks, and even police cars. The celebrated comedian Dick Gregory joined the children and parents at the construction site, but the police, facing a barrage of stones and bottles, arrested him along with at least sixty-six others.[22]

CORE activists returned to the site on August 12 and tried to block the movement of loaded trucks and bulldozers in and out. The police again arrested Dick Gregory and fifty-five others. The *Chicago Tribune* reported, "Many of the pickets were teen-agers and women and small children." The majority of the adults chose to spend the night in jail rather than pay bail; the juveniles were released into the custody of family members.[23] While these protests did not stem the construction of Willis wagons, school board president Clair Roddewig soon announced that school boundaries would be reevaluated, an inventory of classrooms would be undertaken, and a new transfer plan would be developed.[24]

That same month over two thousand men, women, and children made the trip from Chicago to Washington, DC, for the March on Washington. They rode on the Freedom Trains that brought tens of thousands to the nation's capital in support of the civil rights bill recently introduced in Congress. On the podium along with Roy Wilkins, John Lewis, Bayard Rustin, A. Philip Randolph, Daisy Bates, and Rosa Parks, was Mahalia Jackson, the most famous gospel singer in the country and Chicagoans' adopted daughter. Although she was born in New Orleans, at age 16 Jackson fled an abusive guardian and settled in Chicago in 1926, joined church choirs, and soon captured the attention of Thomas Dorsey, considered the "Father of Gospel Music." The two sang together and eventually made gospel records that sold in the millions. At the March on Washington, when Jackson was called upon and she began to sing the spiritual "I've Been 'Buked and I've Been Scorned," a profound hush fell over the assembled crowd.

> You may talk about me sure as you please,
> Talk about me sure as you please,
> Children, talk about me sure as you please,
> Your talk will never drive me to my knees.

I've been 'buked and I've been scorned,
I've been 'buked and I've been scorned,
Children, I've been 'buked and I've been scorned,
Tryin' to make this journey all alone.[25]

In Chicago on August 29, the day after the successful march, and following up on school board president Roddewig's promise to CORE demonstrators in July as well as the settlement reached in *Webb v. the Chicago Board of Education,* the school board approved a new limited transfer plan for the high schools. It allowed the top 5 percent of students in schools without an honors program to transfer to schools with honors courses. But no sooner was the plan announced than white parents began to complain vociferously that the high schools on the list were already overcrowded. On Monday, September 9, over seven hundred white parents showed up at Bogan High School to protest the policy, and the next day they made their opposition known at city hall and the board of education building.[26]

Unlike his responses to the protests coming from Black parents and students, Superintendent Willis acted immediately on the white parents' complaint and removed from the list fifteen of the twenty-four schools with honors programs, including Bogan High School. When school board members told him to reinstate those schools and the African American parents obtained an injunction to compel him to act, Willis refused and evaded the court order. Rather than carry out the court order, Willis submitted his letter of resignation to the school board on October 4, 1963. While most Black Chicagoans welcomed the news, white leaders and businesspeople immediately came to Willis's defense and put great pressure on school board members not to accept Willis's resignation. Upon learning of this decision, CCCO's Lawrence Landry immediately called for a *system-wide* school boycott on Tuesday, October 22, 1963, to protest the decision to retain Willis.[27]

FREEDOMS WORTH FIGHTING FOR: BOSTON AND CHICAGO

Up to this point, the school boycotts and sit-ins organized by students, parents, and community leaders in Chicago had involved only one school at a time. However, in Boston, a system-wide school boycott was organized in

June 1963 to protest the poor conditions in Black secondary schools and the racial exclusion instituted by public school officials. De facto segregation in housing was not so much the issue in Boston. As parent activist Ellen Jackson observed, "You could live on the same street and have a white neighbor, as I did, and you went to one junior high school and she went to another junior high school. So it was a dual pattern. . . . It was not de facto at all." Ruth Batson, Mel King, and other local NAACP leaders went before the Boston School Committee on numerous occasions, decrying the deteriorating physical structures, the overcrowding, and lack of up-to-date books and other curricular materials in the schools assigned to African American children.[28] Jonathan Kozol's bestseller *Death at an Early Age* exposed the overcrowding, poor conditions, and lack of resources for African American public-school students. Published in 1967, the book is based on Kozol's experiences as a teacher in the Boston public schools in the early 1960s.[29]

On "Stay Out for Freedom Day," June 17, 1963, many children and teenagers agreed to participate in the boycott. It was estimated that 3,500 Black students absented themselves from Boston public schools that day and instead many attended workshops in churches and community centers, in what would be later be termed *freedom schools*. The original freedom schools were opened in the era of emancipation by African Americans themselves, religious missionary and philanthropic societies, and the federal government. Booker T. Washington is often quoted as having noted that during the Civil War and Reconstruction, "you had a whole race of people trying to learn to read," and much of that instruction took place in freedom schools. In the 1960s, freedom schools were opened in Boston, Chicago, New York, and other cities where system-wide school boycotts were carried out.[30]

Boston Celtics star Bill Russell was a major supporter of the boycott there, and on the day of the strike he toured the freedom schools and spoke with the teenagers. The *New York Times* reported that Russell "held audiences at nine different centers spellbound with an appeal to be proud of their color" and be "ready to accept opportunity." White students also attended the freedom schools, and "they joined heartily in chants of freedom songs, accompanied by rhythmic hand-clapping." At the freedom school opened at the St. Mark Social Center, Episcopal bishops Anson Phelps

Stokes and James K. Matthews, known for their antiracist activism, spoke to more than 250 teenagers "about the freedoms they were fighting for."[31] Only teenagers attended Boston's freedom schools, because although this was a system-wide boycott, it was confined to students in junior and senior high school. No elementary school students were asked to strike.

Virtually all 3,500 Black secondary students and at least 20,500 other Bostonians participated in the strike on June 18, 1963. Over three hundred children and teenagers showed up at the freedom school at St. Mark's Congregational Church, so the overflow had to be taken by bus to other freedom schools in the city.[32] Later that year the reelection of Louise Day Hicks, an outspoken opponent of school desegregation, to the Boston School Committee in November 1963, as well as the failure of school officials to move on the demands of the Black parents and community prompted a second school strike on February 26, 1964. It was estimated that up to 40 percent of the Black secondary *and* elementary school students participated and over twenty thousand in total, and produced one positive and important outcome.[33] Massachusetts governor Owen Peabody formed a "blue ribbon" committee to investigate "racial imbalance" (segregation) and discrimination in the state's public school systems, which led to the passage of the Racial Imbalance Act by the state legislature in August 1965, calling upon "all school committees to adopt as education objectives the promotion of racial balance and the correction of existing racial imbalance." Even though Boston's school officials labeled it a failure, boycott organizers considered the second protest an important success.[34]

In Chicago in October 1963, Lawrence Landry of the CCCO called for a system-wide boycott of the public schools, but unlike the first one in Boston, it sought the participation of both secondary and elementary school students. Many of the complaints coming from parents, students, and community activists leading up to strike in Chicago were also being registered in New York City, Cleveland, Milwaukee, and other cities. For Black parents and local community leaders, the boycott was the end result of failed negotiations with school officials over the poor conditions, overcrowding, and racial exclusion practiced system wide. The children and teenagers participated in these boycotts because they hoped the protests would lead to improved educational opportunities and resources. By the end of the decade, when it became clear that no integration and little de-segregation was going to take place in these public school systems, Black high school students organized protests and brought about educational change and curricular improvements in the predominantly Black elementary and secondary schools. These high school students had joined in the marches, rallies, and boycotts for quality integrated education while attending elementary school. As high school students, they organized their own boycotts and other protests.[35]

In 1963, Chicago's Freedom Day Committee included representatives from within the school system and from community and political organizations. Lawrence Landry was an activist in Chicago's Friends of SNCC chapter and participated in CORE-sponsored sit-ins and school boycotts on the South and West Sides. NAACP leaders came on board after Mayor Daley refused to comment publicly on Willis's reinstatement. On Freedom Day, October 22, 1963, 224,000 students—50 percent of the total enrollment—participated in the first system-wide school boycott in Chicago. Similar to Freedom Day in Boston, several thousand children and teenagers attended the freedom schools opened in churches, community centers, settlement houses, and other locales throughout the city. The CCCO popularized its thirteen demands, which included the firing of Superintendent Willis, "a basic policy of integration of staff and students," "disclosures of present classroom use and racial composition of pupil enrollment and school staffs," and "the elimination of the neighborhood school policy."[36]

In the late afternoon on October 22 an estimated six thousand adults, children, and teenagers, led by a Boy Scout drum and bugle corps, marched through the streets and along Michigan Avenue to city hall and then to the board of education building. Robert McKersie, an instructor at the University of Chicago Business School, participated in this antiracist protest and recalled, "From several blocks away I could hear the chanting:

"What do we want?"
"Freedom!"
"When do we want it?"
"Now!"

"Feelings of both excitement and unease gripped me as I reached City Hall and saw the line of people two by two, circling the building." McKersie spotted a friend among the marchers. "I fell in step by his side. . . . Now that I was inside, I relaxed and even began to enjoy myself. The sensation was one of exhilaration—a feeling of accomplishment." After circling city hall several times the marchers moved on to the board of education building where the rally was held and McKersie heard "fiery speech after fiery speech."[37]

The next morning the Freedom Day Committee proclaimed the success of the boycott. They had planned on one hundred thousand students participating, and the actual number was twice that figure. Local NAACP leader Rev. Carl Faqua charged that the protest served as "a mandate to Mayor Richard Daley and the Board of Education to get rid of Dr. Willis." On the other hand, Superintendent Willis called the boycott "a failure" and suggested that the protest's leaders were hurting the students' education. Nonetheless, on that day in Chicago, and on days there and in other cities where system-wide school boycotts took place, local districts lost state funding. "The boycott . . . hit the school board's pocketbook," observed a reporter for the *Chicago Tribune*. "Willis estimated that it cost the board $470,000 in state aid funds based on average daily attendance as determined by [a complex] formula."[38]

Negotiations between representatives from CCCO and the school board took place early in November 1963, only to be interrupted by the shocking news of the assassination of President John F. Kennedy in Dallas, Texas, on November 22. The country went into deep mourning, and when the negotiations resumed in December, it became clear that the school board was not willing to seriously address CCCO's thirteen demands. Instead, the board issued a statement on February 13, 1964, declaring "racial and ethnic diversity" was "healthier for . . . the nation as a whole, however, we see no single overall step or action by which diversity can be brought immediately to all our schools by the Board of Education alone."[39]

Angered by the board's statement, Lawrence Landry and others called for a second system-wide strike on February 25, 1964, and established the Freedom Day II Committee. This time some opposition to the announced boycott surfaced, coming from local politicians, ministers, and representatives of various community groups outside and inside the CCCO. Indeed, Mayor Daley recruited Black aldermen Kenneth Campbell and Claude Holman to undertake specific actions to convince parents and local leaders not to support a second school strike.[40] Within the CCCO, however, a slim majority voted to move ahead with the protest. Again, churches, community centers, and other venues were recruited as sites for the freedom schools. And just days before the boycott, school board president Clair Roddewig announced his resignation. Roddewig was the one board member who met regularly with Black parents and CCCO leaders and participated in the protracted negotiations. Roddewig said the retirement was for personal reasons, but most commentators agreed that it was the ongoing conflict with Superintendent Willis over implementing the board's policies, especially those meant to promote school integration. Measures aimed at fostering racial integration were ignored by Superintendent Willis.[41]

To head off a second boycott, Mayor Daley, unlike before the first strike, offered to serve as mediator for the two sides. When there was no response, Daley had Black congressman William Dawson and aldermen Campbell and Holman launch a campaign to stop it and flooded Black neighborhoods with thirteen thousand petitions asking for pledges from parents and religious leaders to "help stop the school boycott."[42] Police officials announced they would arrest anyone who attempted to block or harass a child or teenager entering a public school on the day of the strike. Albert Raby, the new CCCO director, and Lawrence Landry, chair of the Freedom Day II Committee, pledged that would not occur. Alderman Campbell claimed that 85,000 people had signed the anti-boycott pledge and predicted (inaccurately), "they will fall far short of the 100,000" striking children and teenagers.[43]

The second boycott in Chicago took place on Tuesday, February 25, 1964, a few weeks after the first hugely successful public school boycott in New York City, where an estimated 370,000 students stayed out. In Chicago, the second strike is credited with over 170,000 absences. While this was a 22 percent decline in participation compared to the October 1963 protest, it was significantly above the 100,000 targeted. Indeed, in anti-boycott leader Campbell's district, 90 percent of the children and teenagers were absent. Many of those students attended one of the 112 freedom schools opened in churches and community centers and staffed by volunteers from the churches, Kendall College, Northwestern University, the University of Chicago, and other universities. There were few picket lines at specific schools, but some schools were completely empty, and others were reported to have only two or three students.[44]

Teenagers were interviewed about the boycott by *Chicago Tribune* reporter William Juneau who concluded that "most of the youngsters expressed the view that the boycott would help the fight for civil rights." In the over a hundred freedom schools set up, the students "were taught Negro history and 'the meaning of freedom and equality.'" Emma Smith, 18 years old and a student at Du Sable High School, felt that "the first boycott was fine but the second one was not so hot." Emma and her sister Yvonne Smith went to classes at Du Sable on the day of the second boycott: "We have to get our own education if we want to get ahead." However, 14-year-old Joyce Burnett "stayed out of school to let the board of education know that something must be done." "I'm fighting for my rights," she told Juneau, "and the boycott will help."[45]

Lawrence Landry and CCCO leaders viewed the second boycott as a success as well and suggested that the larger than expected turnout was a repudiation of the Black politicians in Mayor Daley's machine who had a vested interest in maintaining segregation because it allowed them to remain in office. "The choice was between freedom and Daleyism" and the children and teenagers chose "freedom." Superintendent Willis issued a statement afterward condemning the boycotts. "The spectacle of having large numbers of youngsters involved in illegal acts has extremely dangerous implications for every American. . . . Violation of attendance laws in this state and elsewhere [does] a great disservice to those allegedly being helped, the school children."[46]

The CPS-sponsored report issued by education researcher Philip Hauser in March 1964 confirmed what Black parents, children, teenagers, the CCCO, and community leaders were complaining about and what the Coons report concluded: 86 percent of Black students attended 90 percent or more Black schools; and 86 percent of white pupils were enrolled in 90 percent or more white schools. But even more important to Black children and teenagers, Hauser documented "the comparative inferiority of the black schools in overcrowding, physical facilities, and the experience and education of the faculty." In his findings and conclusions Hauser called for the adoption of practices that would pair Black and white schools and facilitate pupil transfers. In May 1964, Superintendent Willis and the new school board president, Frank M. Whiston, did not address the school pairings recommendation, but did announce a new "permissive transfer policy" and included a list of overcrowded and underutilized public schools. On May 28, 1964, the *Chicago Defender* headline read, "Willis Throws in Towel, Okays City-Wide Integration of Schools."[47]

The Chicago Freedom Movement began moving in another direction after Dr. King and SCLC decided in August 1965 to target Chicago for the next campaign. James Bevel, Bernard Lafayette, and other SCLC organizers arrived in the city and began working with CCCO's Lawrence Landry, Al Raby, and others on fair housing objectives targeting the racially discriminatory practices of Chicago's real estate industry. The conditions in Chicago public schools for African American children and teenagers did not improve during the period that SCLC and CCCO began mounting open-housing mass marches and demonstrations protesting racial exclusion in the city and some of its suburbs.[48] Black Chicagoans on the South and West Sides faced high rents, lack of municipal services, landlord neglect and negligence, and dilapidated and unsanitary conditions that needed to be addressed. While James Bevel, Jesse Jackson, James Orange, and other SCLC organizers were successful in getting teenage gang members to stop fighting each other and to participate in civil rights demonstrations, Black teenagers in the public schools were often thwarted in their attempts to transfer to underutilized white schools, and those few who were allowed to transfer usually did not stay long because they were often entering "hostile territory."[49]

Many Black parents, teenagers, and children who came to realize that public schooling was not going to be *integrated* decided to organize to demand changes and improvements in the *quality* of public education for African American students in Chicago. When school officials failed to act on those demands by 1968, Black high school students organized boycotts and other nonviolent direct-action protests.[50]

MEETING THE NEEDS OF THE CHILDREN: NEW YORK CITY

Following the US Supreme Court's 1954 *Brown* decision, those parents and community organizations interested in reducing racial segregation in public education in New York City organized the Intergroup Committee on New York's Public Schools. Its objective was to promote public school desegregation. The New York Board of Education also established its own Commission on Integration at the end of 1954. In September 1955, Junior High School (JHS) 258 opened in the Bedford-Stuyvesant neighborhood in Brooklyn and the student enrollment was over 98 percent Black, while the enrollment in JHS 61, under construction in nearby Crown Heights, was projected to be 90 percent white. Rev. Milton Galamison, pastor of Siloam Presbyterian Church in Brooklyn; Winston Craig, chair of the local NAACP's educational committee; union leader Annie Stein; and the Intergroup Committee launched a campaign to rezone the local district to desegregate both JHS 258 and JHS 61. Through meetings, petitions, and conferences attempts were made in 1956 to convince the school board to rezone the Brooklyn district to bring about the desegregation of JHS 258, but they all failed. Historian Adina Back documented this campaign and found that Superintendent William Jansen and school board members opposed integration plans and "fundamentally disagreed with the rezoning proposals the integration leaders put forward."[51]

In Harlem, in 1958, nine Black mothers seeking freedom of choice for their children and improved educational opportunities outside of Harlem launched a boycott of Junior High Schools 126, 130, and 136. The school board eventually brought charges against the "Harlem Nine" for violating the state's compulsory education laws, but these were later dismissed. And in turn, the mothers sued the school board for "the perpetuation of racial segregation in the five school districts in Harlem." In the compromise that was eventually worked out, the boycotting students were not allowed to enroll in the schools their mothers preferred, but entered JHS 43, another predominately Black school, which "offered special guidance services and cultural programs."[52]

Given the deteriorating physical plants, overcrowding, double shifts, and lack of adequate curricular resources in racially isolated public schools, the

Brooklyn NAACP's schools committee in 1960 morphed into the Parents' Workshop for Equality in New York City Schools under the leadership of Rev. Galamison and Annie Stein. The goal was to "nurture leadership skills in parents and [allow] them to become speakers, writers, negotiators, and organizers for the parent group." The Parents' Workshop pursued the expansion in quality integrated public education by urging school officials to build public schools in locations that would promote "racial balance."[53] The parents group placed before the New York City Board of Education the many complaints about the conditions in predominantly Black public schools and lobbied for an open enrollment policy that would allow students in overcrowded schools to transfer to those that were under enrolled. Put into effect in April 1961 for the 1961–62 school year, it proved inadequate because over half of the transfer applications were rejected due to lack of space.[54]

The parents of students whose applications for transfer were rejected at the beginning of the 1961–62 school year decided to mobilize and, with the assistance of the Parents' Workshop, organized a boycott at three schools, two in Brooklyn and one in Manhattan. After a five-day strike, children in two schools were allowed to transfer to the schools of their choice, and the Higher Horizons Program was announced. It would provide students in overcrowded, under-resourced schools with "special services, smaller classes, remedial services, extra counseling, and greater parental involvement." Historian Clarence Taylor documented the quality integrated education movement in New York City and found that civil rights activists did not view the Higher Horizons Program as a substitute for school integration but as an attempt "to divert attention from the issue of integration."[55]

In the face of the demands for public school desegregation, white school officials in New York City continued to push the neighborhood school concept—children should attend the public school closest to their residence—as did those in Chicago, Boston, and other cities. And despite complaints from parents and community leaders, the school board continued to build schools within African American and Puerto Rican neighborhoods, emphasizing that the new schools would relieve overcrowding. And while the pupils attending the newly built schools received improved educational resources and programs, conditions in the older schools remained the same.[56]

The Harlem Parents Committee (HPC), organized early in 1963, sought to address the conditions in these older public schools that Black children and teenagers attended. Under the leadership of Isaiah Robinson and Thelma Johnson, the HPC joined with the Parents' Workshop, CORE, the Urban League, and the NAACP in August 1963 in forming the New York Citywide Committee for Integrated Schools. Similar to the CCCO in Chicago, this new coalition group made its position clear: "We can no longer permit the public school system to function while the needs of our children are not being met."[57] Rev. Galamison became the spokesperson for the group and met with Superintendent Calvin Gross, school board president James Donovan, and other school officials later that month, alerting them that if negotiations failed, a mass demonstration and school boycott would be organized. School officials promised to produce a timetable for desegregating the school system by December 1, 1963.

That month a reporter for the *Amsterdam News,* the city's most widely read Black newspaper, asked a group of students from JHS 139 in Harlem if they were willing to participate in a school boycott, similar to the one in Chicago on October 22. The students explained, "We have rats and roaches in our classrooms." "Some of our seats at our desks are broken." "When it rains, the rain leaks through the top floors." "We're so crowded that we have to use the auditorium for classrooms." "Sometimes we find roaches in our food in the cafeteria." "Our toilets are stopped up." "Our lights are so dim, on dark rainy days, we can hardly see our hands in front of our faces." Many of these same conditions were found in other older public schools in Black neighborhoods throughout the city.[58]

No integration plan was produced in December 1963 and Superintendent Gross even rejected the idea of "involuntary transfers" of Black and white children to promote integration. In response, members of the City-wide Committee voted to organize a system-wide boycott of the public schools on Monday, February 3, 1964. Church, community, civil rights, and teachers' organizations were mobilized and began producing literature to be distributed, which identified locations for freedom schools, and making plans for a children's march on city hall.[59] In an attempt to head off the projected strike, Superintendent Gross issued in early January 1964 a progress report on the open enrollment program. The Citywide Committee found this report to be thoroughly inadequate, and Galamison and members of CORE's Brooklyn branch and the Harlem Parents Committee staged a sit-in at 110 Livingston Street, the school board building, on January 3, 1964. When the antiracist activists were being carried out by police, over two hundred demonstrators outside jeered, "New York City has become just like Birmingham!" Eighteen teenagers and twenty adults were arrested, including Rev. Galamison.[60]

Civil rights activists from Cleveland, Chicago, Boston, and New York who were engaged in the Quality Integrated Education campaigns came together in Manhattan on January 12, 1964, and pledged to make February 1964 "Stay Away from School Month." The National Association for Puerto Rican Civil Rights announced its support for a boycott, as did the more conservative New York branch of the National Urban League.[61] Civil rights leader Bayard Rustin, who organized and carried out the highly successful March on Washington the year before, was recruited to oversee planning for the New York City boycott. Rustin immediately began soliciting volunteers and meeting with church and community leaders to gain their commitment to rally their memberships for the strike. A last minute meeting between the Citywide Committee and school officials turned into a "disaster," and the school board issued a statement insisting that all public school teachers must be present on February 3. If they stayed out, the school board threatened that the teachers not only would lose a day's pay but they also would be disciplined for "neglect of duty."[62]

On Freedom Day, most teachers did show up, but 464,361 students, 44 percent of the total enrollment, did not. The normal daily absence in New York City public schools (NYPS) was 10 percent of the one million pupils, or 100,000. The boycott added 360,000 to that number. In twenty-degree weather, picket lines were set up outside three hundred school buildings, and at least 3,000 children and teenagers marched on 110 Livingston Street, carrying signs declaring "Jim Crow Must Go!," "We Demand Quality Education," and "We Shall Overcome." The marchers in the Bronx went to the office of Governor Nelson Rockefeller, on West Fifty-Fifth Street, and set up a picket line. The public schools in African American and Puerto

Rican neighborhoods were virtually empty except for the teaching staff and administrators. And despite threats that came from NYPS officials, 8.03 percent (3,537) of the 43,865 teachers were absent. The United Federation of Teachers (UFT) did not publicly endorse the boycott, but announced its support of any teacher who decided not to cross the picket lines.[63]

At George Washington High School in Upper Manhattan, there were fifty students and teachers picketing in front when a group of white teenage boys gathered on a corner near the school and began chanting, "Two-four-six-eight, we don't want to integrate!" The police chased them away. Seventeen-year-old Eugene Ward declared, "Equal education is an urgent need and the [school] board has got to realize the public is not going to stand for second-rate, segregated education any longer."[64] The boycott organizers predicted there would be over 8,000 on the picket lines, but even in the freezing cold weather, over 2,600 showed up. In the Bronx, Puerto Rican protesters outside public schools carried signs declaring, "*Integración es un gran educación.*"[65]

Thousands of striking children and teenagers attended the hundreds of freedom schools that opened in all five boroughs. Entertainer Dick Gregory told the children in a Lower Manhattan freedom school that "they would have to be the 'little soldiers' in the battle for Negro freedom."[66] Seventeen-year-old William Washington, a senior at Taft High School and a teacher at the freedom school opened at the John Kennedy Community Center in Harlem, emphasized to the younger children that "the boycott is part of the civil rights movement." Marie Lillenstein organized the freedom school opened at Temple Methodist Church in Manhattan, while college student Turyan Bayles headed the one on the campus of Yeshiva University in the city. Pastor John Collins opened a freedom school at Jefferson Park Methodist Church where the sixty to seventy students in attendance were taught by divinity students from Union Theological Seminary. Following the *Freedom Guide* distributed to freedom school organizers, it offered "a program on Negro–Puerto Rican history and an explanation of their role in the civil rights campaigns."[67]

Milton Galamison, Bayard Rustin, Thelma Johnson, and other organizers declared the boycott "a tremendous success." Rustin, who had organized the March on Washington, believed the February 3, 1964, public school boycott in New York City was "the largest civil rights protest in the nation's history." And he was right.[68] More important, why were the first Chicago and the first New York City school boycotts so successful? It was mainly because over 570,000 children and teenagers recognized the racial injustices and inequities in the public school systems and supported the demands for quality integrated education. On the picket line, a reporter for the *New York Times* interviewed "a white student at the Bronx High School of Science [who] stopped chanting 'Jim Crow must go' long enough to explain that she felt the integration problem was the most important one facing the nation." She said, "It's up to the young people to show the adults how we feel."[69]

School board president, James P. Donovan, was quoted as saying the boycott was "a fizzle. . . . All these people proved is how easy it is to get children to take a holiday instead of going to school." He also believed that the boycott only "showed that parents could be frightened into keeping their children at home by a campaign of intimidation and threats of possible violence." CORE chairman James Farmer replied, "If this is a fizzle, we want more like this." School officials continued to label the boycott "illegal" and "hurtful to the children," and with the coming of the "white backlash," little movement was made on system-wide school desegregation. Individual students could apply to be transferred to a school outside their neighborhood, but a policy and practice of opening schools in locations that would promote integration, and even pairing two public schools to increase integration, generated public opposition.[70]

Parents and Taxpayers (PAT) was formed by white parents and political leaders in March 1964 to oppose integration of the public schools, and thus school board members were even more reluctant to attempt to desegregate all-white public schools. PAT's leaders promised to organize a boycott of their own if a far-reaching school integration program was adopted and implemented. At the same time, the lack of an immediate response from school officials to the demands for school integration prompted Rev. Galamison to call for a second NYPS boycott, as had also occurred in Chicago. This announcement came as a surprise to many on the Citywide Committee, and some opposed the idea. When they met on February 9 a lengthy debate ensued, and the majority supported a second school boycott. Within days, however, thirteen NAACP chapters withdrew from the Citywide

Committee. Bayard Rustin also opposed a second boycott, and instead participated in the March for Democratic Schools in Albany, New York, on March 10, 1964, where an estimated three thousand NAACP and CORE members and other antiracists lobbied state legislators and met with Governor Nelson Rockefeller. Others, however, moved ahead with the second strike. The Parents' Workshop and the Harlem Parents Committee mobilized women and mothers to spread the word, and as was the case with the first boycott, it was the women who carried it out.[71]

The second boycott took place on Monday, March 16, 1964, and was not as effective as the first, but over 165,000 children and teenagers participated. The protest had its greatest effects on public schools in the Harlem and Bedford-Stuyvesant neighborhoods. Police officers were stationed in large numbers outside schools being picketed. The police estimated that there were 980 protesters at 160 schools. Most of those picketers were high school students, and at some schools the policemen outnumbered the protesters. "Outside the George Washington High School in Upper Manhattan, about 25 students marched on the picket lines and urged their classmates to stay out"; however, the *Times* reporter saw a "a Negro girl who hurried past the line" into the building. She shouted, "My mother would kill me if I did."[72]

Unlike the cold and snow on February 3, 1964, the weather on March 16 was perfect, and after the freedom schools closed, about twenty-five hundred children, teenagers, and adults marched through the streets, flanked by police, to city hall where they held a rally. The *Times* reported, "Hundreds of teen-agers, many still carrying their books and in a holiday mood, massed outside the hall. They sang civil rights songs and chanted slogans." Then over seven hundred marchers "took the now familiar route of school protesters. They marched from Manhattan across the Brooklyn Bridge to the Board of Education Building at 110 Livingston Street." There they were joined by marchers coming from Rev. Galamison's Siloam Presbyterian Church in Brooklyn, which served as the headquarters for the protest. The speakers at the rally included Rev. Galamison, Oliver Leeds, Brooklyn CORE chairman, and Malcolm X, the Muslim leader, who declared that "the protest was intended to expose one of the most hypocritical school systems in the country."[73]

While there was no immediate response from school officials following the second boycott, meetings were held with boycott leaders. The report "Desegregating the Public Schools of New York City" was issued in May 1964 by the New York State Department of Education's advisory committee. The three well-respected advisors concluded that given the current and expanding African American and Puerto Rican enrollments, "total desegregation is simply not attainable in the foreseeable future." However, "with thoughtful planning, bold policies, and vigorous action, there are sound reasons to believe that the spread of segregation can be slowed, its severity reduced, and the effectiveness of school programs greatly improved."[74] Historian Clarence Taylor suggested that Superintendent Calvin Gross was not interested in formulating "bold policies" that could be controversial, and he only recommended "the creation of four pairings and three junior high school rezoning schemes, with no further integration measures for the coming year." The school board issued its own statement promising to "take steps to desegregate the schools by September 1964 and produce subsequent desegregation plans."[75]

These announcements helped to reinforce the white backlash. Parents and Taxpayers and the Joint Council for Better Education (JCBE), which were all-white anti-integration groups, had emerged in 1964 and led the opposition to even "four pairings," labeling it "forced integration," because it would involve the "involuntary transfer" of white students from highly desirable all-white schools to not-so-desirable integrated ones outside their immediate neighborhoods. PAT and the JCBE threatened to call a system-wide boycott at the beginning of the 1964–65 school year if the involuntary transfers were carried out. In March 1964, the New York Supreme Court ruled that every student had the right to attend the school nearest his or her home. This was soon followed by the introduction of several bills into the New York State Assembly prohibiting assignment of students to public schools based on race and against the involuntary transfer of students to schools outside their neighborhood.[76]

The leaders of PAT and JCBE made it known that if the involuntary transfer program was put in place, the group would organize a two-day, system-wide school boycott on Monday and Tuesday, September 14 and 15, 1964. James P. Donovan, president of the school board, attempted to head off the strike through negotiations with PAT; however, up to five hundred thousand circulars were distributed in predominantly white areas asking parents to keep their children home. On the first day of the boycott, 175,000 students above the normal absences stayed home. The hardest hit schools were those where white students had been involuntarily transferred outside their neighborhoods. It was estimated that 2,000 picketers were outside 125 schools, carrying signs that read "Give Us Back Our Neighborhood Schools!" and "Our Children Have Civil Rights Too." When Frederick Ruess, a PAT branch leader, was asked how he thought the boycott went, he replied, "Damn good." PAT chair Rosemary Gunning declared, "The Board of Education is now going to have to reconsider its future plans."[77]

On the second day of the boycott, 133,000 students above normal absences stayed home, and over the two-day period, the school system lost another $1.5 million in state funding that was based on daily attendance figures. There were at least 1,900 picketers outside 95 schools, with the largest number of absences in Queens and South Brooklyn. While only 2,300 Black and white students were affected by the school pairings and involuntary transfers, the white backlash had its effect.[78] Civil rights demands were placed on the back burner, and the antiracist advocates who organized Operation Shutdown targeted only selected schools rather than the entire system. Five schools were boycotted on January 19, 1965, and a freedom school was opened at Church of the Intercession in Harlem.[79]

Rev. Galamison, who led the earlier system-wide boycotts, called for strikes at six hundred selected schools, but the proposition generated little support. Historian Clarence Taylor found that the school board "paid no attention to the demonstrations, simply because the organizers had little support. . . . By 1965 the vigorous campaign for integration, led by Galamison, had come to an end."[80] But it was children and teenagers' participation in the boycotts that allowed these nonviolent protest campaigns to achieve some degree of success, including the mounting of "the largest civil rights protest in the nation's history." The social activism on display encouraged young crusaders in Cleveland, Milwaukee, and other cities to participate in civil rights protests, and eventually to pursue their own educational advancement campaigns in the latter half of the decade.

Chapter 6

Every Child a Freedom Soldier

Cleveland, Milwaukee, and Mississippi

*We have rejected the concept that youngsters should not
participate in civil rights demonstrations. They are
not being forced to do anything against their will.
In fact, most of the motivation for the Civil
Rights struggle has come from the youth.*

James Farmer, chair, CORE (1963)[1]

WHEN CIVIL RIGHTS ACTIVISTS arrived at the Brett Elementary
School in Cleveland on January 29, 1964, to protest the "intact busing" of
African American students and teachers from the overcrowded Hazeldell
Elementary School, they came under attack from a mob of whites carrying sticks, stones, baseball bats, and various weapons. The police stood on
the sidelines and did nothing. While the students arriving by school bus
were allowed to enter the building, the Black and white protesters were
subjected to racial slurs and epithets until they made a hasty retreat.[2] Beginning early in 1963 in Cleveland and Milwaukee, as in Chicago and New
York City, protest marches, picketing, sit-ins at board of education headquarters, and setting up picket lines at overcrowded and under-resourced
Black public schools took place on a regular basis. However, with empty
classrooms in school buildings in white neighborhoods in Cleveland and

Milwaukee, public school officials addressed the overcrowding in the Black schools with intact busing, a practice that angered Black *and* white parents and community leaders.

ATTACK ON INTACT BUSING: CLEVELAND

In Cleveland, the African American population increased from 147,808 in 1950 to 279, 352 in 1965, with 99.1 percent concentrated in Black neighborhoods on the East Side, leading to severe overcrowding in already poorly resourced public schools. The all-white public schools on Cleveland's West Side often had underutilized space. As in Chicago and other cities, rather than allowing African American children to transfer to all-white public schools, the administrators in Cleveland initially converted auditoriums, gymnasiums, libraries, and storerooms into classrooms and began constructing mobile classrooms in the school yards of Black public schools. The lack of classroom space meant that in September 1961 over twelve hundred children in Cleveland remained on the waiting list to enter kindergarten classes.[3]

To address the overcrowding, the Ohio Department of Education in 1957 authorized school officials in Cleveland to establish the Relay Program, which was comparable to the double shifts found in New York, Chicago, Philadelphia, and other cities. This meant that one group of elementary or secondary pupils attended school in the morning and another group attended in the afternoon. In Cleveland, however, the double-shifts were found only in the all-Black public schools on the East Side. Believing that their children's education was being shortchanged, African American parents in September 1961 organized the Relay Parents March to Fill Empty Classrooms after learning that there were about 165 *empty classrooms* in public schools located in white neighborhoods. Inspired by the sit-ins and other nonviolent direct-action protests taking place in the South, Black parents formed picket lines in front of Cleveland's board of education building throughout September and October 1961 to demand public school integration.[4]

Faced with ongoing demonstrations and continuing negative publicity, school officials in Cleveland decided to end the Relay Program in the spring of 1962. This was considered a victory for the mobilized Black parents in the Hazeldell neighborhood. However, the demand to allow African American students to transfer to all-white schools was opposed by white parents and groups, such as the North American Alliance for White People, that made it clear they did not want African Americans to attend "their schools." To relieve the extreme overcrowding in the Black schools, administrators decided that beginning in September 1962, Black students and teachers would be bused to all-white schools, but they would not be integrated into the curricular or extracurricular activities there. Historian Leonard Moore documented the quality integrated education movement in Cleveland and reported that Black parents "were outraged on realizing that the school board had altered the busing program to minimize contact between black and white students all in an attempt to appease angry white parents." This meant that "once the bused students arrived at the receiving school with their teacher, they had to remain in that particular classroom the entire day." The Black students could not eat lunch in the cafeteria and were banned from assemblies, physical education classes, and school-wide extracurricular activities. Finally, Black students had access only to the restroom at one designated time per day and were not allowed to see the in-school nurse.[5]

Initially, all the bused students were from the Hazeldell School, so the Relay Parents changed the name of their group to the Hazeldell Parents Association (HPA). As was the case in Chicago and New York City, the Cleveland NAACP, Urban League, CORE, and various Black and white civic organizations in December 1962 forged a coalition, which they named the United Freedom Movement (UFM), and sought to challenge the school board's policies and practices. Led by Harold Williams and Rev. David Zuverik, negotiations with Superintendent William Levenson and school board president Ralph McCallister to end intact busing went on for weeks. However, Levenson argued that transporting entire classes "was the easiest thing to do; we do not want to [antagonize] anyone any more than necessary by attempting to integrate." School board members agreed and refused to make any changes. Frustrated by this response, the UFM delivered an ultimatum: the Black students bused to the receiving schools must be integrated into the host school's classes and extracurricular activities by September 1963. School officials, however, ignored the UFM's demand.[6]

Intact busing continued in the new school year, so on Sunday, September 29, 1963, the UFM held a mass rally at Cory Methodist Church and voted to pursue nonviolent direct-action protest and outlined plans to set up picket lines in front of the board of education building. The next day over 250 protesters marched in front of the school board's headquarters, carrying signs declaring "End Intact Busing" and "Integration Now!" The activists returned each day during that week. The protest generated enormous negative publicity and moved the school board to make some changes.[7] The school board agreed to form a Human Relations Committee, which would oversee the integration of the students being bused into the host school's activities at the beginning of the second semester, January 15, 1964. However, the school officials' version of integration meant that only 20 percent of the 940 bused pupils would engage with other students for about forty minutes each day, and the rest of the time they would remain separated, as was the case during the first semester. When UFM member and parent Betty Eckland learned what the school board president was recommending, she charged, "McCallister is not going to get away with this. The board [passed] those resolutions" stating that the bused students would be "integrated" into the host schools' activities, "and they are going to stick with them."[8]

On Wednesday morning, January 29, 1964 when UFM and HPA activists showed up at the Brett Elementary School and began their protest and picketing, not only were activists attacked with sticks, stones, and baseball bats by the white parents and residents, but one Black man was knocked to the ground and pummeled. Then another white man brought out some menacing dogs. "They tried to make the dogs attack the pickets," a journalist reported. "The hecklers marched through the line saying 'sic-em; sic-em.'" While this confrontation was taking place, several UFM members staged a sit-in at Superintendent Levenson's office in the school district headquarters. They stayed for several hours, but he never appeared.[9]

The following day, January 30, when the activists arrived at Memorial Elementary School, located in an Italian American neighborhood, they were met by a huge mob of over fourteen hundred residents, some carrying weapons. They attacked the protesters as well as the Black reporters from the *Cleveland Call and Post*, Allen Howard and Kenneth Temple, who were kicked and beaten while the white policemen stood by and did nothing.[10] Black and white journalists had been attacked in Little Rock, Arkansas; Birmingham, Alabama; Oxford, Mississippi, and other places in the South while covering civil rights demonstrations and received little or no protection from local law enforcement officers or the FBI.[11] But Cleveland was not the only northern city where the police stood by and allowed white rioters to brutally attack nonviolent civil rights protesters. In Boston, Chicago, Philadelphia, Detroit, and other northern cities, many white police officers and administrators held the same racist views as the white rioters and believed that violence and brutality were justified to preserve white supremacy. In the southern states, it was white supremacist laws that the police and local constabulary upheld; in the Northeast, Midwest, and West, it was a matter of unmerited white privilege and supremacy.[12]

In the midst of this violence the Cleveland school board issued a statement declaring, "We are integrating classes and by next September we are preparing to accomplish complete integration." Not trusting the statement, on Tuesday, February 4, 1964, one day after the massive school boycott for integrated public education in New York City, UFM members staged a sit-in at Cleveland's board of education building. Police were brought in to remove them and in doing so injured several protesters. UFM activists May Myrick and Hazel Little were thrown down the building's concrete stairs. "I was dragged down three flights of stairs by the police," Little revealed. "And when they got me to the bottom, they threw me in a corner." She asked to be taken to the hospital, but they refused and instead took her to the police station, jailed her, and charged her with obstruction of justice and assault on a police officer. Myrick was also arrested and taken to jail and complained that in the cell a matron asked her to remove her clothes to be examined "while policemen and other males were present."[13]

Cleveland mayor Ralph Lochner had little official control over the school system and had not intervened in the disputes over school integration. But the bad publicity from the protests, the police brutality, and arrests at the board of education building led to efforts to bring school officials and UFM representatives together. Again the negotiated agreement, approved by the school board on February 9, 1964, called for "the integration of the transportation classes forthwith and a discontinuation of the transportation class system by any means the board deems necessary and proper." While the "transportation class system" ended, the board caved in to white parents' objections to integrated schooling, and only a small number of Black students were allowed to remain at Brett and Memorial Schools.[14]

UFM leaders came to consider the possibility of organizing a public school boycott in Cleveland, given the successful school protests that month not just in New York City but closer to home in Cincinnati, Ohio. NAACP and CORE leaders in the Queen City had been complaining about not only de facto segregation and overcrowding in the all-Black public schools but also about the absence of African American teachers in the school system. Negotiations with school officials broke down and civil rights leaders called for a boycott on Tuesday, February 11, 1964. Although there was not enough time to open many freedom schools, on the day of the boycott, over 18,000 students were absent. Normally about 8,500 students were absent per day, out of a total enrollment of 83,500 students. Later that day Lloyd Trotter, Cincinnati NAACP leader, declared, "We think the boycott has been very successful"; and school officials agreed to work with a "conciliation team" of civil rights leaders to address hiring practices and segregation in the school system.[15]

MARTYRS FOR THE CAUSE

In Cleveland, however, basically to further appease white parents, the school board announced on February 26, 1964, that three new schools would be constructed on the city's East Side. Upon learning of this decision, the UFM immediately held a meeting and the representatives of the various organizations voted unanimously for a resolution calling on the school board to enact "a moratorium on the construction of new schools." But when the resolution was presented to school board president James McCallister, he snapped, "Who appointed [UFM] dictator of policy for the people of Cleveland?" He pointed out that the school board had already purchased the land and was moving ahead on the construction projects. But given the size of the parcels of land purchased and the inappropriateness of the chosen sites (one was right beside a highway), UFM members and African American parents understood the new schools were to be built to limit the future possibility of public school integration.[16]

Without the benefit of the report being prepared by the school board's own Human Relations Committee on system-wide integration, work on the new buildings began in March 1964.[17] Then on Monday, April 6, fifty UFM members decided to set up a picket line at the Lakeview school construction site and attempted to block the movement of materials and equipment in and out. One protester, Booker T. Eddy, was almost run over when he crawled under a slowly moving truck. The police dragged him out and arrested him, along with nineteen others, charging them with trespassing and disorderly conduct. The picketers returned the next day, Tuesday, April 7, and tried to block the movement of large equipment into the Lakeview site. The day before, the activists had gathered in a ditch to prevent further digging and had to be dragged out by the police. Employing the same tactic the next day, one protester, Rev. Bruce Klunder, a white minister and CORE activist, was lying in a shallow ditch but was run over by a bulldozer and was crushed and killed. The workman operating the bulldozer claimed he did not see him. Some protesters tried to attack the driver, but the police pulled them away. This was the first death associated with the numerous school boycotts and protests that took place in 1963 and 1964 involving hundreds of thousands of children, teenagers, and adults.[18]

When the news spread about Rev. Klunder's death, rioting erupted on Cleveland's East Side in the Glenville area that evening. It was considered at that time the worst "civil rights violence in the city's history." Over three hundred police were called out to disperse crowds of young people who were attacking and looting stores. Tear gas was fired into large crowds after the police ordered them to disperse. *Cleveland Plain Dealer* reporter George Battan witnessed the rioting. "Outbreaks of violence and vandalism raged in the school site neighborhood and extended down side streets and along Lakeview Road." He found the "police were ducking rocks and scuffling on walks and in streets in the riotous atmosphere." The police were finally able to restore order after midnight. Thirteen people were injured, including eight policemen; and thirty-six young people were arrested, including twelve females, and taken to jail.[19]

Over two thousand people attended Rev. Klunder's memorial service at Cory Methodist Church on April 10. When Ruth Turner, chair of Cleveland's CORE, announced plans for a system-wide school boycott on April 20, 1964, the mourners clapped loudly and shouted their approval. Mayor Ralph Lochner obtained an injunction against further demonstrations at school construction sites; he then met with UFM and school board members and negotiated a two-week halt of construction at the three sites while a panel of experts evaluated "the segregation problem."[20] However, school board president James McCallister ignored the agreement reached with Mayor Lochner and announced that construction would continue at all three sites, angering the activists and ultimately generating more support for the school boycott.[21]

In Cleveland, on Monday, April 20, the boycott was carried out in much the same way as the earlier school strikes in Chicago, New York City, and Boston. Marchers targeted the school district headquarters for picketing and a rally in the afternoon. Locations and teachers were recruited for freedom schools, and curricular materials on African American history and culture were assembled and distributed. "Every child . . . a freedom soldier," declared Ruth Turner, and in the freedom schools, "he will learn something about himself and his struggle."[22]

Church congregations raised funds for teaching materials, while high school students spread the word, distributed flyers, and organized rallies. Over eighty freedom schools were opened, and the teachers included college students and teachers, social workers, and clergy. "There is a spirit among the kids here," observed *Cleveland Plain Dealer* reporter Robert G. McGruder. He interviewed several freedom school students, and 13-year-old Beverly Morris believed "the kids listen to the teachers to learn what the movement is all about." Her classmate Gail Minor said she was there "to show her displeasure at segregated schools." Cory Methodist Church was not prepared to accommodate the eighteen hundred children who showed up there. Class sizes had to be doubled and "a huge room on the second floor held four classes with over 200 students." In most freedom schools, "lessons of the day emphasized Negro history and literature, the civil rights movement, and Negro biographies."[23]

It was estimated that up to twelve thousand children and teenagers attended the freedom schools. Each child who attended received a "Freedom Certificate" indicating their participation in this demonstration of "democratic education." Unfortunately, in the second tragedy of the public school protests that took place across the nation in 1964, 5-year-old Randy Adkins was hit by a bus as she crossed the street clutching her Freedom Certificate from the freedom school. She died shortly after. Randy's parents and others viewed her as a martyr, like Rev. Klunder, in the movement for quality integrated education.[24]

The UFM considered the boycott a success because 92 percent of the sixty thousand Black students, who made up 50 percent of the school system, were absent that day. But there was still no movement on the part of the school board to reconsider the decision about school construction sites that clearly contributed to racial isolation in the public school system. The UFM then turned to the courts to prevent the school board from continuing the school construction projects. One lawsuit, filed on behalf of twenty Black children, challenged Cleveland's segregated education as a violation of the Supreme Court's *Brown* decision. The lawsuits were eventually dismissed, but the resignation of school board president James McCallister in 1964 came to be considered a victory because he was replaced by Paul Briggs, former chair of the Ohio Commission on Civil Rights. Historian Leonard Moore found that although there was little desegregation in Cleveland before the court-ordered, cross-town busing program in the 1970s, the new school board president "began to [address] many of the complaints of black parents: . . . adopted integrated teaching materials, revised the curriculum; implemented a human relations program; . . . and opened libraries in every elementary school."[25]

ATTACK ON INTACT BUSING: MILWAUKEE

On Monday, February 3, 1964, members of Milwaukee CORE and the NAACP chapters organized picket lines around the Twelfth Street School, the Twentieth Street School, and the Sherman School, with some carrying signs declaring "Stop School Segregation Now!" At the Twentieth Street School about 180 Black students were arriving by school bus, and state assemblyman Isaac Coggs from Milwaukee announced, "We're going to march around the schools first to try and end de facto segregation, and we're going to have other demonstrations to try and stop it." At the Sherman School, as the fourth graders arrived, "pickets marched in a tight circle between the buses and the entrance forcing the children to walk between the demonstrators." The day before, Sunday, February 2, over 350 men, women, and children had participated in the March for Integrated Schools, and the next day, almost a hundred showed up on picket lines at public schools to denounce the intact busing program.[26]

As was the case in Cleveland, rather than allowing Black students attending extremely overcrowded schools to transfer to under-enrolled, all-white schools, school officials in Milwaukee transported the teachers and Black pupils "intact" to an all-white school that had empty classrooms. In Milwaukee the practice began as early as 1957, when both Black and white students were transported, usually on a temporary basis until their neighborhood school was renovated or a new one was built. But by 1962, it was only African American children who were being transported, and this led to ongoing civil rights activism.[27]

Many of the same factors that led up to the school boycotts in Boston, Chicago, New York City, and Cleveland were found in Milwaukee in the early 1960s. The post–World War II Black migration meant that between 1950 and 1960, the Black population increased 300 percent, from 21,772 to 62,458, and African Americans were confined to the city's Inner Core, where the public schools became seriously overcrowded. Though there had been all-Black public schools in the city for decades, a long-term struggle was waged in the late 1940s to hire Black teachers. However, the first Black principal, Grant Gordon, was not appointed until 1960; the second, Ardie Howard, in 1965.[28]

The Wisconsin department of education conducted an investigation of the Milwaukee public schools in 1961 and found that the overcrowding and lack of resources in predominantly Black schools meant that important "educational opportunities offered to children attending the Fifth Street

School, Fulton Junior High, and North Division Senior High School," all Black, were "shockingly inferior" compared to those in all-white elementary and secondary schools.[29] The next year the state department of education investigated Fulton Junior High School after several white teachers were attacked by students. The teachers wanted to reinstate the use of corporal punishment against students, but the investigator, Robert Van Raalte, concluded that those teachers "unwilling to accept the challenges presented" by the "migrant crisis" should be replaced. He concluded, "High quality classroom instruction is the most potent force available to change pupil behavior."[30]

School officials in Milwaukee also addressed the perceived need for "cultural adjustment" for the children of southern migrants by offering "compensatory education programs" beginning in the late 1950s. Historian Jack Dougherty argued that Milwaukee public schools were at the forefront of this educational strategy. "With intellectual support from the nation's leading academics and financial support from the Ford Foundation," northern urban school districts "laid the groundwork for a strategy that would eventually be adopted by the federal government in its grand scale effort to eliminate poverty through public education: Title I of the Elementary and Secondary Education Act of 1965." Milwaukee was among the cities that participated in the Great Cities School Improvement Program and in 1959 received a grant from the Ford Foundation to assist "in-migrant" students. Dougherty and other researchers found that within five years, compensatory education became the preferred way to deal with the "Negro Problem" in Milwaukee's and other urban public-school systems.[31]

Compensatory education programs achieved widespread acceptance among academics and school administrators in the 1960s because this new approach placed the blame for academic underachievement squarely on African American children and their families. Most white and some Black social scientists considered African American cultural practices "pathological versions" of European American culture, and thus the children born in the rural South but now entering urban public school systems were considered "culturally deprived." In the early months of 1963, as part of the commemorations of the centennial of the Emancipation Proclamation, Milwaukee mayor Henry Maier's Commission on Community Relations released its report, *The Negro in Milwaukee: Progress and Portent*. Rather than racial discrimination and economic exclusion, the authors blamed the Black migrants coming from the South for the educational problems:

> We must realize that Negroes of low income, still unaccustomed to life in a Northern city, do not have a long heritage of culture and an ethical tradition on which to build their lives. They seem to lack a sense of family intimacy and interdependence; as a result, their families often do not instill into the children good behavior patterns. Not everybody is fortunate enough to be born into families with these principles. In time, of course, Negroes will learn them.[32]

This inaccurate, patronizing, and demeaning perspective on educational disadvantages was given broad and lasting credence when Daniel P. Moynihan's widely publicized report *The Negro Family: A Case for National Action* was published in 1965.[33] Some social scientists viewed the report as another example of blaming the victim and were highly critical of its findings and conclusions. Nonetheless, "cultural deprivation" provided justification for the federal and state governments' funding of supplemental educational programs and projects in urban public school districts.[34]

In July 1963, when the Junior Bar Association of Milwaukee asked attorney Lloyd Barbee, president of the Wisconsin NAACP, to speak, the members expected to hear an account of the NAACP's role in the Birmingham Crusade that took place earlier that year and about current plans for the upcoming March on Washington on August 28. But that didn't happen. Born in Memphis in 1925, Lloyd Barbee served in the US Army during World War II. Supported by the GI Bill, he attended LeMoyne College in Memphis and afterward won a scholarship to attend the University of Wisconsin Law School. After graduation Barbee remained in Madison, worked for the state government, and soon headed the NAACP branch there. Active in the campaigns to gain employment of African American educators in the Milwaukee public schools, he moved there in 1961 and was eventually elected president of the Wisconsin NAACP.[35]

"If the *Brown* decision means anything," Lloyd Barbee told the lawyers, "it means that school segregation is unconstitutional wherever it exists, north or south." He called on the Wisconsin superintendent of public instruction to intervene and order Milwaukee public school officials "to act affirmatively" and pursue effective strategies to advance quality integrated education. Barbee was from the younger generation of civil rights activists who celebrated the hiring of African Americans as public school teachers in Milwaukee as a victory, but who also viewed racial integration as not just a means for Black advancement but an end in itself. While he served as head of the Madison branch, Barbee attended an NAACP leadership conference in 1961, led by attorneys Robert Carter and June Sharlogoff, and was encouraged to take on the campaign for integrated public schooling that the Milwaukee NAACP had failed to mount.[36]

The Milwaukee NAACP's lack of activism had been challenged earlier by Charles Sherard, an autoworker and president of the local chapter of the Negro American Labor Council (NALC). In 1962, Sherard's group launched picketing in front of grocery stores in Black neighborhoods where no Black workers were employed. The majority of those on the picket line were teenagers. While the NAACP branch president Clarence Parrish's complaints to business owners about job discrimination did result in the hiring of Black workers, the NALC's emphasis on nonviolent direct-action protests would prevail in the school campaign.[37]

The members of the Milwaukee school board did respond to Lloyd Barbee's charge that they were perpetuating segregated education in the system and should be supporting quality integrated education for all children. The school board convened the Special Committee on Equality of Educational Opportunity to investigate these charges. However, school board president John Foley chose corporate attorney Henry "Buck" Story to chair the subcommittee and in so doing guaranteed the interests of the white corporate establishment would guide the inquiry. The Story Committee, as it became known, went on to examine the operation of the "neighborhood school concept" in Milwaukee's public schools. Story told Barbee and others that school officials had no responsibility to address segregated schooling that resulted from housing patterns. The school board has only an "educational responsibility," and "no functional responsibility to eliminate the conditions of housing and employment which are the source of such handicaps" as poverty and racial discrimination.[38]

The Story Committee held public meetings as part of its investigation of the public schools in Milwaukee's Inner Core to determine the effectiveness of compensatory education programs introduced earlier. Barbee disputed this emphasis, viewing the compensatory education programs as "half a loaf," and considered integrated schooling another important objective. Barbee, Wesley Scott and Gwen Jackson of the Urban League, and Clara New of the Northside Community Inventory Conference (NCIC), a grassroots organization, testified before the Story Committee, some placing less emphasis on integration than others. But for Clara New and a few others "this [was] not an either/or situation"; there was "the need for a massive program" in compensatory education, and the efforts to achieve "complete integration" should be supported.[39]

This testimony before the Story Committee was given in late October 1963, right after the successful school boycott in Chicago, Milwaukee's almost contiguous sister city. What was happening in the Chicago public schools to try and stem the increasing racial segregation and the efforts to remove Superintendent Benjamin Willis were well-known among Milwaukee's leaders, parents, teenagers, and children. The headline in the *Milwaukee Journal* "Negro Pupils Join Boycott; Thousands Stay Out of Chicago Schools to Protest Policy" was not quite accurate, since thousands of white students also participated in the strike and attended the freedom schools.[40] Moreover, Black and white teenagers in Milwaukee had earlier demonstrated their commitment to nonviolent direct-action protests to challenge racial discrimination. In March 1963, members of Milwaukee's NAACP youth council launched picketing in front of Marc's Big Boy Restaurant because the owner, Ben Marcus, failed to hire any African Americans as workers. The young people maintained the picket lines for three days until the first Black workers were hired at the restaurant.[41]

In Cleveland, the practice that triggered picketing and other direct action protests was the intact busing of entire classrooms of Black students to all-white public schools and segregating them there. The UFM mounted demonstrations at the Brett and Memorial Elementary Schools, and eventually the school board ended the practice. In Milwaukee, African American parents believed that the intact busing there was *worse* than in Cleveland because the students were bused to the receiving school, then

When Juanita Jackson (fourth from the left) became director of the NAACP's youth department in 1935, she recommended that the youth councils across the country join in the campaign to free the Scottsboro Nine.

In 1947, the NAACP youth department held a national conference in Houston, Texas, where members also participated in civil rights marches.

The nine courageous teenagers who agreed to enroll at Little Rock's Central High School often met in the home of Daisy Bates (top row, second from right), president of the Arkansas NAACP branch, to plan activities.

In the Birmingham campaign in May 1963, children as young as 6 marched to the downtown area. They were arrested and taken to makeshift jails, where they remained until they were bailed out.

The children and teenagers who demonstrated in the streets of Birmingham in May 1963, even after they were jailed, often sang "We Shall Overcome" and other freedom songs to raise their spirits.

The first district-wide public school boycott was held in Boston in June 1963 and included only secondary school students. The second boycott there, in February 1964, included all grade levels. Parents, students, and teachers met at freedom schools opened at St. Mark's Congregational Church (above) and elsewhere in the city.

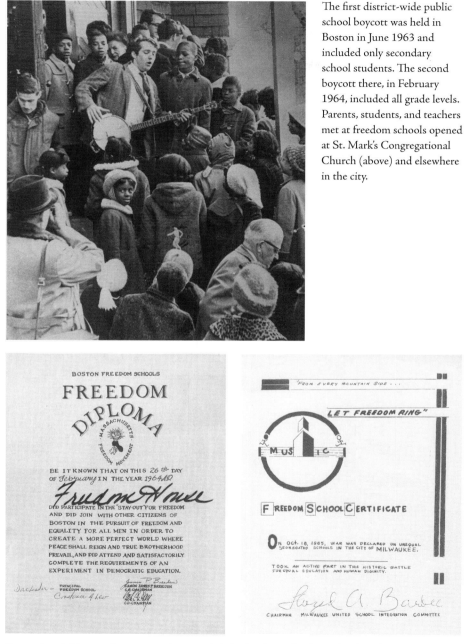

Boycotting children and teenagers who attended the freedom schools on the day of the strike were often rewarded with a Freedom School diploma or certificate. The diploma shown is from Boston; the certificate, from Milwaukee.

An estimated 224,770 students participated in the first public school boycott in Chicago in October 1963, calling for an end to racial segregation and the resignation of school superintendent Benjamin Willis. Thousands marched through downtown streets chanting "Freedom Now!"

On the eve of the first public school boycott in New York City, in February 1964, children and teenagers met with parents and community leaders at Rev. Galamison's Siloam Presbyterian Church to make posters for the marches.

An estimated 360,000 students went on strike in New York City in February 1964. Despite the cold weather, the protesters demonstrated in the streets, held rallies at city hall, and marched to school board headquarters in Brooklyn.

In Cleveland in the early 1960s, overcrowded conditions in Hazeldell public schools were addressed through the "intact busing" of Black teachers and students to all-white schools with available class-room spaces. Bused Black students were segregated *within* these schools and prohibited from using the facilities or interacting with other students.

In Cleveland, on April 7, 1964, at a CORE protest at a school construction site, 27-year-old Rev. Bruce Klunder was accidently runover by a bulldozer and killed. His death sparked widespread rioting that evening. The public school boycott in Cleveland took place later that month.

The Milwaukee United School Integration Committee (MUSIC) was formed in February 1964 to challenge "intact busing" and organized a public school boycott in May on the tenth anniversary of the Supreme Court's *Brown* decision. Flyers announcing the strike were circulated throughout the city (left). On "Freedom Day," picket lines went up at many schools, over twelve thousand students were absent, and thirty-two freedom schools were opened throughout the city.

The rioting associated with the "long hot summers" of the 1960s began in July 1964 in Brooklyn and Harlem. Violence erupted on Columbia Avenue in North Philadelphia in August 1964 following the arrest of a Black woman at a traffic intersection. Subsequent investigations revealed the majority of the rioters there and in other cities were teenagers and young adults.

Black children and teenagers in Selma in January and February 1965 organized their own marches and demonstrations in support of the voting rights campaign. Over two hundred who marched on the county courthouse were arrested and taken to local jails, where they were held for days before being released.

The Selma to Montgomery March took place following the unprovoked attack on nonviolent protesters on the Pettus Bridge on "Bloody Sunday," in 1965. Lynda Blackmon and other children and teenagers joined Martin Luther King Jr., Coretta Scott King, and hundreds of others who arrived in the state capital where Dr. King delivered his famous speech "Our God Is Marching On."

In May 1965, when Philadelphia NAACP leader Cecil B. Moore launched demonstrations at the all-white Girard College, thousands participated. Moore asked teenage gang members to support the protest campaign and to serve as marshals on the picket lines.

In August 1965, Dr. King spoke to hundreds gathered at the Girard College walls to call for the school's desegregation. King declared, "The Girard College wall is like the Berlin Wall" in Germany; it is "symbolic of the cancer that must be removed before there will be freedom and democracy in this county." The first fatherless Black boys were enrolled at Girard in September 1968.

(Additional photos and educational resources are available at www.youngcrusaders.org.)

bused back to their former school for lunch, then bused back to the host school for the afternoon classes, and then returned by bus to their home school at the end of the day. Lost class time due to unnecessary bus travel was a major issue for Black parents, students, and leaders in Milwaukee.[42]

The city's leading Black newspaper, the *Milwaukee Star*, ran a series of articles and photos in 1963 of the Black students being separated from the white students in the host schools. Historian Jack Dougherty found that "intact busing created dramatic visual representations of Milwaukee-style segregation, and Barbee's supporters seized on the issue." Marilyn More-heuser, a former nun and *Milwaukee Star* reporter and managing editor, wrote a series of articles exposing the conditions for African Americans in the public schools, and she worked closely with the coalition of Black and white organizations that came together in January 1964 to form the Milwaukee United School Integration Committee (MUSIC).[43]

The precipitating event leading to the formation of MUSIC occurred on Tuesday, January 21, 1964, when Lloyd Barbee walked out of the school committee's meeting after the chairman, Buck Story, decided that Barbee's allies—CORE's Richard McLeod and the NCIC's Cecil Brown—would not be allowed to speak at the proceedings. In front of newspaper reporters and television cameras, Barbee marched out, followed by McLeod and Brown. "Then two men lifted Barbee on their shoulders and carried him down the hall," the *Milwaukee Journal* reported, "and were followed by others who were singing . . . 'We Shall Overcome.'" Barbee told the media present that the NAACP and other groups would take "direct action" against the school board for practicing "de facto segregation in the public schools."[44] Martin Luther King Jr. came to Milwaukee the following week, spoke, and held a fund-raising rally. King told those assembled that "a school boycott is a creative way to dramatize the whole [integration] issue."[45]

The NAACP and CORE's March for Integrated Schools took place on Sunday, February 2, 1964, and the next day they formed picket lines in front of three "receiving schools" engaged in intact busing. The march and picketing brought no change in school board policies, and Superintendent Harold Vincent and committee chair Buck Story continued to defend their adherence to the "neighborhood schools" concept.[46] Similar to what occurred with the formation of the Coordinating Council of Community Organizations in Chicago, the Citywide Committee for Integrated Schools in New York City, and the United Freedom Movement in Cleveland, the representatives of the NAACP, CORE, the Urban League, and other Black and white social and political organizations came together to form MUSIC. They announced at the end of February that they were organizing a school boycott in Milwaukee to take place on May 18, 1964, coinciding with the tenth anniversary of the *Brown v. Board of Education* decision. As in the earlier school boycotts, MUSIC made arrangements for the striking children and teenagers to attend freedom schools on the day of the strike.[47]

Milwaukee city officials threatened to prosecute parents whose children participated in the boycott and any public school teachers who promoted nonattendance on that day. Nonetheless, Mildred Harpole, a reading teacher in the public schools, worked with MUSIC to identify thirty Black churches to provide space for the freedom schools and recruited three hundred volunteer teachers. Harpole believed it was imperative to open freedom schools on the day of the boycott. "I didn't feel that it was productive for the students to sit at home or be in the streets during the boycott." Journalist Marilyn Moreheuser developed the curriculum used in the schools and made sure it did not suggest that this was a "day of rebellion against the school system and authority," but it was a "positive program" that emphasized civil rights demands and African American history. As was the case in freedom schools in other cities, the young crusaders would also learn freedom songs emphasizing that they were "gonna sit at the welcome table one of these days."[48]

High school student Vada Harris supported the efforts to integrate the Milwaukee public schools, and rather than attending the all-Black North Division High School, she sought out and obtained a transfer to Riverside High, a predominantly white school. Harris volunteered to work with MUSIC, and on Freedom Day she taught Black History in the freedom school at her parish school, St. Boniface, where Father James Groppi was rector. Harris had studied Black History at that school. In 1966, Black high school students launched the Textbook Turn-In campaign that spread to schools across the country. In her senior year at Riverside High, in 1967, Harris organized the textbook turn-in protest there against the absence of

Black History in the assigned textbooks and other readings. She and other Black students turned in their textbooks at the principal's office at Riverside High, and that same year African American students in public and private schools in Chicago, Boston, Philadelphia, and other cities organized boycotts and other protests and demanded courses in Black History.[49]

On Freedom Day in Milwaukee, Monday, May 18, 1964, picket lines were set up in front of many school buildings, and it was estimated that twelve thousand children and teenagers participated in the boycott and 60 percent of the Black students in the public schools. Over four thousand Black and white students attended the thirty-two freedom schools opened throughout the city and named for John F. Kennedy, Martin Luther King Jr., Marian Anderson, James Baldwin, and other important figures. Opal Whatley sent her four children to the Crispus Attucks Freedom School held at Mount Moriah Baptist Church. "This is our day," Whatley proclaimed. "We're fighting for our rights." Over two hundred high school students attended the Frederick Douglass Freedom School at Christ Presbyterian Church, and one girl who was interviewed declared she was there "because the school board won't do anything." "If we didn't boycott," she added, "they'd think the kids didn't care."[50]

St. Matthew Christian Methodist Episcopal Church served as MUSIC's headquarters. Over eight hundred children and teenagers attended the freedom school there, and entertainer and civil rights activist Dick Gregory spoke to the students and teachers. "What you do here will help in Chicago, and from one end of the country to the other, and all over the world," Gregory told them. "The great thing about this is not black against white, it is right against wrong." College students and professors, local ministers, social workers, and even public school teachers taught in the freedom schools. The public school teachers "came in here expecting to get arrested because they were not going to school," MUSIC leader Marilyn Moreheuser pointed out. "That's an indication of real courage." At the end of that day, so many thousands of young people showed up at St. Matthew's Church for the "Freedom Day Hootenanny and Rock Concert" that it had to be moved to the pavilion in Garfield Park.[51]

Barbee and MUSIC viewed the boycott as a success in demonstrating broad community support for school integration. Indeed, Ms. Val Phillips, the sole African American on the board of aldermen in Milwaukee, declared, "The boycott was the greatest demonstration of Negro unity in the history of the city."[52] Unfortunately, as was the case in other cities, the school board's main response to the protests was to provide more resources in the form of compensatory education programs for the public schools in Milwaukee's Inner Core. Therefore, MUSIC filed a lawsuit, *Amos et al. v. Board of School Directors, City of Milwaukee*, on behalf of forty-one Black and white children, accusing school officials of maintaining segregation through "school zone boundaries, construction decisions, transfer policies, intact busing, and teacher assignments."[53] Through the end of 1964, MUSIC volunteers were involved in the extensive research for this lawsuit and Lloyd Barbee's successful campaign for a seat in the Wisconsin State Assembly from Milwaukee's Sixth District.

Members of the NAACP youth council in Milwaukee attended the freedom schools and were on the picket lines throughout the school protest campaigns. Early in 1965 Father James Groppi, a vice president of MUSIC, agreed to serve as the youth council's advisor. At the construction site on Milwaukee's South Side for McDowell Elementary School, the youth council set up picket lines in May 1965 because they believed the school would only contribute to public school segregation. When confronted by the police, many of the teenagers were arrested. In subsequent protests at public school construction sites, Father Groppi and several other Black and white clergymen were arrested along with young people.[54]

By the end of 1965, however, there were few changes in the school system, and MUSIC launched a new round of protests in pursuit of quality integrated education, including a second school boycott in October 1965 when an estimated seven thousand students went on strike, and even a third in March 1966 at only North Division High School in which five hundred students participated. By that date, as the *Amos et al.* lawsuit dragged on, MUSIC became more preoccupied with legal research and strategies and less with mass protests. In 1966, social activism among young people shifted to the open housing marches led by Father Groppi and the NAACP youth council, which culminated in the passage of Wisconsin's fair housing law in 1968.[55]

FREEDOM SUMMER AND THE MISSISSIPPI FREEDOM SCHOOLS

Black History was the major topic of discussion in the freedom schools opened in Boston, Chicago, New York City, Cleveland, and Milwaukee in 1963 and 1964 and became one of the most important subjects included the curriculum for the Mississippi freedom schools opened during SNCC's 1964 Freedom Summer campaign. In 1962, the Southern Regional Council, a civil rights leadership group, launched the Voter Education Project (VEP) to provide funds for voter registration drives. Bob Moses, SNCC's lead organizer, established the Council of Federated Organizations (COFO) in February 1962 to bring together the national and local groups engaged in civil rights activism throughout the South. The VEP helped to register over three hundred thousand Black southerners by 1964, but fewer than four thousand African Americans were on the voting rolls in Mississippi.[56]

SNCC's and COFO's organizing efforts in the Magnolia State were often stymied by opposition coming from law enforcement officers, local registrars, and members of the Ku Klux Klan and other white supremacists. Black SNCC organizers working in Mississippi were targeted, and Herbert Lee, Louis Allen, and five others associated with the voting rights campaign were murdered in 1963 and 1964. Moses and organizer Lawrence Guyot decided that SNCC should recruit northern white students to work in Mississippi; they realized that "wherever white volunteers went, the FBI follows." SNCC organizer Stokely Carmichael agreed. "While these [white volunteers] are here, national attention is here. The FBI isn't going to let anything happen to them. They let the murderers of Negroes off, but already [white] men have been arrested in Itta Bena [Mississippi] just for threatening white lives." Thus Moses and SNCC organizers decided to recruit Black and white college students to come to Mississippi for Freedom Summer.[57]

Over five hundred college and university students made the trip to Mississippi in the summer of 1964 and worked on voter registration campaigns, taught in freedom schools, and staffed SNCC's community centers known as Freedom Houses. After receiving training in June 1964 at Western College for Women in Oxford, Ohio (now part of Miami University), the brave volunteers began arriving later that month. Funds to support the summer project were raised by New York City's Friends of SNCC, the VEP, and other civil rights groups in northern cities and states. Unfortunately, the project got off to a bad start when three SNCC workers—James Chaney, Andrew Goodman, and Michael Schwerner—went missing in June after going to Philadelphia, Mississippi, to investigate the burning of a Black church and were arrested by the local police.[58]

James Chaney (Black) was 21 years old and from Meridian, Mississippi. He had joined SNCC in 1963 and organized voter education classes. Michael "Mikey" Schwerner was born in 1939 in New York City and was a graduate student in social work at Columbia University when he joined CORE. He and his wife, Rita Levant Schwerner, had just arrived in Meridian, Mississippi, in January 1964. Andrew Goodman was born in New York City in 1943 and was attending Queens College studying to become a social worker. The FBI sent dozens of agents to participate in the search for the missing men. After weeks of searching, their bodies were discovered in an earthen dam outside the town on August 4, 1964. Entertainer Dick Gregory offered a reward of $25,000 to anyone providing information leading to the arrest and conviction of the murderers, but local white residents kept their secret.[59]

Local registrars in Mississippi had prevented African Americans from voting in the delegate selection process for the upcoming Democratic National Convention in Atlantic City. In response, civil rights activists formed the Mississippi Freedom Democratic Party (MFDP) in June 1964 and held their own election—the Freedom Vote—for delegates to attend the Democratic Convention in August. Freedom Summer volunteers were able to register over sixty-three thousand voters who participated in the MFDP election, and the party sent sixty-two "Freedom Democrats" to the convention. However, President Lyndon B. Johnson refused to allow the Black and white MFDP delegates to replace the all-white delegation from Mississippi for fear of losing white southerners' support. When they were offered only two at-large seats, the MFDP delegates rejected it and walked out of the convention.[60]

SNCC and COFO had much more success with the opening of the freedom schools. Since 1962, SNCC organizers had been soliciting books, magazines, maps, and other materials for the libraries in the Freedom

Houses. Additional curricular materials were requested for use in the freedom schools. COFO announced that the freedom schools would "provide politically emerging communities with new young leadership, and constitute a real attack on the presently stifling system of education existing in the State." The schools would create "an educational experience for students which will make it possible for them to challenge the myths of our society, to perceive more clearly its realities, and alternatives, and ultimately, new directions for action." The children and teenagers would be taught to become "active agents in bringing about social change."[61]

Forty-one freedom schools were opened throughout Mississippi in the summer of 1964. The children and teenagers received training in citizenship, leadership development, African American and civil rights history, art, drama, music, typing, and foreign languages. Homer Hill attended the freedom school in Clarksdale and recalled that "the teachers put a library in the school and many of the books were on black history. Richard Wright, . . . Langston Hughes, [and] Frederick Douglass' writings" were included with "a wide range of books and plays." Rather than memorizing information, the students engaged in discussions and were "given the opportunity to role-play, dramatize and reenact the lessons they learned." The students in teacher Wally Roberts's freedom school class in Ruleville told him, "What we want you to do is to help us become Freedom Fighters. We want to go on picket lines and do protests."[62]

Thelma Eubanks was 15 years old in 1964 and attended the freedom school in McComb every day it was open. "We were introduced to black authors who we didn't know anything about at the time. Richard Wright and James Baldwin. I thought they were good." This was a summer of many firsts for Eubanks. "This was the first time I really heard black success stories. And the freedom school was the first time I had a social relationship with whites." This was important because "it just made me know that everybody in the world wasn't like [white] southerners."[63] Using donated mimeograph machines, the students printed their own newspapers, entitled *Freedom Star*, *Freedom's Journal*, or *Freedom Train*, and used them to raise the political consciousness of children and adults in the area. The newspapers were distributed when the students went out canvassing as part of the voter registration drives. Eddie J. Carthen was 12 years old and recalled,

"Canvassing was tough work. . . . We'd have certain days we'd go out and canvass all day."[64]

While attending the summer program and afterward, freedom school students participated in civil rights protests. In Indianola, they engaged in a sit-in to desegregate the public library and local restaurants; in Cleveland, Mississippi, when the students organized a picket line and distributed voter registration materials, they were arrested. And in Ruleville, when several freedom school students tried to obtain service at a local restaurant, shots were fired at them by white segregationists.[65] After attending the freedom schools during the summer, some students volunteered to desegregate all-white public schools in their area. Thelma Eubanks, who was arrested several times for participating in civil rights protests, desegregated all-white McComb High School in the fall of 1964.[66] Other freedom school alumni organized boycotts of the substandard Black public schools in the state. In Jackson, Mississippi, "we were able to organize the three high schools," recalled Hezekiah Watkins. "I'm told that 90 percent of the student body walked out." As they marched down a highway, the police arrived and arrested some of them. "It happened, and we made history that day."[67]

In Shaw, Mississippi, the students boycotted all-Black McEvans High School in September 1964 over the lack of educational resources; and in January 1965 at Henry Weathers High School, serving Sharkey and Issaquena Counties, over four hundred students walked out after they were told to remove the SNCC breast pins they were wearing. This boycott inspired other protests, and in Indianola in February 1965, as the young crusaders walked along the highway protesting racial discrimination, they were attacked by police using billy clubs and cattle prods. Fifty-three students were arrested. Historian Jon N. Hale found that during Freedom Summer the freedom school students "were not just educated to work in civil rights campaigns, but they organized among themselves and demanded social and educational change."[68] As will be discussed, throughout 1965 and 1966, thousands of elementary and high school students participated in sit-ins, boycotts, school walkouts, and other direct action protests in Mississippi, Alabama, Louisiana, and in many northern and western states, demonstrating their strong commitment to the ongoing civil rights campaigns.

PART III
From Civil Rights to Black Power

Chapter 7

Police Brutality, Black Self-Defense, and Student Activism

*I went to jail a lot. We marched downtown [in Selma]
because we were tired. Tired of going in Kress' and you
could order something, but you had to take it outside.
We were tired of that. We were tired of being put in
the back all the time. When we went to the movies,
they had a colored side and white side. The white
side was always better. We were tired of this.*

Towanna Hinkle, 16 years old (1965)[1]

"ONLY THREE-HUNDRED OF US were permitted to march all the way to Montgomery," Lynda Blackmon Lowery recalled. "Of the marchers going the whole distance, I was the youngest of them all." There were 18- and 19-year-olds who journeyed over the three days from Selma to the Alabama capital, "but I was one day short of my fifteenth birthday."[2] When the voting rights protests were taking place in Selma, especially between January and March 1965, hundreds of children and teenagers marched, and scores were arrested and victimized by police brutality. Dallas County, Alabama, Sheriff Jim Clark, and Selma's director of public safety, Wilson Baker, generally brutalized and jailed civil rights protesters and intimidated and threatened violence against African American residents. While there have been many accounts of the civil rights protests in Selma, the emphasis is usually placed on "Bloody Sunday," March 7, 1965, and the subsequent Selma to Montgomery March. What has not been highlighted is the contribution that children and teenagers made in the marches, sit-ins, picketing, and other demonstrations *before* the brutal police attack on the Edmund Pettus Bridge. Indeed, as was the case with the massive school boycotts in the northern cities, the success of the protest at Selma was due very much to the extensive engagement and mobilization among children and teenagers.

The police brutality on display on Bloody Sunday was much too famil-iar to Black adolescences and young adults in American cities and towns. Before and after the Selma march, police brutalization and killing of Afri-can Americans led to calls for the establishment of civilian review boards to investigate citizens' complaints against the police and to recommend disciplinary action when warranted. Unfortunately, few were created, and even where citizens' advisory committees existed, they had no authority to discipline or punish the officers. Thus, when the local Black population reached a critical mass, many teenagers and young adults participated in violent disturbances and rioting sparked by police murders or rumors of murders. Police brutality, price gouging by store owners, and employment discrimination were among the reasons given for the "long, hot summers" in the 1960s.

"WE ARE MOVING TO THE LAND OF FREEDOM"

Bill and Amelia Boynton were among the few teachers or other Black pro-fessionals who challenged the racist practices in Selma in 1963 by working with SNCC organizers Bernard and Colia Lafayette. In most places in the South, African American public school teachers chose not to engage in the civil rights campaigns or try to register to vote for fear of losing their jobs.[3] The Dallas County Voters' League (DCVL) had been formed in the late 1920s to address Black voter registration, but after the president, C.J. Adams, was threatened and forced to leave, Bill Boynton succeeded him until his death in May 1963. Frederick Reese headed the group be-tween 1963 and 1965. But there was little success in the voter registration drives. While over twenty-eight thousand Black citizens were eligible, Amelia Boynton pointed out, "in [February] 1963 there were 180 registered

Negroes in [Dallas] County, though clinics and schools had been held for several years." African Americans made up 57 percent of the population in Dallas County, and therefore Black voting strength was considered a threat to white supremacy. Legalized and extralegal anti-Black violence was carried out to maintain whites' control in Dallas County.[4]

As a result of the DCVL and SNCC's organizing efforts, however, Bernard Lafayette reported that in 1963, "between February and September, we got about 2000 people to go down and try to register and about 600 of them actually got registered." The Lafayettes returned to Tougaloo College in September 1963, and Worth Long, James Love, and later Silas Norman became the SNCC organizers in Selma. In the fall of 1964 Lafayette reported, "James Bevel and SCLC moved into Alabama and began to build on making Selma a national issue of Voter Registration." Amelia Boynton prevailed upon and finally convinced Dr. King and his SCLC colleagues to come specifically to Dallas County and Selma to participate in the voting rights campaign. The reality that young SNCC organizers had been working in Selma for months became a source of tension and conflict once SCLC officially arrived.[5]

The Emancipation Day commemoration on January 2, 1965, signaled Dr. King's official arrival in Selma. With over seven hundred people present at Brown Chapel African Methodist Episcopal (AME) Church, King denounced local efforts to "freeze voter registration at their present undemocratic levels." Civil rights activists would first appeal to white political leaders in Alabama, but if they do not act, "we will seek to arouse the Federal Government by marching by the thousands to places of registration." And he made it clear, "We must be willing to go to jail by the thousands. We are not asking, we are demanding the ballot."[6]

Bettie Fikes and other high school students had been conducting sit-ins at the Dairy Queen and Woolworth's in Selma throughout 1964, but they wouldn't let Lynda Blackmon participate because she was too young. Blackmon only served as the "gopher" to make reports to parents and other adults once the teenagers were arrested. "But all that changed on January 2, 1965." Dr. King and SCLC were planning a youth march for January 18, 1965, and Blackmon was going to take part. She recalled that every time a Black resident went to register to vote, his or her photo was taken. "Someone would take a picture and then show it to the person's boss. White people could fire black people wherever and however they wanted." But the children and the teenagers were not as vulnerable to threats and intimidation; "that's why civil rights leaders needed us children to march."[7]

A series of youth rallies and workshops on nonviolence were held and led by James Bevel. On Thursday, January 14, Dr. King met with the young people, and the following day forty high school students petitioned the SCLC organizers to officially assist with the upcoming march. On Monday, January 18, over three hundred protesters gathered for the march from Brown Chapel; at least half were teenagers. Those who stopped along the way to obtain service at store lunch counters were usually accommodated. Eight-year-old Sheyann Webb had attended the meetings and rallies and decided that she would miss school on January 18 and join the protest. The marchers set out headed for the courthouse. Walking two abreast along the sidewalk with her neighbor Margaret Moore, Webb recalled, "We passed the Selma City Hall where a group of white people stood watching us. Some of them laughed, I remember, but I didn't hear any shouts or jeering." At the courthouse the marchers stopped and began singing freedom songs. Amelia Boynton asked Sheriff Clark if they could enter the building. He responded, "You stay inside once you get there." Boynton went in and waited for a while and then came out at lunchtime as the staff was leaving. "When the sheriff saw her, he just got mad." He grabbed Boynton by the neck and "ran her down the street to the sheriff's car and had her arrested and taken to the city jail."[8]

Then the deputies came forward, and one shouted, "Y'all are under arrest." The marchers were pushed and shoved, sometimes struck with a cattle prod. "I saw some of the [deputies] use the cattle prods and saw men and women jump when the electric ends touched against their bodies. . . . We were being moved like cattle." At city hall a police officer asked Webb why she was there and not in school. "Who told you to go to the courthouse with these people?" She answered, "Nobody, I just come." "If nobody told you, then why did you come?" "To be free," she replied. "If you want to be free, then go home." Webb was allowed to leave, but sixty protesters were arrested with Amelia Boynton that day.[9]

Rachel West was 9 years old and attended the rallies at Brown Chapel with Sheyann Webb. Sometimes when they were singing, Dr. King "would call us over where he would be sitting at the altar and lift us up on his lap and we'd sit there with him until it was time for him to speak. I'm sure many of the other people envied us. We'd be sitting there so proud." Rachel West had ten brothers and sisters. Her parents, Lonzy and Alice West, were poor and often had a hard time feeding the large family. "Food was always short and sometimes we were hungry." At some of the rallies at the church, the civil rights workers would bring and pass out lunchmeat sandwiches, milk, and orange juice. "There were lots of kids out there . . . and I remember jumping up and down . . . trying to get to the front of the line worrying that the supply would run out before I got up there." But she made it; "the milk was gone, but there were cartons of orange juice." The major reason for the civil rights activism was voting rights, but there were practical purposes as well: "It helped us get some food."[10]

The young crusaders were particularly inspired by the example of their teachers. In most southern protest campaigns, Black public school teachers stayed on the sidelines, but in Selma, on January 22, 1965, under the leadership of Rev. E. D. Reese, the Black teachers gathered and marched to the courthouse, where Sheriff Clark pushed them out of the way with his nightstick. School superintendent Joseph Pickard was there and urged the teachers to return to the church. The teachers stood there for twenty minutes and were not arrested, so they marched back to Brown Chapel. Sheyann Webb remembered, "When the teachers began coming in" the three hundred children and teenagers "just stood up and applauded." This reception touched the teachers and "inspired them to take part in the drive for voting rights, for freedom. At the same time, they—with their dignity that astounded the white community—inspired many of the children as well as the adults."[11]

Afterward, Judge James A. Hare issued an injunction forbidding demonstrations in front of the courthouse. On Monday, January 25, Rachel West left school and headed for the courthouse, where dozens of singing protesters were being told by Sheriff Clark that this was an illegal assembly and they must disperse. After a few moments, they began singing again. "Shut up! . . . I said stop it right now." Clark then warned, "If you don't stop right now, I'm going to arrest every one of you." The singing stopped for a few minutes, but then someone began again and others joined in. "All right," shouted Sheriff Clark, "Arrest 'em. Move 'em this way. Move 'em this way down the street." The deputies started grabbing people, and over a hundred were arrested. Rachel West ran home to tell her family what had happened.[12]

Then, on January 30, 1965, a cold Saturday morning, James Bevel led about a hundred marchers to the Selma courthouse. Rachel West recalled that "the wind was terrible; it went right through my coat"; Sheyann Webb was wearing only a dress "and her legs were vibrating." The singing marchers stood outside the board of registrars' office. Sheriff Clark came out and told them the office was closed and they had to leave. Bevel told the sheriff that "Negroes had been waiting a hundred years." "They're going to have to wait longer" was Clark's snide reply. The marchers started singing again, and the sheriff pointed to Bevel and shouted, "Arrest him." The deputies moved in and arrested about twenty-five people. West and Webb ran home, while others returned to Brown Chapel.[13]

Dr. King returned to Selma at the end of January and prepared to lead the march to the courthouse on Monday, February 1. He planned to lead one march to the courthouse from Brown Chapel, another would leave from a church in neighboring Perry County, and a third would consist of children and teenagers assembled in another church. "Even though they cannot vote," Dr. King argued, "they have a right to make their own witness and are determined to be freed." That morning King led hundreds of marchers from Brown Chapel to the courthouse, and hundreds were arrested. Dr. King and Rev. Ralph Abernathy were released at first and then jailed again along with 250 others.[14] At the Perry County Courthouse, five hundred children and teenagers had been arrested, and the conditions of their incarceration were life threatening. In *Pillar of Fire*, Taylor Branch reports that in Perry County the deputies "had stuffed several hundred young prisoners into a fifty-by-sixteen stockade." SNCC organizer Prathia Hall witnessed the "brutal conditions": the young people were "crammed on bare concrete, provided water in . . . tubs from which they were obliged to drink 'like cattle or with their hands.'" Many juveniles were released to their parents, but others were taken to a more distant prison farm.[15]

Sheyann Webb and Rachel West were among the one thousand students, "most of them junior high school kids," Webb recalled, who gathered after school on Wednesday, February 3, and marched toward city hall carrying signs declaring "Release Dr. King from Jail" and "Let Our Parents Vote." Public safety director Wilson Baker met them and kept telling them to go home. "Finally, he announced that we [were] all to follow him, that we were under arrest." The children were taken into city hall, and their names and addresses were collected. "Some of us were then told to go home. The others were jailed."[16] The following week Rachel West learned what had happened to those arrested. The sheriff's deputies took them on a forced march that day into the backwoods. Rachel found out that as the teenagers passed the courthouse, Sheriff Clark came out and shouted, "March!"

> A bigger girl, trying to catch her breath and talk, said . . . the deputies pushed and prodded them with their clubs, making them run toward the prison road camp about five miles away. "We [were] run out of town," the girl said. "And when we dropped to catch our wind they'd get after us and threaten to hit us. They kept saying, 'You wanted to march, so march!' They wouldn't let us rest.' . . . Finally, after several miles, the deputies let them go, apparently sure they'd worn all the "marching fever" out of them. "We gonna march again," the girl was shouting. "He ain't gonna stop us. He ain't."[17]

The next day, Thursday, February 11, the teenagers organized a march that was "four times larger than Wednesday's." Lynda Blackmon marched with them, and she was arrested again.[18] "The first time I went to jail I was fourteen and I was scared." There were about a hundred children packed into two cells in the city jail, one for girls and the other for boys. "After that first time, I wasn't so afraid because I was with my buddies and we knew we had each other's back." That Thursday, however, "when the city jail was full, the police took busloads of us kids to a prison camp called Camp Selma. The prison was about five miles away from town." The teenagers were kept there for three days, then they loaded them on a bus and they "took us to another prison camp even farther away." They knew their parents were frightened because the sheriff and his deputies would not tell them where their children were being held. "We were gone for six long days. Finally when our leaders in Selma found out where we were, they demanded our release. The buses brought us back to Selma, and we all ran home as fast as we could."[19]

In nearby Marion, Alabama, the county seat, marches had been taking place for two weeks, and the *New York Times* reported that on February 3 over seven hundred schoolchildren had marched in protest.[20] Marches continued there without arrests, but on February 17 SCLC organizer James Orange was arrested and charged with "contributing to the delinquency of minors," and so another march was organized. State troopers learned of the protest to take place in Marion on February 18, 1965, and swung into action. The police blacked out the photographers' cameras with paint and turned off the streetlights between Rev. James Dobynes's Mount Zion Baptist Church and the county courthouse. Upon leaving the church, the marchers were stopped by state troopers who had blocked the street. Using a bullhorn, police chief C. T. Harris ordered the marchers to disperse or turn around and go back; but when Rev. Dobynes knelt to pray, he was clubbed and dragged away by the troopers. Other troopers went after the other marchers and chased ten or more into Mack's Café, including 82-year-old Cager Lee. As they were beating Lee, his daughter, Viola Jackson, tried to pull the troopers away, but she was beaten as well. When her son, Jimmie Lee Jackson, moved to protect her, he was grabbed, thrown against a wall, and shot twice in the stomach by two troopers.[21]

Jimmie Lee Jackson was taken to the hospital in Selma. Lynda Blackmon and other children and teenagers not only "prayed Jimmie Lee would live" but they also mounted a protest march and Blackmon was again arrested and taken to the city jail. "There were twenty-three girls stuffed into this one cell." But one of the young crusaders, Pat Green, became ill. "We kept calling the jailers and asking for help," but the jailers only gave the girls brooms and told them to clean up any mess. "Pat was moaning and groaning," so Blackmon decided to use the broom handle to break open the window in the cell. "We shouted down that we had a sick girl who needed some help." Soon the jailer returned with two deputies and asked who broke out the window. If no one talked, then they "all were going to the sweatbox." Lynda decided to confess. "I did it." "What's your name?" "Lynda Blackmon." But as depicted in the 1960 film *Spartacus* when Roman soldiers confronted the enslaved rebels, Blackmon recounted that "somebody behind me said, 'My name's Lynda Blackmon.' Somebody on the other side said, 'My name's Lynda Blackmon.' Pretty soon there were about five Lynda Blackmons."[22]

Except for Pat Green and one other girl, they were all taken to the sweatbox, "which didn't have any windows. It was an iron room with a big iron door." There was little air, no beds, no sink, and no toilet; "nothing but heat." Blackmon was unsure how long she was in the sweatbox. "All I know is every one of us passed out from the heat." Lynda came to as other prisoners were carrying her into court. The judge was there. "Y'all smell. Just write your name on a piece of paper and get out of here." Some wrote "Howdy Doody" and "Minnie Mouse"; no one wrote their real name. "By the time I got out of jail that day, Jimmie Lee Jackson had died."[23]

ON THE EDMUND PETTUS BRIDGE

James Bevel came to visit the Jackson family in their home in Marion on February 26 and asked them if SCLC should keep going with the voting rights campaign. Cager Lee, Jimmie Lee Jackson's grandfather, declared, "Oh, yeah!" Back in Selma that evening, Bevel spoke at the mass meeting at Brown Chapel and called on those assembled to go by foot to the state capital to press for full voting rights. The audience response was overwhelmingly positive. "Be prepared to walk to Montgomery! Be prepared to sleep on the highway." Dr. King was in Atlanta then, but he supported the plans to march from Selma to Montgomery to petition state lawmakers for voting rights. King came to Marion on Wednesday, March 3, to deliver the sermon at Jimmie Lee Jackson's funeral and then returned to Atlanta.[24]

When Governor George Wallace learned of the planned march, he initially thought it would not be a problem and agreed to provide an escort of state troopers. However, several Alabama legislators told him of the great likelihood of violence along the route, and that such a march was really not a good idea. So on Friday, March 5, Wallace issued a ban on the march. Dr. King was in Atlanta and was told about the ban, but SCLC's Hosea Williams and others let King know that hundreds of people had already arrived in Selma to participate in the march. Dr. King finally agreed to move ahead and told his colleagues he would work on overturning Wallace's ban.[25]

On Sunday afternoon, March 7, the marchers gathered at Brown Chapel and then headed out across the Edmund Pettus Bridge. Eight-year-old Sheyann Webb and 14-year-old Lynda Blackmon were with them. "I was walking between some young white guy and a black woman," Webb remembered. "I think she must have been from Perry County." Before they left the church, the holy warriors prayed and sang freedom songs. Webb continued, "As we got to the downtown and started toward the bridge, we got quiet."[26] There was a wall of state troopers and the sheriff's posse on horseback, with Sheriff Jim Clark and state trooper Colonel Al Lingo out in front. Sheyann Webb saw "they were wearing blue helmets, blue jackets, and they carried clubs in their hands; they had those gas mask pouches slung across their shoulders." She heard Sheriff Clark "speaking over the bullhorn saying that this was an unlawful march and for us to disperse and go back to the church."[27]

Lynda Blackmon was accompanied by her friends. "I was with Jimmy Webb and fifteen of my buddies. Jimmy was our group leader." After the bullhorn announcement, "Jimmy Webb said, 'Let's pray,' and we went down on our knees. That was normal." Blackmon was still on her knees when she heard "pop, pop, pop." Then "all of a sudden a cloud of gas was burning my lungs, and my eyes. I couldn't breath and I couldn't see."[28]

The brutal attack on the peaceful protesters on the Edmund Pettus Bridge on what became known as Bloody Sunday was captured by photographers and on videotape. Viewed first by television audiences nationwide, and then internationally, since that time the startling images of the attack have been used in numerous documentary films about the 1960s civil rights campaigns. When the troopers attacked, Lynda Blackmon was afraid and just stood there, then an unidentified white man grabbed her from behind and began pulling her along the road. "I bit that hand and that's when he hit me over my eye. He hit me twice—hard." She tried to get up, but "he pushed me forward and hit me again, this time on the back of my head." Lynda staggered up and began running, right into the cloud of tear gas, and passed out. The next thing she remembered she was on a stretcher and "some men were loading me into the back of a hearse." She knew she was not dead, so she jumped off the stretcher and started running home. "I sure wasn't going to let them put me in the back of that hearse before my time." On the way back she saw her sister Joanne Blackmon, seemingly lifeless, being carried by a man. "They killed my sister!" But the man told her she had only fainted from the gas. Lynda slapped Joanne to awaken her, but when she saw Lynda she started screaming. "I knew the tear gas had messed up my face, but I didn't realize I was covered with blood."[29]

The family of Rachel West had been asked to remain behind in the church, but as soon as the marchers disappeared from view, Rachel and several of her classmates ran through the side streets and tried to catch up with them. They didn't make it. "All of a sudden I heard screaming and shouting," West recalled, "and I stopped to see what was happening." The mounted troopers were approaching, and Rachel began to run toward her home as the horsemen were heading down her street. Frank Soracco, a civil rights worker, saw what was about to happen. Soracco "came by me and was moving fast. And I must have been crying out because he stopped and just swept me up and carried me under the armpit and kept moving. . . . This one horseman was right behind us, and there were several others coming on fast." Soracco deposited Rachel inside her house and continued upstairs and locked himself in the bathroom. The white civil rights marchers had been targeted, and "the horsemen were mad at them. They wanted to kill them, I was sure, especially the way they had chased the guy who carried me in."[30]

Those who were attacked or had witnessed the state troopers' rampage went back that evening to Brown Chapel depressed and disappointed. Some were crying because "they felt that they had been beaten down . . . again." "Now there was a bunch of kids there." Sheyann Webb was with Rachel West and "we were just sitting there crying." Later that evening, however, someone in the congregation started moaning and humming a freedom song, and pretty soon "it just started to catch on, and people began to pick it up." "Ain't Gonna Let Nobody Turn Me Around" was the song, and soon everyone in the church was singing "Ain't gonna let George Wallace turn me around," "Ain't gonna let Jim Clark turn me around." The singing became louder and louder; soon they were clapping their hands and crying for joy. People hearing the singing came in from the streets. "Just all of a sudden something happened that night and we knew in that church that—Lord Almighty—we had really won, after all. We had won!"[31]

After Dr. King announced that a new march from Selma to Montgomery would take place on Tuesday, March 9, hundreds more began pouring into town to participate.[32] Because King had not received assurances that the march was officially sanctioned, and wanting to avoid another bloody incident, he led the marchers to the Pettus Bridge and up to the waiting state troopers and police deputies; he prayed and then turned the marchers around and returned to Brown Chapel. King was awaiting the federal court order rescinding the ban on the march. James Forman and other SNCC leaders who had not been told what Dr. King planned to do were angered and let King know. Their attention soon shifted that evening when they learned that James L. Reeb, Orloff Miller, and Clark Olsen, Unitarian Universalist ministers who had come to Selma to march, were attacked by several white men as they left Walkers' Café. Rev. Reeb from Boston died in the hospital from head injuries two days later. Rev. Reeb's murder focused even more national attention on the march, and people from throughout the country soon descended on Selma.[33]

Three thousand marchers finally set out on Sunday, March 21, accompanied by national guardsmen.[34] Lynda Blackmon was one of the teenagers who actually made the four-day trip. She spent the first night in a tent on a farm with 150 other females; and the next day, she recalled, "was March 22, 1965—my fifteenth birthday." In her memoir *Turning 15 on the Road to Freedom*, Blackmon describes the water-logged journey culminating in Montgomery with the evening concert on March 24. It included Harry Belafonte, Sammy Davis Jr., Pete Seeger, Nina Simone, Tony Bennett, Peter, Paul, and Mary, and other famous entertainers. The next day twenty-five thousand people assembled at the capitol, where Dr. King gave his much-celebrated speech "Our God Is Marching On!" "We are on the move now," he declared. "The bombing of our homes will not dissuade us. We are on the move. The beating and killing of our clergymen and young people will not divert us. We are on the move. . . . We are moving to the land of freedom."[35] Lynda Blackmon was in Montgomery that day. "My buddies were there, kids I went to jail with so many times." She listened to the speakers, and then, as she later recalled, "I went home and back to school. But I was a different person. We still had mass meetings, but we didn't march or go to jail anymore."[36]

HIGH SCHOOL STUDENT ACTIVISM AND BLACK SELF-DEFENSE

The violence and brutality that state troopers and sheriff deputies unleashed on nonviolent protesters on Bloody Sunday had become all too familiar to most Americans, especially Black children and teenagers who were (or were not) engaged in the nonviolent direct-action protests in the early 1960s. As with the Children's Crusade in Birmingham, the police brutality in Selma had been captured and disseminated by television news programs, radio, newspapers, and other media, and there was a range of responses to the police attacks on the marchers crossing Selma's Pettus Bridge. For example, on Sunday, March 14, 1965, it was estimated that twenty-five thousand people in Boston, sixteen thousand in San Francisco, fifteen thousand in Washington, DC, and fifteen thousand in Harlem rallied to protest the unprovoked violence and brutality in Selma.[37]

Most of the students at all-Black Jackson High School in Jonesboro, Louisiana, had seen the news reports of the violent attack in Selma and were quite disturbed by it when they arrived at school on Monday, March 8, 1965. Then a rumor began to spread that physical education teacher Frederick Kirkpatrick, a member of the Deacons for Defense and Justice, a Black self-defense group, was going to be fired because of his social activism. Bloody Sunday was terrible enough, recalled Annie Johnson, a student at Jackson High, this rumor "kind of just put a little icing on it and stirred it up a bit. The kids went nuts over it." The angry students left their classes and began congregating in the halls discussing how to respond. At some point during these discussions the glass in the trophy case and the panes covering the framed photos of Principal J. R. Washington and school superintendent J. D. Koonce were smashed. Given the disturbance, Principal Washington contacted school district officials and was given permission to close the school for the rest of the day.[38]

The significance of Black self-defense groups such as the Deacons for Defense protecting nonviolent civil rights activists has been well documented in works by historians Christopher Strain, Hasan Kwame Jeffries, Akinyele Omowale Umoja, and others.[39] At times, these self-defense groups had to protect Black high school students engaged in civil rights activism. Historian Simon Wendt, in *The Spirit and the Shotgun: Armed Resistance and the Struggle for Civil Rights,* devoted a chapter to "God, Gandhi, and Guns in Tuscaloosa." He described how the Black men in the unnamed self-defense group had to rescue a group of high school students who were being threatened by a white mob outside the Druid movie theater in Tuscaloosa. The 1964 Civil Rights Act had just been passed, and these young people in Alabama decided to "test the compliance of the city's movie theater and its restaurants." On the afternoon of July 6, 1964, a group of Black teenagers had managed to desegregate the Druid Theater, but when they were leaving, they were attacked by angry whites hurling stones and bottles. Police officers arrived, but they had difficulty controlling the mob. One of the teens went back into the theater and telephoned Joseph Mallisham, the leader of the Black self-defense group, who immediately assembled a "two-car convoy manned with armed blacks to rescue them." When they arrived, the teenagers jumped into the cars, and as they sped away, other defensemen joined the convoy. But Wendt tells us the vehicles were being fired upon by Klansmen all along the route. "Poor marksmen, they missed, and several black men rolled down their windows and returned fire. The stunned white assailants, not expecting armed resistance, fled quickly."[40]

In Jonesboro, Louisiana, the Deacons for Defense and Justice was formed in 1964 and worked closely with CORE organizers operating in northern Louisiana parishes. Frederick Kirkpatrick had arrived as a teacher at Jackson High School in 1963 after having played football and graduated from Grambling University. Soon after, Kirkpatrick became one of the leaders of the Deacons.[41] When the students at Jackson High walked out of their classes upon hearing that Kirkpatrick was to be fired, they decided to remain on strike and came up with a "list of demands" for school officials. They called for the renovation of the gymnasium, the building of an auditorium, and expansion of the library's resources and the curriculum "to include auto mechanics and clerical skills; and they wanted 'Negro history courses.'" The next day the students showed up outside the school carrying protest signs and "singing freedom songs" and remained there that day and the next. On Thursday, March 11, school officials announced that Jackson High was closed but said it would reopen on Monday, March 15.[42]

Jonesboro's white leaders then decided that the students' boycott and picketing at Jackson High had to end, and on Friday, March 12 the police officers and their posse showed up, blockaded the streets surrounding the school, and prepared for an attack. When Deacon Olin Satcher came upon the police blockade, he asked what was going on, but was violently assaulted by a police officer who then arrested him. When Deacon Ernest Thomas came on the scene, a police officer told him to leave. When he asked for the officer's name, Thomas was grabbed, placed in handcuffs, and threatened with violence. "You better not move or I'll have hair flying everywhere," the policeman barked. At that point Thomas was arrested for "threatening a police officer and resisting arrest" and taken to jail. But the Deacons knew that by challenging what was about to happen, they "had deterred police officers and vigilantes from attacking the defenseless students."[43]

The following week the students remained on strike and were manning the picket lines around Jackson High. One morning the police and firemen showed up at the school and stopped the fire truck close to where the students were picketing. The firemen began to prepare to open water hoses on the teenagers, similar to what Sheriff Bull Connor had done to the young crusaders in Birmingham two years earlier. Historian Lance Hill's account of what happened next is based on his interview with CORE organizer Fred Brooks, who was on the picket line that day along with the high school students.

> Brooks . . . watched helplessly as the crisis deepened. Suddenly a car pulled in front of the school. The doors swung open and four Deacons, led by [Ernest] Thomas, stepped out and began calmly loading their shotguns in plain view of the police. . . . The firemen walked toward the students with their hoses in tow. Then Brooks . . . remembered one of the Deacons giving the order: "When you see the first water, we gonna open up on them. We gonna open up on all of them." The Deacons then turned to the police and issued a deadly serious ultimatum. "If you turn that water hose on those kids, there's going to be some blood out here today." The police officers warily eyed the four Deacons standing before them, shotguns loaded and readied, faces grim and determined. Prudence prevailed. The law enforcers retreated and ordered the fire trucks to roll up the hoses and depart.[44]

On Sunday, March 14, 1965, as tens of thousands marched in cities and towns throughout the country protesting the police brutality in Selma on Bloody Sunday, CORE chairman James Farmer appeared on the television news program *Issues and Answers*. He called on federal marshals and FBI agents to go to Jonesboro and other Louisiana cities and towns and arrest police officers engaged in brutal attacks on civil rights workers and nonviolent protesters.[45]

The students at Jackson High maintained their boycott, and on March 26 hundreds of Black students and parents marched on the school board building in Jonesboro in protest over the shooting murder of Detroit teacher Viola Liuzzo, who had been driving civil rights activists between Selma and Montgomery. This huge protest and the escalating tensions throughout the state due to the Deacons' increasing militancy prompted Louisiana governor John McKeithen to enter the stalled negotiations between the Jonesboro school board and Black students, parents, and the Deacons. Lance Hill reported that by Saturday, March 27, 1965, "McKeithen had conceded virtually all the boycotters' demands. He agreed to additional textbooks and water fountains, library improvements, new landscaping and playgrounds." And subsequently "voters approved an $800,000 bond issue for a new gymnasium."[46]

"THE TYPICAL RIOTER WAS A TEENAGER OR YOUNG ADULT"

Law enforcement officers in Louisiana and other southern, northern, and western states continued to carry out brutal attacks on African American men, women, and children in 1965, but the unarmed and armed resistance was mounting and often led to rioting, numerous injuries, and loss of life. Before the 1960s in most northern or western cities and towns, there was not a critical mass of young Black people to defend themselves or to mount an insurgency. Indeed, that could be suicidal. Throughout the nineteenth and early twentieth century, African American men, women, and children were victimized in white-on-Black "race riots" that in some places turned into pogroms and "racial cleansing." This racial violence often resulted in precipitous flight or involuntary migration by Black refugees seeking "the warmth of other suns."[47]

In Harlem, New York City, however, that critical mass of young people had been reached in the 1930s, and on Tuesday, March 19, 1935, African American youths rioted upon hearing the rumor that a 16-year-old boy, accused of stealing a penknife from the Kress variety store on 125th Street, had been taken by the police into the basement of the store and beaten to death. An angry crowd gathered outside the building and began hurling trash cans and bricks through store windows on the streets between Fifth and Eighth Avenues. Later investigations revealed that racially discriminatory employment practices created extreme poverty for Black families in New York City during the Depression. At the same time, the researchers found that the city's police officers "were overzealous in arresting black youth." The police operated like an "occupying army" and the young people and adults "complained of constant brutality." The only fatality in this violent disturbance in 1935 was the police shooting and death of 16-year-old Lloyd Hobbs, who was innocently returning home from a movie.[48]

In 1943, as in 1935, an unfounded rumor sparked the insurgency in Harlem on Friday, August 1. People were told that a white police officer had killed a Black soldier who was protecting his mother and another Black woman from another policeman who was trying to arrest them. The soldier, Robert Bandy, punched the policeman and turned to run. The officer drew his pistol and shot the soldier in the leg, and he was taken to the hospital; Bandy was not killed. However, over five thousand police officers were eventually called out to stop the looting and vandalism that erupted in Harlem between 125th and 145th Streets and along Seventh, Eighth, and Lenox Avenues. Order was restored within twenty-four hours, but six African Americans were killed, hundreds were injured, and 550 people were arrested.[49]

With newspaper and television coverage of civil rights campaigns in the South in the 1950s, children and teenagers nationwide learned of the murders, bombings, Klan attacks, and violent outrages being perpetrated against nonviolent civil rights activists and ordinary Black citizens almost on a daily basis. As was discussed in chapter 2, many Black youths growing up in the 1950s attributed their political awakening to the murder of Emmett Till, after seeing photos of the teenager's disfigured face and mangled body. Some also subscribed to the Black nationalist beliefs and practices of the Nation of Islam, which preached self-defense and practiced separation from white people in the United States.[50]

In the early 1960s the speeches of Nation of Islam minister Malcolm X galvanized many Black youths and contributed to the new militancy in the streets and on high school and college campuses.[51] Sociologist J. Herman Blake, writing in 1969, pointed out that most of the proponents of Black Nationalism and Black self-defense during that decade had come under the influence of the Nation of Islam, many through the eloquence of Malcolm X and other Muslim ministers. While most young African Americans did not subscribe to the view that there should be "total separation" between Blacks and whites in the United States, Blake also noted that "the break between Malcolm X and the Nation of Islam in early 1964 had a profound impact on . . . the development of black nationalism among countless numbers of blacks who supported the Muslim emphasis on black consciousness and racial solidarity."[52] At the same time, the unjustified and violent attacks on civil rights activists, the burning and bombing of Black churches and schools, and the ongoing brutalization by the police and other law enforcement officers also helped to ignite the new Black insurgency.[53]

In 1964, the wave of Black rebellions began on Tuesday, March 24, in Jacksonville, Florida, when the arrest of civil rights demonstrators led to disturbances by Black high school students. Responding to a bomb threat, police and firemen arrived at New Stanton Senior High School and tried to arrest one of the students. The policemen and their vehicles were pelted with bottles, cans, and stones, and violent conflict erupted and spread into the downtown area. During the looting and vandalism that lasted two days, a Black woman was shot and killed while driving her car through the riot area.[54] And as described in chapter 6, on the evening of April 7, 1964, rioting erupted in Cleveland when the young people learned that Rev. Bruce Klunder had been run over and killed by a bulldozer while protesting the construction of a new public school in the Lakeview section.[55]

In New York City, the so-called Harlem fruit riot in April 1963 laid the groundwork for deadly disturbances the following year. Three Black teenagers, accused of turning over a fruit cart on 129th Street, were caught by the police. *New York Times* reporter Junius Griffin, at the scene, noted that the teenagers who witnessed the incident "jeered the patrolmen, and reinforcements were summoned. Policemen emerged from patrol cars with pistols drawn and nightsticks swinging." As one police officer was viciously beating one of the teenagers, Frank Stafford, a Harlem resident, went up to the officer and asked, "Why are you beating him like this?" The policemen then turned on Stafford and began beating him. The officers took Stafford, Fecundo Acion, another eyewitness to the attack, and three teenagers to the police station, where they were again brutalized. Stafford had to be taken to the hospital and remained there for two weeks. Junius Griffin reported that many young people were beaten at the scene, and "four policemen were injured. Several persons were arrested. Charges of police brutality were made by Harlem residents."[56]

Nineteen sixty-four is considered the first year of the long, hot summers during the decade. On Thursday, July 16, in the Yorkville section of Manhattan, 15-year-old James Powell was shot and killed by off-duty police lieutenant Thomas Gilligan, who claimed that the teenager lunged at him with a pocket knife, though what actually happened was never confirmed. Nonetheless, several hundred teenagers who, along with James Powell, had been attending the nearby Robert Wagner Junior High School's summer courses soon gathered at the scene. When police reinforcements showed up, the students began hurling garbage-can lids, bottles, and bricks at the officers, and several youths were taken into custody but later released. The next morning protesters organized picketing in front of Wagner Junior High carrying signs that declared "Stop Killer Cops!," "End Police Brutality," and "We Want Legal Protection!"[57]

Over 250 people attended James Powell's funeral service on Saturday, July 18, and then they organized a march along Seventh Avenue to Officer Gilligan's Twenty-first District headquarters, calling for the police lieutenant's firing or at least his suspension. When the police tried to disperse the crowd in front of the station, fighting broke out. And as the police began to make arrests, bottles, cans, and other debris rained down on them. Street fights and looting began, and by that evening flaming Molotov cocktails were added to the mix. When a patrolman's car was hit, the officers began firing into the air and the riot was on, continued into Sunday and Monday, and spread to the Bedford-Stuyvesant section of Brooklyn.[58] In

their book *Race Riots: New York 1964,* Fred Shapiro and James Sullivan concluded "the Gilligan-Powell case was the spark which . . . flamed into the
Harlem and Bedford-Stuyvesant riots. . . . For six nights, mobs roamed the
streets in two boroughs. As many as 4,000 New Yorkers dedicated themselves to attacks on police, vandalism, and looting of stores. When it was
all over, police counted 1 rioter dead, 118 injured, and 465 men and women
arrested."[59]

In 1964, the precipitating events that led to violent disturbances and
rioting in Rochester, New York; Jersey City, Elizabeth, and Paterson, New
Jersey; and Dixmoor, Illinois, did not always involve teenagers; however,
young people between the ages of 15 and 24 comprised over 50 percent
of those arrested by the police during the disturbances. As with the 1963
Harlem fruit riot, that same year in Philadelphia it was the police killing of
24-year-old Willie Philyaw on October 29 that portended the way Black
residents would respond to rumors of police violence the following summer. Those residents who witnessed the shooting saw Philyaw flee from a
police officer after having been accused of stealing a watch from a drug-
store. Shortly afterward, a crowd of young people began throwing bricks
and bottles at police vehicles and into nearby store windows and started
looting. Swift action by the Philadelphia police force prevented the disturbance from escalating.[60]

Not so on August 28, 1964, when police officers pulled Odessa Bradford
from her car for blocking an intersection in North Philadelphia and tried to
arrest her. A crowd formed and surrounded the paddy wagon. They began
hurling bricks and trash cans at the police and into store windows. Rioting
erupted and continued for three days, fed by the rumor that "a pregnant
black woman's been beaten and shot to death by a white policeman." Two
people were killed, 339 injured, including 100 police officers, and 308 were
arrested.[61] In Chicago the following summer, there was a similar incident.
After a Black woman was struck and killed by a fire truck, a protest rally
was organized and soon sparked rioting. Over 150 policemen were called
out to battle rioters on August 14 and 15, 1965. Though no deaths occurred,
twenty-four people were arrested and seventy-five were injured, including
eighteen police officers.[62]

Also in August 1965, rumors set off seven days of deadly rioting in Los Angeles. On August 11, 1965, a traffic incident led to the arrests of Ronald and Marquette Frye and their mother, Ruby Frye, who was accused of attacking one of the police officers. After the three were placed in the police vehicle, it was alleged that someone in the crowd spat at the policemen. Rather than leaving the scene, two officers got out of the car, confronted the large group, grabbed a young woman, and arrested her. The onlookers became "irate" and began stoning the police car. Rumors soon spread not only that the Fryes had been beaten at the police station but also that the young woman arrested was pregnant and died in police custody. Once the violence erupted, block after block of stores were looted in the Watts neighborhood, and eventually the National Guard was brought in to restore order. Considered one of the deadliest riots in US history, over a thousand national guardsmen joined the Los Angeles Police Department (LAPD) in arresting over four thousand people; over thirty were killed and hundreds were injured.[63]

Dr. King was profoundly disturbed by the violent disturbances taking place that summer of 1965. During the Watts riot, several Los Angeles ministers contacted him and asked him to come to the city to try and help end the conflict. Dr. King, along with Bayard Rustin and Andrew Young, decided to go to Los Angeles, where he met with Mayor Sam Yorty, police chief William Parker, and Governor Edmund "Pat" Brown and surveyed the damaged neighborhoods. King visited Westminster Community Center in Watts, but while there he was heckled by militant Black teenagers. When he tried to talk to the young people, they began shouting, "We won! We won!" But King asked them, "How can you say you won when thirty-four Negroes are dead, your community is destroyed, and whites are using the riot as an excuse for inaction?" "We won," they said, "because we made them pay attention to us."[64]

Following the insurgency, Governor Brown formed a commission to investigate the violent disorders in the City of Angels. The group was headed by John McCone, a successful businessman who had held several positions in the US Defense Department and served as director of the Central Intelligence Agency between 1961 and 1965. Submitted in December 1965, the

McCone Report blamed the teenagers and young adults for the rioting, because they were frustrated due to "the glowing promise of the Federal poverty program" whose projects "did not live up to their press notices." The teenagers listened to "the exhortations [by their leaders] to take the most extreme and even illegal remedies to right a wide variety of wrongs, real and supposed."[65]

Rather than addressing the numerous charges of brutality and misconduct leveled against the LAPD, the McCone Report emphasized "the dull, devastating spiral of failure that awaits the average disadvantaged child in the urban core, [whose] home life all too often fails to give him the incentive and the elementary experience [to prepare him] . . . for school. . . . Frustrated and disillusioned, the child becomes a discipline problem, leaves school [and] slips into the ranks of the permanent jobless, illiterate and untrained, unemployed and unemployable." The "failures of the Negro community" caused the social problems affecting the youth; and the recommendations called for "expanded job training," "preschool education," "remedial courses" and "improved law enforcement to prevent crime and to handle citizen complaints to improve community relationships."[66] Missing from the McCone Report was a call for the establishment of a civilian police review board charged with the investigation of complaints of police misconduct or mistreatment and empowered to discipline law enforcement officers found guilty of brutality and the unnecessary use of force.

POLICE VIOLENCE AND DEMANDS
FOR CIVILIAN REVIEW BOARDS

On Saturday evening, July 24, 1965, 20-year-old Teddy Jones and 17-year-old Anna Lucas, along with about 150 teenagers, were outside Coney Island Park in Brooklyn after it closed, dancing to the music from a radio. A Black policeman, Arthur Crichlow, came up and told the couple to leave the area, even though another police officer had said they could dance awhile longer. "One cop tells you one thing, one cop tells you another," replied Teddy Jones. Patrolman Crichlow did not like this response and the two began to argue. "Okay, I'm taking you in on a discon [disorderly conduct] charge."

According to Anna Lucas, after handing over his wallet for identification, Jones tried to get it back, and the policeman grabbed him by his shirt. "Teddy was talking pretty loud, but he wasn't cursing or nothing." Then Crichlow shouted, "Don't embarrass me in front of all these people." The officer took out his nightstick and "hit Teddy across the brow of his left eye." Jones was then taken to the police station and from there to Coney Island Hospital, where six stiches were sewn into his forehead. Then he was sent back to the police station. At criminal court on Sunday afternoon, the judge commented that Jones did not look well and postponed the hearing. They took Jones to Kings County Hospital, where he was diagnosed with a skull fracture, underwent surgery, but died from his injuries.[67]

"The tragedy of Teddy Jones," declared Aryeh Neier, executive director of the New York Civil Liberties Union, "underscores the need for a civilian review board to judge complaints of police brutality. So far there has been no real response to the case from the police." In the December 1965 *New York Times Magazine* article titled "Necessary Force—Or Police Brutality?" journalist Thomas R. Brooks mentioned the recent police killings in Newark, Philadelphia, and St. Louis, as well as New York City, where all the victims were African Americans, and "it's practically unheard of for a policeman involved in the killing of a citizen to be punished." This meant that among the reasons given for the ongoing rioting—merchants' price gouging, discrimination in housing and employment—"the first is police brutality." Unlike most cities in 1965, New York had a civilian complaint review board, and that year it received 231 complaints from 208,844 arrests, an average of eight per week. But only one policeman had ever been dismissed after an investigation. Brooks concluded, "Clearly there is a crisis. Police brutality—or rumors of it—was the catalyst in the riots this summer" in Watts, Chicago, and other cities, and "it could set off more rioting in the future."[68]

The demands for the establishment of civilian police review boards became a civil rights issue, and CORE, the NAACP, and local civil rights organizations launched marches and demonstrations to try and persuade elected officials to create them. But the real need was for the *empowerment* of civilian review boards. For example, in Philadelphia, the Police Advisory

Board had been established in 1958. Historian Matthew J. Countryman pointed out that Mayor James Tate had issued an order in June 1964 requiring "all citizens' complaints against the police to be forwarded to the Police Advisory Board" and even authorized the NAACP to place local attorneys in police stations during the summer "to investigate charges of police brutality." While some considered Philadelphia police chief Howard Leary "the most enlightened policeman in America," this did not prevent regular clashes between African Americans, especially teenagers, and the police that culminated in the August 1964 riot.[69]

Riots and violent disturbances occurred in Chicago and Cleveland in July 1966, in Cincinnati and Tampa in June 1967, and Detroit and Newark in July 1967, and President Lyndon Johnson appointed Illinois governor Otto Kerner to chair a federal commission to investigate and prepare an analysis of these ongoing "civil disorders." Issued in March 1968, the Kerner Report concluded, "Our nation is moving toward two societies, one white, one black—separate and unequal." It recommended that rather than "blind repression or capitulation to lawlessness," social and economic improvement "requires a commitment to national action—compassionate, massive and sustained, backed by the resources of the most powerful and richest nation on this earth."[70]

Longstanding social and economic grievances and police brutality triggered civil disturbances, the report asserted, and white citizens needed to accept the reality that "to some Negroes, police have come to symbolize white power, white racism, and white repression. And the fact is that many police do reflect and express these white attitudes." The commissioners found these violent disturbances "were usually ignited by a minor incident fueled by antagonism between the Negro population and the police." There was "an accumulation of unresolved grievances" against local police departments. In addition to the "high level of dissatisfaction" among Black residents, "confidence in the willingness and ability of local government to respond to Negro grievances [was] low." The investigation also revealed that "the typical rioter was a teenager or young adult, a lifelong resident of the city in which he rioted, a high school dropout; he was, nevertheless, somewhat better educated than his nonrioting Negro neighbor, and was usually unemployed or employed in a menial job." And these young people were usually well informed about local and national politics, but were "highly distrustful of the political system."[71]

The chapter "The Police and the Community" in the Kerner Report includes an analysis of the "problem of grievance mechanisms." In most locations, civilian complaints against the police were rarely investigated, but there was "substantial evidence that policemen . . . have little fear of punishment for using unnecessary force because they appear to have a degree of immunity from their departments." Specific procedures needed to be adopted that had the potentiality of "gain[ing] the respect and confidence of the entire community." The commissioners believed that police departments should undertake "thorough investigation of complaints" and pursue "prompt, visible disciplinary action where justified."[72]

There is little or no evidence that urban police departments felt pressured to move in the direction recommended in the Kerner Report. After it was submitted in March 1968, the ongoing disturbances culminated in nationwide "civil disorders" following the assassination of Martin Luther King Jr. on April 4, 1968. While police brutality was documented and condemned, the Kerner Report also blamed the rise of Black Power for the "incitement and encouragement of violence." "Strident appeals to violence, first heard from white racists, were echoed and reinforced, in the inflammatory rhetoric of black racists and militants." The Kerner commission concluded that a "doctrine of black power and violence" was being preached by "extremists" who "crisscrossed the country" and whose "rhetoric was echoed by local 'militants' and organizations," creating "the ugly background noise of the violent summer."[73]

The Black Panther Party for Defense, the US Organization, and various Black student organizations springing up on college campuses in 1966 and 1967 were often the source of the "ugly background noise" filling the public sphere. Black Power was often framed by these groups in terms of Black self-defense, particularly against unprovoked racial assaults and police violence.[74] Teenagers usually made up the majority of active members in most Black Power groups, and they volunteered to work on the projects and programs that older leaders had organized, just as the children and teenagers had done with the NAACP, SCLC, CORE, and SNCC projects and campaigns in the late 1950s and early 1960s.[75]

Similarly, after 1966, African American teenagers embraced Black Power with the understanding that the social and economic discrimination and police harassment they experienced should be challenged. African American students' Black Power protests served as models of social activism for brown and white teenagers who launched the Student Rights Movement. It would address the lack of relevant course material and the oppressive restrictions on apparel, ideological diversity, and free speech in most US secondary schools, colleges, and universities in the late 1960s.

Chapter 8

Civil Rights, Black Power, and Increasing Youth Militancy

*In the actual courses in Central High [in Peoria,
Illinois], there is discrimination against black people
in general. Especially when the teachers talk about the
history of the country. When you study America, they
say, "America—land of the free, home of the brave."
I know that "brave" is the white man; and "free"
is the white man. I see blacks asking for freedom,
but they don't get it. The black man is not free to do
anything. . . . They just say these things. They want
other countries to get a good impression of America.*

James Brown (1970)[1]

ON FRIDAY AFTERNOON, November 17, 1967, an estimated thirty-five
hundred African American students from at least twelve high schools
converged on Philadelphia's board of education building at Twenty-First
Street and the Parkway. From the beginning of the 1967–68 school year, as
part of their "Black Power demands," the high school students had been
calling for the addition of Black History courses to the curriculum. But
they also sought relief from overcrowded classrooms and physical improvements and renovation of the school buildings. In October 1967, a bill had
been passed by the Pennsylvania House of Representatives requiring the

inclusion of information on African Americans and other minority groups in required history courses offered in public schools throughout the commonwealth. Earlier in the fall semester, students at Simon Gratz, Benjamin Franklin, William Penn, and other high schools organized demonstrations in front of the school buildings in support of their demand for the teaching of Black History, but on November 17, they decided to bring their case to Superintendent Mark Shedd and members of the school board.[2]

While several teachers were inside the school board building engaged in negotiations with Superintendent Shedd about the new courses, the police arrived on the scene and began arresting students. Police commissioner Frank Rizzo called out the police force and was present at the protest. When some students tried to resist arrest, the police attacked them with their night sticks, and a full-scale riot erupted that soon spread into Center City, the downtown area, where fleeing students broke store windows and vandalized cars. Twenty-two people were injured during the violent confrontation and fifty-seven students were arrested. School board president Richardson Dilworth accused Frank Rizzo of triggering the violence, but a court order was issued banning further demonstrations at public high schools, something Rizzo thought was long overdue. The unprovoked police attack on peaceful high school students was condemned by Black and white parents, teachers, and community leaders.[3]

The large-scale student demonstration in Philadelphia, inspired by local and national Black Power advocates, was comparable to the picketing, boycotts, and other protests organized by high school students in Chicago, Pittsburgh, New York, Memphis, and other cities and towns throughout the United States in the late 1960s. In other words, while the objectives of many social activists shifted from ending de facto and de jure segregation to the pursuit of Black Power and community control, children and teenagers were the first ones to take up both causes. Indeed, neither civil rights objectives nor Black Power demands would have been addressed without the participation of the young crusaders. This becomes apparent when we examine the children and teenagers' engagement in civil rights and Black Power campaigns in Philadelphia, Chicago, and other cities at the end of the civil rights era and the emergence of Black Power.

TEENAGE GANGS AND THE
GIRARD COLLEGE PROTESTS IN PHILADELPHIA

Children and teenagers in Philadelphia played a variety of roles in one of the longest school desegregation campaigns outside the South, and their contributions are inestimable. Girard College, founded in 1848 at the bequest of financier Stephen Girard, was located in North Philadelphia on a forty-five-acre tract. It provided housing and elementary and secondary education for at least twelve hundred boys ages 7 to 18 years. Beginning in 1869, the school was overseen by the Board of City Trusts, a public agency. Under the terms of Stephen Girard's will, the college was to enroll "poor, white orphan boys," but even before the Supreme Court's *Brown* decision, city attorneys petitioned the trustee board to allow nonwhite boys to enroll. When the trustees voted to uphold Girard's will and restrict admission to white boys, attorney and city councilman Raymond Pace Alexander filed a lawsuit in September 1954 on behalf of two Black 7-year-olds, Robert Felder and William Ash Foust, for admission to the school.[4]

The Orphans Court and the Pennsylvania Supreme Court upheld the trustees' decision, but in April 1957 the US Supreme Court ruled in response to an appeal that "since the Board of City Trusts operates Girard College as an agency of the State of Pennsylvania . . . its refusal to admit Foust and Felder to the college because they were Negroes was discrimination by the state. Such discrimination is forbidden by the Fourteenth Amendment."[5] The school's trustees and alumni then returned to the Orphans Court and asked for the appointment of thirteen "private trustees" to administer the school. Once this was done, Girard College could be considered a "private institution."[6] City solicitors and NAACP attorneys appealed the Orphans Court's action, but in January 1958 it was upheld by the Pennsylvania Supreme Court, and the US Supreme Court refused to review the lower court's ruling.[7]

Cecil B. Moore, a militant but well-respected attorney, was elected president of the Philadelphia NAACP in January 1963. Soon after, he launched a series of civil rights protests and began setting up picket lines at construction sites for public buildings where no nonwhite workers were employed.

Working with members of the local CORE branch, picket lines were set up at the site for the new Municipal Services Building in Center City and at the Strawberry Mansion Junior High School site in North Philadelphia. Then, in July 1963, the NAACP protests expanded to the main post office at Thirtieth Street, where African American workers complained of discriminatory promotion practices, and in December 1963, to the Trailways Bus Terminal in Center City to demand employment for African Americans as bus drivers. Moore encouraged teenagers to join the protests and recruited North Philadelphia gang members to serve as "marshals" on the picket lines.[8]

From the nineteenth century, Philadelphia and other US cities had innumerable youth gangs that claimed and patrolled a local territory, not allowing members of other gangs or the unaffiliated to intrude. Gang wars were commonly sparked by rivalries and invasions of another gang's territory, and some gangs' engagement in petty criminal activities generated police surveillance and arrests. The Susan Parrish Wharton Memorial Settlement House, known as the Wharton Centre, opened in North Philadelphia in October 1931, and the staff engaged in "preventive work" with teenage gang members in the neighborhood. This included providing recreational activities, counseling, and employment guidance. In 1953, the Centre launched "Operation Street Corner," which supported the hiring of college students to serve as "gang workers" to provide assistance and advice to juveniles interested in improving their educational and employment options. The Wharton Centre staff assisted Cecil Moore in recruiting teenage gang members to participate in the civil rights protests in North Philadelphia.[9]

Eighteen-year-old Henry Reddy was a member of the Moroccans, a North Philadelphia street gang, in 1964. When Cecil Moore set up picket lines at the construction site for the Strawberry Mansion Junior High, Reddy and other Moroccans walked the picket lines and monitored the demonstrations. Then early in 1965, Moore announced that his next target would be Girard College and pledged to surround the school's ten-foot-high stone walls with protesters until fatherless "black" boys were allowed to enroll. On Saturday, May 1, 1965, Reddy was among those who marched with Cecil Moore from Center City to Girard College, where the protesters were met by over nine hundred police officers. There was no confrontation then or when the protesters returned to the walls on Sunday and Monday, May 2 and 3. Cecil Moore announced, "If they don't unlock Girard College, we'll be in court, either as criminal defendants or civil plaintiffs."[10]

On Tuesday evening, May 4, at around 7:00 p.m., Henry Reddy and seven other teenagers brought a ladder to the Girard College wall and began scaling it. But they were soon spotted by the policemen on patrol. Once taken into custody, the teenagers were taken downtown to the Police Administration Building and charged with trespassing, breach of the peace, inciting a riot, and disorderly conduct—all for attempting to scale a wall. When Cecil Moore arrived at police headquarters, he paid the teens' bail and told the reporters present that trespassing was not the crime, "racial segregation is the real crime."[11] After this incident Henry Reddy volunteered to work with Moore to recruit other gang members to join the picket lines at Girard College.

The NAACP maintained protests around Girard College every day for the next eight months, and thousands of men, women, and children joined the demonstrations. On Tuesday, August 3, 1965, Martin Luther King Jr. arrived at the Girard College walls and addressed the crowd: "At this stage in the twentieth century in the city that is known as the 'cradle of liberty,' the Girard College wall is like the Berlin wall" in Germany, King declared. "This wall, this school is symbolic of a cancer in the body public that must be removed before there will be freedom and democracy in this country." In December 1965, Moore suspended the demonstrations when Pennsylvania governor William Scranton authorized state-appointed attorneys to file a lawsuit on behalf of seven Black boys who had been denied admission to Girard College.[12]

The teenagers who were active in the Girard College protests decided to form their own civil rights organization, called the Young Militants and led by 18-year-old George Brower. In addition to working with Moore and the NAACP, the teenagers played an active role in the rallies and programs organized by Philadelphia's branch of SNCC and subsequently with the Black People's Unity Movement (BPUM) and the Philadelphia Freedom Organization. Early in 1964 high school student Charyn Sutton joined Philadelphia's Student CORE chapter, one of the few in the country. She hoped to go to Mississippi to work in SNCC's Freedom Summer campaign, "but they were requiring that you had to be eighteen."[13] After graduating and enrolling for one year at Brandeis University and then working for the National Student Movement's (NSM) tutorial project, Sutton headed south. She joined the staff at SNCC's headquarters in Atlanta and worked on Julian Bond's successful campaign for the Georgia House of Representatives. Sutton returned to Philadelphia in 1966, joined the SNCC staff there, and helped organize the Philadelphia Freedom Organization, modeled after the Lowndes County Freedom Organization in Mississippi. According to Sutton, the goal was "to use the southern model to get people registered to vote and . . . involved in electoral politics."[14]

In June 1966 when Stokely Carmichael declared that the goal for SNCC in future campaigns would be Black Power, the announcement was music to the ears of the Young Militants—Barry Dawkins, Eugene Dawkins, and Carole West—and BPUM organizers John Churchville, Walter Palmer, and Rev. Paul Washington. However, Frank Rizzo, at the time deputy police commissioner, viewed Black Power as an escalation in Black militancy that needed to be checked. Not only was there increased police presence at Girard College and other protest sites, Charyn Sutton recalled there was also stepped-up police surveillance by Rizzo's newly formed "civil disobedience squad." But she found that "a lot of the surveillance operations were so obvious that it seemed that the effort was not as much to . . . get information on us, as to terrorize us and frighten us, to give us the sense that we're being followed . . . always being traced."[15]

Then on Saturday, August 13, 1966, the police, "heavily armed," raided SNCC's main office, the NSM Freedom Library, and the apartments of SNCC's Fred Meely and George Brower of the Young Militants. Four people were arrested. Deputy police commissioner Rizzo claimed that there were "storehouses for arms, ammunition and dynamite," but they actually found only two sticks of dynamite (but no blasting caps) in Brower's apartment. Rizzo also alleged that those arrested were "plotting to blow up Independence Hall." SNCC's Stokely Carmichael and James Forman came to Philadelphia later that month to participate in a Black Unity Rally at Rev. Paul Washington's Church of the Advocate in support of the arrested

SNCC workers and Young Militants. Within a few weeks, the police were forced to drop the charges against those arrested in the raid due to "lack of evidence."[16]

US district court judge Joseph Lord ruled on September 2, 1966, that Girard College's denial of admission to Black orphan boys violated Pennsylvania's public accommodations laws; but the Girard College trustees and alumni immediately announced they would appeal the decision. At that point Cecil Moore promised to "ring the wall with pickets" that would include "hundreds of teenagers and members of tough North Philadelphia street gangs."[17] Over the next twenty-one months, rallies and picketing continued around the Girard College walls, and teenage gang members provided the security for the marchers. Finally, on May 20, 1968, the US Supreme Court upheld the lower court's ruling that given the "state's involvement" in overseeing the institution, it would have to abide by the state's antidiscrimination laws. On September 11, 1968, 9-year-old Theodore Lewis Hicks, the last of the seven original plaintiffs still eligible for admission, enrolled at Girard College along with three other fatherless Black boys.[18]

TEENAGE GANGS AND CIVIL RIGHTS: CHICAGO STYLE

The use of teenage gang members to serve as marshals and security guards for civil rights marches and picket lines in Philadelphia, as well as the shift in Black high school activism from engagement in civil rights protests to Black Power demands, had its counterpart in Chicago between 1966 and 1970. Elementary and secondary school students participated in the system-wide boycotts organized by the Coordinating Council of Community Organizations (CCCO) in 1963 and 1964, and attended the freedom schools opened throughout the city. There they learned how participating in school strikes contributed to the local and national Civil Rights Movement. When Martin Luther King Jr. decided to take his movement to Chicago and began marches and demonstrations for fair housing in the city and surrounding suburbs, he met with leaders of the teenage gangs on the South and West Side and recruited them for his civil rights crusade. Yet, as was the case in Philadelphia in 1967 and 1968, Black high school students in

Chicago pursued Black Power by organizing boycotts, marches, and demonstrations to demand the hiring of more Black teachers and administrators and the addition of Black History courses to the curriculum.

Even before August 1965 when Dr. King and his SCLC colleagues agreed to launch a pilot program of nonviolent direct-action protest in the North, Bernard Lafayette had moved to Chicago and was working for the American Friends Service Committee (AFSC) to bring nonviolent tactics and conflict resolution techniques to local teenagers. In the summer of 1964, Lafayette worked with students at John Marshall High School to organize Students Organized for Urban Leadership (SOUL). Robert Gore, a member of SOUL, recalled that with Lafayette's assistance, "we were organized to deal with conflicts among young people in the community. We were training them in nonviolence." The student group worked closely with the Citizens Committee to End Lead Poisoning, creating informational materials and canvassing the West Side neighborhood explaining the dangers of lead poisoning. In November 1964, Lafayette organized a workshop on nonviolence in Palestine, Illinois, led by Rev. James Lawson and attended by CCCO members and community leaders and almost a hundred young people, many with gang affiliations.[19]

The deadly riot in Los Angeles in the summer of 1965 finally convinced Dr. King to take his nonviolent civil rights campaign to Chicago. As was mentioned earlier, when he arrived in Watts on August 17, 1965, to find out if he could be of assistance in restoring order and normalizing police-community relations, he was rebuffed by some local leaders and Black youths.[20] This convinced King of the need to take his movement to the urban North, and at the SCLC meeting in Atlanta later that month, King cast the deciding vote for the Chicago campaign. Prize-winning biographer Taylor Branch summarized the Windy City's advantages: "King chose Chicago for the music of Mahalia Jackson, the transplanted heartland of Mississippi, and in part because the Al Raby coalition [CCCO] pushed hardest for help." King wanted Black Chicagoans to "pick up their souls," and he soon sent James Bevel and twelve others to help them do just that.[21]

SCLC's James Bevel, James Orange, Al Sampson, and Andrew Young were placed in charge of the youth-related work in Chicago early in 1966, and they focused on recruiting juvenile gang members to participate in the demonstrations. Al Sampson met with members of the Blackstone Rangers and with the help of former basketball star Larry Patterson, recruited them for training in nonviolence. Then James Bevel and Andrew Young met with thirty gang members at a church in Woodlawn on the South Side. After Dr. King and his family moved into an apartment on Chicago's West Side in January 1966, several members of the Conservative Vice Lords showed up to talk, and they subsequently took Dr. King on a tour of the neighborhood. "We were labeled a gang," one of the Vice Lords declared, "but we always considered ourselves protectors of the community." In their conversations with King, "we had ideological struggles . . . about the best method for addressing the problems in the community, was it violence or nonviolence?"[22]

The culmination of SCLC's gang recruitment activities occurred on June 11, 1966, at an all-day meeting at the Blackstone Sheraton Hotel, which the gang members called the first "Turf Masters" convention. Eighteen gangs were represented and staff from the American Civil Liberties Union (ACLU), the YMCA, and the Urban Training Center attempted to answer a relevant question raised by one of the gang members: "Where does nonviolence come in when police [are] beating you in the head?" Some of the presenters tried to address the question, and some focused on the need to gather evidence that could be used to take to court, if necessary. Dr. King countered, "We don't need guns. We don't need knives. We don't need Molotov cocktails. We have something more powerful." He wanted the teenagers to know that "power in Chicago means getting the largest political machine in the nation to say yes when it wants to say no."[23]

The participants agreed to set up a council made up of two representatives from each gang and one adult from each of the various community organizations and with committees on health, education, welfare, employment, and recreation. SCLC organizer Bernard Lafayette saw this as a welcome change: "We looked on [gang youth] not as a menace to the community but as a resource." James Orange was pleased when "those guys just sat down and started talking about working together. From that period on, we worked with these guys." Unfortunately, James Meredith, the first African American to graduate from the University of Mississippi, had been shot on June 6, 1966, while on his "March against Fear" in Mississippi.

SCLC made arrangements for eight gang leaders to accompany them on the bus ride from Chicago to Mississippi to continue Meredith's March, and it was there that they and many others were introduced to the call for "Black Power" as an alternative to "Freedom Now."[24]

Members of the Blackstone Rangers, Gonzato Disciples, and Vice Lords were in attendance when Dr. King addressed a rally of thirty thousand at Soldier Field on July 10, 1966, just days after rioting had occurred following the police shooting of an unarmed teenager in the Puerto Rican community on Chicago's near North Side. And two days after the Soldier Field rally, a riot erupted on the city's West Side when two teenagers seeking relief from the over ninety-degree heat were arrested after they reopened a fire hydrant that the police had turned off. A crowd gathered at the site, police reinforcements arrived, and then seven more young people were arrested. Rock throwing, window smashing, and looting broke out, along with random gunfire and continued into the next day. The Kerner Commission reported that after two days of rioting the police and forty-two hundred national guardsmen restored order, but one man and two teenagers were killed by stray bullets, eighty were injured, and 533 people were arrested. As was the case in earlier riots, "most of the participants were teenagers."[25]

When things finally settled down, James Bevel and the SCLC organizers began making plans for their first open housing march to take place in Gage Park, a Chicago suburb, on Friday, August 5, 1966.[26] James Orange recommended that the gang members serve as marshals. Bevel put together a workshop on nonviolence for the teenagers before the demonstrations, and later recalled, "We collected their weapons, weapons we didn't even know they had." James Orange reported that during the marches "the worst thing that can happen is to let the gang kids get together." They decided to separate members of the same gang and "pair them off" with those in others, and as a result, "they got to know each other," Bevel recalled. "After the first two or three marches . . . they saw who the enemy was." Dr. King declared, "I saw [gang members'] noses being broken and blood flowing from their wounds; and I saw them continue and not retaliate, not one of them, with violence."[27]

The summer of 1966 witnessed the emergence of Black Power and Black Power demands, and young gang members in Chicago and other cities found this much more appealing than SCLC's nonviolent approach. Ultimately, only the Blackstone Rangers, Conservative Vice Lords, and Black Disciples continued working with Dr. King and civil rights organizations in Chicago after 1966. For example, gang members worked in 1968 and 1969 with the Coalition for United Community Action (CUCA), headed by former SCLC organizers Rev. C. T. Vivian and Rev. Jesse Jackson. A coming together of sixty organizations, CUCA sought to close down construction sites that employed no African American or Hispanic workers, which was in violation of the federal government's new affirmative action directives.[28] C. T. Vivian recalled, "We organized demonstrations at the building sites." And the gang members were there. "We were saying, 'You're not giving us jobs, so it's time you [white workers] got out of here.' We did it nonviolently, but those guys in those unions were afraid we weren't. They would leave work and work would stop." CUCA negotiated with Mayor Daley the creation of the "Chicago Plan," which provided union jobs and union cards for young Black workers.[29]

At the same time, when the gang members marched with civil rights groups, there was no commitment to nonviolence. At these events gang members and other teenagers carried walking sticks and other weapons and made it clear they were prepared to use them.[30] Nonetheless, after 1969, there was an overall decline in civil rights activism and gang activity in Chicago. Historian Simon Balto argued that with the formation of the police department's Gang Intelligence Unit, the promulgation of more aggressive surveillance, and the increase in "stop and frisk, . . . physical abuse, threats, and intentionally exacerbating intergang conflict," there was significant fragmentation in juvenile street gangs in Chicago in the 1970s.[31]

BLACK POWER, BLACK HISTORY, AND HIGH SCHOOL STUDENT ACTIVISM

The Black students' march on Philadelphia's board of education building on November 17, 1967, demanding the inclusion of Black History courses in the school curriculum had counterparts in several other cities in the late 1960s. Complaints about the depictions of African Americans, Mexican Americans, and other racial minorities in history textbooks and other materials used in US elementary and secondary schools became part of the national conversation in 1964. *New York Times* education reporter Fred M. Hechinger, writing in October of that year, registered "the chronic complaint of minority groups . . . that textbooks ignore minorities' own distinctive past and contributions to majority culture." Hechinger recommended that publishers "respond to the demands of the Negro for civil rights by aiming at a fuller understanding of African history and the history of the Negro in the United States." "Traditionally," however, textbooks "have been edited with a view to the total market, including the Southern States." As a result, it was difficult to "provide much complimentary detail about the Negro in American life."[32]

In May 1966, when state education officials in California decided to adopt the textbook *Land of the Free: A History of the United States* by John Caughey, John Hope Franklin, and Ernest May, the book came under attack from Max Rafferty, the state's education secretary, University of Southern California professor Emery Stoops, the John Birch Society, and other conservative groups claiming that it was "slanted in the direction of civil rights . . . with high praise for militant groups and with condemnation of the great majority." *Land of the Free* committees were formed throughout California that year and circulated attacks on the book for (among other things) spending too much time discussing "Negro slaves and freedom" and Revolutionary War hero Crispus Attucks, and for declaring that Rosa Parks should be remembered as a "freedom fighter." Despite these attacks, *Land of the Free* was approved for use in California's secondary schools in December 1966.[33]

Black students and parents' protests against the distortions and absences in history and social studies texts soon led to a congressional investigation. Harlem congressman Adam Clayton Powell Jr., chair of the House Committee on Education and Labor, charged that "something should be done about racially distorted and offensive textbooks . . . which depict minority groups solely in an inferior and subjugated position—or even worse, ignored altogether." Powell held hearings in August 1966 to investigate the issue, and in his testimony before the committee, Howard Howe, the US Commissioner of Education, admitted that "we should no longer let this problem be swept under the rug." However, because the federal government had no power to force state and local action, "our efforts should be to encourage voluntary action by states and localities by getting information into their hands."[34]

In the late 1960s, Black junior and senior high school students, their parents, and community activists kept the pressure on local officials and school boards. In Harlem at the beginning of the 1966–67 school year, Black students at two junior highs and one elementary school organized demonstrations and were "threatening to boycott . . . to get African and American Negro history into the curriculum and Negroes into supervisory posts in Harlem schools." Earlier in 1966 when an attempt was made to remove Robert Poynter, the only Black teacher at Harlem's PS 175, demonstrators closed the school twice, "blocking the sidewalk so teachers could not pass." Activists promised the same for the beginning of the 1966–1967 school year.[35] However, the boycott at PS 175 was avoided after representatives of CORE, the Parent Teacher Association, and concerned parents held a series of meetings with school officials, who ultimately agreed to add "the teaching of African and American Negro history at the school."[36]

Many young people in Boston, New York City, Chicago, and other northern and southern cities were first exposed to Black History when they attended the freedom schools opened during the system-wide boycotts that began in June 1963. When SCLC's Bernard Lafayette organized the group SOUL at Chicago's John Marshall High School in the 1964–1965 school year, in addition to receiving training in nonviolent direct-action protest tactics, the students echoed the ongoing demand for the inclusion of Black History courses at the school. Unfortunately, two years later, there still were no Black History courses. The Marshall Association for the Advancement of Black Students had been formed in 1967, initially to try to remove, or at least discipline, a bigoted white teacher. Marshall High student James Smith recalled, "If a student came into class with his hair natural, the teacher would give him a hard time. . . . Right in front of the class, the teacher would say 'man, you're a dummy, you can't learn anything.'" Completely misinformed about Black History, this teacher claimed that all Black leaders were "communists," that the Black vote in Chicago "could be bought," and often made other disparaging remarks in class about African Americans. Though the teacher was not fired, James Smith would go on to organize school boycotts there and system-wide in 1968.[37]

Teenagers sparked and/or participated in rioting in Cincinnati, Newark and northern New Jersey, and Detroit in the summer of 1967 when thousands of national guardsmen had to be deployed to restore order.[38] Then, in November 1967, rioting erupted on Chicago's South Side after African American students at Englewood High School organized walkouts and picketing when Principal Thomas Van Damm "reassigned" Black teacher Owen Lawson to another school "for political reasons." Lawson taught history and social studies, emphasizing in his classes African peoples' contributions to US and world history. He also served as advisor to the Afro-American History Club. The students and their supporters believed that Lawson was removed because his lectures were "too militant" and had "Black Power overtones."[39]

Local community groups supported the students' walkout, and on its second day, November 20, 1967, over three hundred students and activists surrounded Englewood High, carrying picket signs declaring, "We Want Lawson and Black History," as numerous policemen in squad cars stood by. Inside the school, Rev. John Porter of Christ Methodist Church met with Principal Van Damm and district superintendent Michael R. Fortino, who claimed Lawson's transfer was due to his "administrative incompetence" and "not for political reasons." Van Damm also mentioned that "we are trying to establish a permanent course on Negro History here and Lawson was one of the persons drawing up the curriculum." However, Lawson was only a "full time basic" (FTB) substitute teacher with no permanent assignment, and Van Damm would not reinstate him at Englewood High. Lawson was told to report to the board of education building for assignment to another post, and on the second day of the protest, Principal Van Damm was forced to close the school early because too few FTBs showed up for work. The members of the FTB organization carried out a "sick-in" that day in solidarity with fellow FTB Owen Lawson.[40]

On the third day of demonstrations outside Englewood High, several teenagers started throwing stones at the police cars and were chased into a nearby luncheonette. As the police dragged the students out, those outside watching began to shout and cry out about the brutality displayed and started throwing rocks and bottles at the police. A melee erupted and trash cans and rocks were hurled into store and restaurant windows. Twenty-one people were arrested, mostly juveniles, and local businesses reported thousands of dollars in damage.[41]

That same day, November 21, 1967, at Waller High School on the near North Side, the African American students walked out of their classes upon hearing a rumor that a Black teenager's leg was severed when white students pushed him onto the elevated train tracks. Fighting began in the school cafeteria and moved into the streets, where students hurled rocks through store windows and threw bottles at police when they showed up. African American students at nearby Cooley Vocational High School heard the rumor about a teenager losing a leg and decided to join in the rioting, breaking store windows and looting display items. The police on the scene arrested eighty-two people, including forty-six teenagers, and twelve policemen and civilians were injured. At least sixty police officers were deployed at the two schools the next day with only about 40 percent of the students in attendance.[42]

In April 1968, at Hirsch High School on the South Side, fifteen hundred students organized a walkout to protest Operation Snatch and the cancelling of Afro-American Day. Historian Dionne Danns noted that "Operation Snatch was launched by administrators as a way to discipline students loitering in the hallways." Students not in their classrooms could be snatched and detained by teachers and held until the class period was over; then the student would be charged with an "unexcused absence."[43] On Tuesday, April 2, students began leaving the school after a five-gallon gas can exploded outside the cafeteria. Principal William Kelleher dismissed classes and agreed to meet with the representatives of student activists the next morning. At that meeting Kelleher said Operation Snatch would be reconsidered; and the Afro-American Day was not really cancelled, merely postponed "because we wanted it to be a cultural and educational event that the students would be proud of."[44] Shortly after, Kelleher announced that Operation Snatch was "no longer a functioning program" and he would meet with "human relations experts" to address the students' other complaints.[45]

DEATH OF A KING

The deaths in Memphis, Tennessee, of sanitation workers Echol Cole and Robert Walker, crushed inside a garbage truck in February 1968, prompted a labor strike not just to demand replacement of faulty equipment but also for union representation and increased wages for the city workers. In the early 1960s students at colleges in the Bluff City participated in sit-ins that led to the desegregation of most restaurants, stores, and other public places; but there was a lull in social activism until 1967 when the calls for Black Power resulted in the formation of the Black Organizing Project (BOP), led by Charles Cabbage and Coby Smith. This coalition group wanted to establish a "Black United Front to coordinate and implement all black community politics" in Memphis and sought "community control over education, finances, . . . and land ownership." The BOP's youth branch, the Invaders, targeted "specifically high school students and college underclassmen" for membership. Historian Shirletta J. Kinchen reported that the males-only group sought members between ages 13 and 22, but in early 1968, "the majority of the group's makeup consisted of Carver High School students and graduates."[46]

After the sanitation workers in Memphis went on strike and union representatives and city officials were deadlocked, Rev. James Lawson, head of the local ministerial group Community on the Move for Equality, invited Dr. King to the city to participate in the ongoing demonstrations. Kinchen documented the Black workers' activism and found that the young people "became an essential component of the strike. After sanitation workers, high school and college students were constant fixtures at the downtown marches." King gave a speech in Memphis to an estimated seventeen thousand people on March 18, 1968, and vowed to return to lead another demonstration on March 22. King encouraged the participation of the Invaders in the march, which was rescheduled for Thursday, March 28.[47] That day, with King, Lawson, and Ralph Abernathy in the lead, the crowd started down Main Street when soon they began to hear the sound of crashing glass. Teenagers in the back of the line of marchers had begun breaking windows and looting stores, and policemen in full riot gear were confronting the marchers. A horrified King asked to be taken back to the Lorraine

Motel where he was staying, telling the others, "I will never lead a violent march."[48]

After order was restored, several ministers and journalists blamed the Invaders for what became known as the Beale Street Riot, but BOP's Charles Cabbage denied the charge and told Dr. King and others that Rev. Lawson and the ministers had alienated the Invaders and other young people by not including them in the deliberations for the protest. King left soon after, but returned to Memphis on Wednesday, April 3, and met with Cabbage, James Smith, and the Invaders at the Lorraine Motel and promised the teenagers financial support if they agreed to serve as marshals at the next peaceful march. However, the next day, April 4, 1968, Dr. King was standing on the balcony of the Lorraine Motel when he was struck by an assassin's bullet and was killed. The nation and the entire world were shocked by the heinous political murder. Nonetheless, Coretta Scott King decided she would fulfill Dr. King's promise, and, just four days after his assassination, she returned to Memphis on Monday, April 8. With the Invaders serving as marshals, she led a massive nonviolent march through the city that drew thousands.[49]

When news of Dr. King's assassination was broadcast, rioting erupted in cities and towns throughout the United States. Over the next three days, thirty-nine people were killed and over fourteen thousand were arrested. In Harlem and other sections of New York City, there was massive looting and arson. In Washington, DC, President Lyndon Johnson had to call out nine thousand federal troops to help restore order after two days of rioting. There were eight deaths and numerous fires attributed to the violence, with over seven hundred people injured, including many law enforcement officers, and at least three thousand people in the District were arrested. In Chicago, Lieutenant Governor Samuel Shapiro asked the president to send federal troops "to combat an insurrection" and the "vandalism, looting, and arson" taking place throughout the city. In addition to the fifteen hundred Illinois Army National Guardsmen brought in on April 5 to work with the four thousand firemen and law enforcement officers, five thousand soldiers from nearby US Army bases were sent to the city.[50]

As expected, absenteeism was high on Friday, April 5, in public and private schools all over the country; but many of those who showed up came to protest. In Chicago, students walked out of their classes at Hyde Park, Hirsh, South Shore, Harper, and several other high schools. At Bowen High School the Black students' request for Black History courses had just been turned down by school administrators, and on April 5 the request for a memorial service for Dr. King was rejected. This sparked a walkout by Black students at Bowen, who joined other teenagers marching, clapping, and shouting through the streets of the South Side. According to one witness, the students "tore up everything in their path on their way home."[51] Mayor Richard J. Daley's Riot Study Committee, created to investigate the disturbances, reported that "the principals of a number of the high schools in the black communities were forced to call upon the police for assistance in quelling vandalism and physical assaults on whites," and all the schools in those areas were eventually closed. And as was the case in other riots during that decade, "a relatively small number of so-called natural leaders among the young blacks of high school age were generally the catalysts and leaders of the April disorders. . . . A few older blacks joined them in this destructive 'leadership' role."[52] These "natural leaders" in Chicago's high schools organized district-wide strikes later that year to promote both civil rights and Black Power objectives.

At William Penn High School in York, Pennsylvania, known as York High, African American students made up 23 percent of the 1,526 enrolled. On the afternoon of April 4 several students were in the middle of planning various activities for Black Pride Day, scheduled for Monday, April 8, 1968. Underclassman Louis Woodyard suddenly rushed into the room sobbing and crying, "They killed King . . . They killed King. We have to do something!" These students then went to all the classrooms and called out to the Black students to let them know what had happened. Former York High students told historian Dwayne C. Wright that they gathered together and decided collectively not to attend classes the next day, but to meet together in the auditorium and hold their Black Pride Day where they could grieve together. York's school superintendent, Woodrow W. Brown, decided to keep the schools open on Friday, April 5, but upon entering York High that morning, the Black students told Principal O. Meredith Parry they were going to use the auditorium all day. Reginald Ellis, a senior, recalled "being very solemn" with Principal Parry. "It wasn't defiance, but it was resolve."

Parry allowed them use of the auditorium, but refused to announce the students' gathering over the school's speaker system. So they went classroom to classroom gathering the Black students to meet in the auditorium.[53]

Deborah McMillan was a senior at York High and recalled that "the students were more interested in doing something." They were angry, and they wanted everyone to know they were going to do something that "was important for us" and to let others know they were "serious about what they were doing." They decided to come up with a "list of demands" and number one was "Black History must be mandatory for all students at William Penn." Other demands included the hiring of more Black teachers, administrators, and guidance counselors; the formal recognition and support for Black student groups on campus; the employment of "Black cafeteria personnel such as cooks" and servers; and the establishment of a "school holiday . . . for the commemoration of Dr. Martin Luther King Jr.'s death."[54]

The students met with and presented their demands to York's school board. At the April 22 meeting, the only African American school board member, Russell Chapman, supported the students' cause, and the board voted five to one in favor of offering "a course on Negro History" in the high school beginning in September 1968. Over the next year, two African Americans were hired as teachers, two as guidance counselors, and several others in staff positions. Julia Muldrow was hired to teach Black History, but the course was not mandatory. It became an elective for upperclassmen. William Penn was the only senior high school in York. In Chicago with numerous high schools, many with predominantly Black enrollments, the students organized walkouts, boycotts, and other nonviolent protests demanding courses in Black History and the hiring of more African American teachers and other school personnel.[55]

BLACK POWER AND HIGH SCHOOL BOYCOTTS IN CHICAGO

In 1963 and 1964, hundreds of thousands of elementary and secondary school students in Chicago had participated in the district-wide Freedom Day boycotts organized by the CCCO, and between 1965 and 1968 there were parent-initiated protests over racial discrimination at specific public elementary schools. In November 1965, for example, the Concerned Parents of Jenner Elementary School called for the removal of Principal Mildred Chuchut because of her perceived racist attitudes and behavior. The Black parents organized a boycott and the protests continued into February 1966 when Dr. King spoke at a rally in support of the strike. "We must emphasize that while Jenner is but a single and bitter example of the system's insensitivity and failure to educate, it is but one thread in a vast fabric of educational and administrative inadequacy that is woven about this entire city." Principal Chuchut was finally replaced in April 1966. Similar efforts were mounted in Chicago against racist principals at Attucks Elementary School in April 1967 and Crown Elementary School in February 1968.[56]

At Austin High School on Chicago's West Side, the Black student enrollment went from less than 2 percent in 1958 to 48 percent in 1968, but there was still only one Black teacher on the faculty. Riccardo James, then a student at Austin High, believed that "many white teachers held racist attitudes," and he led a walkout of three hundred students on October 7, 1968, demanding the hiring of more Black teachers and administrators. However, when Black students mounted their walkout, white students at Austin High organized a protest of their own and argued that the Black students were "trying to take over *their* school." Riccardo James told the *Chicago Sun-Times* reporter, "Each of us has personal prejudices—it's inevitable. . . . What we wanted to do is to talk about it with the white students." In exasperation, James asked, "How can you get along with someone if you don't know him?"[57]

That same day, October 7, 1968, at Morgan High School there were conflicts between Black and white students in the cafeteria that continued outside the building. Principal James Moore decided to call the police "as a safety measure," and when a policeman intervened in a fight, he was hit and cut over the eye by a student. As patrolman Glen Lanier tried to arrest the student, others tried to prevent it, and several policemen arrived and soon arrested fourteen students. This led to hundreds of students at Morgan High staging a walkout the next day.[58]

At Harrison High School in Chicago's Lawndale neighborhood, African American students formed their first Black Power organization and dubbed themselves the New Breed. In September 1968, they issued a four-page manifesto emphasizing that the students "will not accept the treacherous rhetoric of gradualism, nor fall to the equally frustrating cries of irrational acts. We demand freedom and justice now." In addition to assuming the position as the "liaison and bargaining agency for the student body," the student activists sought "recognition of Concerned People of Lawndale as the parent-teacher organization" and "making the Afro-American history course required of all students." Since Black students made up 54 percent of the thirty-one hundred students enrolled at Harrison High, they sought the "appointment of black administrative assistants for discipline and of black counselors at large." Principal Alexander Burke, however, refused to accept any of the students' demands.[59]

Given this response, Victor Adams and Sharron Matthews of the New Breed organized a sit-in in the school cafeteria, which triggered a walkout by five hundred students on Monday, October 7, 1968. The police were called in and twelve students were arrested, including Adams and Matthews. The boycotting students gathered at nearby St. Agatha Catholic Church and held a rally. Victor Adams had been released by the police, and he addressed the over eight hundred students assembled. "They're always telling us to be peaceful and protest in an orderly fashion," but that's not how the country "gained its independence. . . . What we are going to do is deal with the system." The New Breed was joined by Puerto Rican and Mexican American students in their march on Chicago's board of education building.[60] At Fenger High School on October 8, over 250 Black students gathered in the cafeteria to formulate their demand for a "Negro teacher for the Afro-American history classes." Principal George Triezenberg called the police, but no arrests were made.[61] School officials finally met with a group of Black students, parents, and teachers from Fenger High on Friday, October 11, 1968, but many student leaders left that Friday meeting dissatisfied and decided to get together at the Black Students for Defense office, 251 E. Pershing Road, on Sunday, October 13, to determine their response.[62]

Student leaders from at least twelve high schools came together and formulated a "Black Student Manifesto." Calling itself Concerned Black Students, the group announced citywide public school boycotts beginning on Monday, October 14, 1968, and every Monday afterward until their demands were met. The manifesto called for not just "complete courses on

Black History," but also "inclusion in all courses the contributions of Black persons." The students also demanded the hiring of more Black teachers and administrators, especially in predominantly Black high schools, and the establishment of school holidays to celebrate Martin Luther King Jr. and other African American heroes. They wanted "revised ROTC training for Negroes to train them to repel the constant threats to our community." They also wanted school officials to "use Black businessmen to supply class photos and rings to Black schools."[63]

In its October 15, 1968, front-page headline, the *Chicago Daily Defender* declared "35,000 Stage Peaceful School Walkout." Most of the striking students stayed away from the school grounds, but fire alarms were set off at several schools and thousands of those in attendance were forced to evacuate. The front door of Calumet High School was set afire by a Molotov cocktail. Over three hundred students, led by Black Students for Defense, held a rally at the South Side's Washington Park, which the students renamed Malcolm X Park. At least twenty-four students were arrested at various schools throughout the city. According to board of education figures, over 60 percent of the students were absent that day at Englewood, Cooley Vocational, Harlan, Hyde Park, Lindblom, Phillips, and Waller High Schools. Several dozen students marched on the board of education building where Harrison High's Victor Adams tried to deliver the students' manifesto to James Redmond, but was told the school superintendent was not available.[64]

While most students returned to their classes on Tuesday, October 15, some did not. It was reported that forty students from Gage High School marched on the board of education building to insist that the 150 students who participated in the Monday walkout be readmitted without punishment. At Kennedy High School, the principal, Dorothy Sauer, suspended over a hundred students who walked out on Monday and refused to allow them to enter the building the next day without their parents. Rev. Arthur Brazier, the head of The Woodlawn Organization, announced his group's support for the students' protests and pledged to assist them in pursuing the curricular changes and teacher diversity. Philip Katz, principal of Lewis-Champlain Elementary School, contacted the principals of schools on the South and West Sides and called for the formation of a group to assist the board of education in finding "new solutions" to ongoing school problems.[65]

On the second Monday strike, October 21, an estimated twenty-eight thousand students boycotted Chicago's public high schools and this time they were joined by over seven hundred teachers.[66] At the Senate Theater on Madison Street, at least two thousand Black students attended a noon rally organized by the Black Panther Party, where entertainer Sammy Davis Jr. was scheduled to perform. At Austin High the police were summoned, and three students were arrested for "disorderly conduct" and sixteen others for truancy.[67] That same day, over five hundred Black teachers left their schools early to attend a noon rally at Fellowship Baptist Church. Among the speakers were school administrator Barbara Sizemore, Bobby Wright of the Black Teachers Caucus, Timuel Black of Teachers for Quality Education, as well as Sharron Matthews of Harrison High and Omar Aoki from Lindblom High. The teachers announced their support for the students' demand for "quality education for all students in black community schools." At Harrison and Lakeview High Schools, Puerto Rican and Mexican American students had issued their own manifesto and called for courses on their literature and history and for bilingual programs. They too participated in the boycotts. Rev. José Burgos, president of the Latin American Ministerial Association, announced his group's endorsement of the Black and Hispanic students' educational demands.[68]

Only about ninety-two hundred students at about twenty-nine high schools struck on the third Monday, October 28, mainly because the school board and Superintendent Redmond agreed to meet with representatives of the strikers on Wednesday, October 30. Nonetheless, an estimated 250 Black students participated in a "funeral march" from Civic Center Plaza to the board of education building on LaSalle Street. Six students wore black robes and carried a coffin labeled "Board of Education" and "Daley," which they subsequently stomped to pieces. Several other protesters paraded outside the board of education building for several hours, and it was reported that at least forty-five girls walked out of their classes at Jones Commercial High School.[69]

The meeting with school board members on Wednesday evening, October 30, did not go well. Hundreds of people showed up and dozens of students and several teachers addressed the board, including Puerto Rican parents and students seeking more Spanish language and bilingual courses. The activists began reacting to the board members' statements, but board president Frank M. Whiston wanted to stem the outbursts and maintain control of the meeting. "This is our meeting, not yours," declared James Harvey, representing the Afro-American Student Association. "And we'll respond by applauding when we want." There was another burst of applause and Whiston abruptly ended the board's meeting. The students returned to their meeting places to deliberate and soon announced that "sit-ins would be launched" at public schools throughout the city beginning on Monday, November 4, 1968.[70]

The *Chicago Tribune* soon denounced the "rebel leaders" and their call for sit-ins at public high schools. "The school system can't tolerate seizure of school property and disobedience of school rules by a group of adolescents who, if they are not emotionally sick, are being cruelly misled by adult fanatics." The editor believed "to tolerate 'sit-ins' would invite wholesale vandalism and complete chaos."[71] Superintendent Redmond decided to adopt a "get tough policy," and on Monday, November 4, had two hundred policemen stationed at twenty-three high schools likely to have disturbances. Sit-in demonstrations took place at the administrative offices at Parker, Lindblom, Hyde Park, Englewood, and Chicago Vocational High Schools and involved hundreds of students. At Parker High School an estimated two hundred students barricaded themselves in the lunchroom and refused to leave. The police were summoned, and using billy clubs, they chased the students out of building. The protesters outside who saw this began throwing rocks and cans at the police and then at nearby stores and started looting them. The police arrested eleven Parker High students. At Harlan High, when those sitting in were forced by the police to leave, students held a rally outside the school building and urged local residents gathered outside to join them in the protest.[72]

At least forty students sat in at the principal's office at Hyde Park High, while over three hundred paraded around the school building. Those who refused to leave the area once the police arrived were arrested. At least twenty-five arrests were made. It was estimated that the largest number of student protesters, over four hundred, were at Paul Lawrence Dunbar

High. And while the creation of Black History courses was still the number one issue at DuSable High School, student activist Ora Ferguson participated in the demonstrations because "we want better washrooms, heat in school rooms, and the windows repaired."[73]

African American students went from 21 percent of the enrollment in 1963 to 99 percent in the 1968–69 school year at Calumet High School. Several protests about the deteriorating physical conditions were launched beginning in February 1967. Finally, in December 1968, Black students presented their "manifesto" containing twenty-eight demands to Principal Charles La Force. They called for increases in the number of Black History courses and African American teachers and administrators, greater input from the parents and the community in school issues, and more sanitary conditions in the school's cafeteria and washrooms. On Friday, December 13, 1968, after an unfruitful meeting with the principal, some disturbances broke out in the school lunchroom and soon spread throughout the building. Principal La Force had to close the school. Meetings were held with students, parents, and faculty the next week, and La Force agreed to have parents involved in the decision making at the school.[74] Historian Dionne Danns concluded that the organized protests at dozens of high schools in Chicago in the 1968–1969 school year resulted in greater input from parents and students in school decision making, "the acquisition of insurance for student athletes, the increase and expansion in Black History courses; . . . increased funding for school building repairs, more technical and vocational courses, and curricular changes that reflected Africans' contributions to world history."[75]

HIGH SCHOOL STUDENT ACTIVISM NATIONWIDE

The widespread high school student activism in Chicago was representative of the student rights and antiwar protests taking place throughout the United States in the late 1960s. The National Association of Secondary School Principals released a study in January 1969 that reported that 59 percent of senior high schools and 56 percent of junior high schools had experienced "some kinds of protests" over the previous two years. In February 1969, Columbia University law professor Alan F. Westin gathered information on 349 "high school disruptions" between November 1968 and February 1969. Westin found that 132 incidents involved charges of "racial discrimination," 81 were related to politics and the Vietnam War, 71 were against "dress regulations," 60 against "disciplinary practices," and 17 for "educational reforms."[76]

High school principal turned researcher Kenneth Fish, in his book *Conflict and Dissent in the High Schools*, published in 1970, cited these studies and declared, "High school walkouts, sit-ins, and school closings are a serious concern to parents, citizens, and many students," and emphasized that in his research and personal experience, "most of the conflict in high schools of the United States is related to problems of race."[77] Fish contrasted these findings with the observations of Earl Kelley in his 1962 book *In Defense of Youth* where Kelley asserted that high school students "behave better than they ever did. . . . School discipline and behavior are better than ever before . . . and it is unheard of for a school to be closed because the students are out of control." Kenneth Fish's reality in the late 1960s was quite different. "My experience as principal of a 2,300 student high school which was partially closed down for two days as a result of a week of protests, fighting, and cafeteria disorder has given me an understanding of some of the phenomena and forces of high school conflict."[78]

Of the four case studies Fish presented, three involved African American students and racial discrimination. However, some of Fish's observations about Black students were not entirely accurate. He opined, "Today's black students are different from their counterparts of twenty years ago, owing to social changes of many kinds." Indeed, sociologist Thomas Pettigrew referred to these high school students as "this 'newest' new Negro" and "they have a new race-consciousness and feeling of unity."[79] However, as was documented here in chapters 1 and 2, "race-consciousness and feeling of unity" had been apparent in Black children and teenagers' activism from the 1930s. We now know that some of their "counterparts twenty years ago," and even earlier, launched school boycotts and engaged in civil rights activism in various parts of the country to bring about social and educational change.

Black students' activism, along with the protests and demonstrations taking place on college and university campuses in the late 1960s, spurred high school activism among other students of color and white teenagers as well. These young people pursued their own demands after observing the significant gains achieved through civil rights activism and Black students' protests. For Mexican American students in the Western states, another important influence on teenage activism was the farmworkers movement led by Cesar Chavez, Dolores Huerta, and the United Farm Workers organization. In struggling for union representation, the farmworkers utilized mass protests, demonstrations, marches, and national boycotts to gain support for "La Causa." Many elementary and high school students participated in the union demonstrations and in the historic march from Delano to the California capitol in Sacramento in March 1965. In East Los Angeles, in 1966, Mexican American high school students organized Young Citizens for Community Action (YCCA) to pursue their educational objectives, but soon became more involved in the issue of police brutality. Reflecting the militancy of the Black Panther Party, the teenagers in YCCA renamed the group, the Brown Berets, and in the fall of 1967 began making plans to organize school boycotts over extreme overcrowding, lack of resources, and absence of Chicano history and literature in the curricula in the Los Angeles Unified School District (LAUSD).[80]

When the principal of Wilson High School abruptly cancelled the students' production of the play *Barefoot in the Park* (claiming it was unsuitable material for teenagers), the students staged a walkout at lunch time on Friday, March 1, 1968. College students in United Mexican American Students, the Brown Berets, and Sal Castro, a teacher at Lincoln High School, urged the students at Lincoln, Garfield, and Roosevelt High Schools to walkout on Tuesday, March 5, in solidarity with the Wilson High protesters, and every day to Friday, March 8. The teenagers set up picket lines in the streets near the schools and carried signs declaring "Walk Out Today, Or Drop Out Tomorrow," "Teachers Sí, Bigots No!," "Education, Not Eradication." Mexican American students' boycotts, called blowouts, sought the teaching of Chicano history and literature, offering bilingual courses, serving Mexican food in the cafeteria, and hiring Chicano teachers and administrators.[81]

At Roosevelt High School in East Los Angeles, administrators decided to call in police officers, who surrounded the school and harassed the students as they walked out. Two Mexican American students accused of hurling bottles at squad cars were beaten in front of the school by the police. The beating brought about increased unity between students and Chicano activists in East Los Angeles.[82] The students at predominantly Black Jefferson High School in South Central joined the Mexican American students' blowouts. In December 1968 at Fremont High School, also in South Central Los Angeles, African American students followed the lead of their Mexican American comrades and formed a Black Student Union (BSU). Following a rancorous outburst at a meeting with the faculty, however, violence erupted and four BSU students were suspended and others were arrested. Then over five hundred students joined a strike and demanded more Black faculty and administrators, including the principal, and no disciplinary action against suspended students. LAUSD administrators subsequently agreed to many of the students' demands.[83]

The protests by Mexican American students in California were taken up by Chicano students in Denver and several other Colorado towns and in Texas. In *Young Activists: American High School Students in the Age of Protest*, historian Gael Graham reports that in Crystal City, Texas, in 1969, "the refusal of school authorities to permit Mexican American girls to be cheerleaders galvanized the entire Mexican American population (which was numerically dominant) . . . and allowed a new political party, La Raza Unida, to takeover not just the school board, but the city council as well." As a result of the boycott, Mexican and Mexican American history courses were offered, Mexican American music and cheerleaders were included at sports events, and "the cafeteria used only produce grown by the United Farm Workers."[84]

The protests in Crystal City inspired high school students in other Texas towns. In Uvalde, Texas, for example, Mexican American students launched a blowout in February 1970 demanding improved facilities and resources and better relations with the principal and school staff. Unfortunately, local white politicians decided to call out the Texas Rangers to intimidate the teenagers, and "parents of the boycotters were either fired or threatened with dismissal from their jobs." Graham reports that Mexican American students staged a blowout and marches in the Lower Rio Grande Valley, but "the school administration refused to consider their list of fifteen demands" and instead "expelled some sixty students." It was only through the intervention of the federal district court at the request of the Mexican American Legal Defense and Education Fund that these students "were reinstated and their records cleared."[85]

Mexican American students at Roosevelt High School in East Los Angeles organized another blowout in March 1970 because of school officials' failure to move on the student demands made earlier. But this time two hundred white students at Beverly Hills High School staged a protest in support of the Mexican American students' demands offering evidence of the solidarity that had developed among teenagers seeking "student rights" and "student power." White teenagers had learned from the activism of African American, Chicano, and Puerto Rican students that organized protest could bring about change in educational policies and practices. Gael Graham concluded that the activism of students of color "affected a much broader constituency among students and could sometimes unify students across races and against teachers and administrators." However, there was also "white backlash." "Many whites believed that compulsory integration required only chilly toleration of the newcomers' presence," she reported. "They did not intend to incorporate minority students into the fabric of school life, let alone reweave that fabric into a new pattern."[86] Students in public schools across the country wanted "the right to dress as they pleased, publish and distribute their own newspapers, form their own extracurricular clubs, and invite outside speakers to campus." The achievement of these goals would benefit all high school students.[87]

The clashes as well as the solidarity between Black and white high school students were clearly on display in Waterbury, Connecticut, in a boycott by over a thousand students at three high schools. On September 27, 1968, forty African American students at Crosby High School went on strike because of a "dispute over the teaching of Negro history." However, that same day, "about 150 whites walked out . . . to protest use of a textbook on Negro history in a course on American history." Some white students also complained that "black students went unpunished for misbehavior." Nonetheless, both Black and white striking students "would stay away until an agreement was worked out . . . involving the schools' dress code."[88]

CONCLUSION: CHILDREN, TEENAGERS, AND SOCIAL CHANGE

In the 1930s and 1940s, NAACP youth councils organized demonstrations in support of the antilynching bill pending in Congress and for the freedom for the Scottsboro Nine. The boycott organized by students at all-Black R. R. Moton High School in Prince Edward County, Virginia, in April 1951 led to the NAACP lawsuit *Davis, et al. v. School Board of Prince Edward County, Virginia*, which was included in the monumental *Brown v. Board of Education* decision in 1954. The Montgomery bus boycott was launched in December 1955 by local Black ministers, leaders, young people, and adults and was justified by their religious faith. Gladis Williams, a high school student in Montgomery at that time, recalled, "We would have a prayer" before leaving the churches or halls to take to the streets. "Got to have a prayer before we go to do battle."[89] The Little Rock Nine demonstrated grace under pressure as they entered hostile territory at Little Rock's Central High School during the 1957–58 school year. And the tens of thousands of elementary and high school students who participated in the Youth Marches for Integrated Schools in May 1958 and April 1959 understood the religious basis of their commitment to social justice and educational change in the United States.

The teenagers in the NAACP youth councils in Kansas, Oklahoma, and North Carolina in the 1950s laid the groundwork for an antiracist student movement launched in Greensboro, North Carolina, in February 1960. While hundreds of Black and white college students participated in the sit-ins and other nonviolent direct-action protests, high school students in Chattanooga, Tennessee; Baton Rouge, Louisiana; and other southern cities joined the picket lines and sit-ins and were arrested throughout 1960 and 1961. Sixteen-year-old Brenda Travis was arrested and sent to reform school and came to be considered a freedom fighter following her participation in a sit-in at the bus terminal in McComb, Mississippi, in 1961. NAACP leader Medgar Evers declared, "Brenda's in the reformatory because she is sick and tired of discrimination and segregation. She's the symbol of the fight for freedom down here."[90]

In CORE's Freedom Rides into the South between May and December 1961, at least 25 percent of the participants were teenagers. In the Albany

Movement in 1961 and 1962 where thousands marched for months, the teenagers who were arrested and jailed by Sheriff Laurie Pritchett often sang freedom songs to raise their spirits, and it became known as "the Singing Movement." While few African Americans were registered to vote in Albany in 1962, the Children's Crusade in Birmingham in May 1963 inspired children and teenagers throughout the country to join in civil rights activism by participating in boycotts, sit-ins, marches, and demonstrations. In Boston, Chicago, New York City, Milwaukee, Cleveland, and other cities, hundreds of thousands of children and teenagers participated in district-wide school boycotts and attended freedom schools where they learned that participating in school strikes was an important contribution to the antiracist campaigns for "quality integrated education."[91]

The participation of young crusaders in civil rights campaigns was crucial for their success. It was children and teenagers who desegregated all-white public and private schools. From the 1930s the youngsters organized their own protests with little or no input from adults, and often achieved their objectives, especially after 1966 and the advent of Black Power. The mobilization to obtain courses in Black History and to hire more African American teachers and administrators was carried out by high school students themselves who devised and issued their own manifestos. The civil rights and Black Power activism of African American high school students in the 1960s served as models for Puerto Rican, Mexican American, and white students who recognized that they too were victims of unjust policies and discrimination and began mobilizing for student rights. While there appeared to be less and less religious fervor expressed by the young student activists at the end of the decade, they nonetheless believed their movement was a crusade that would profoundly affect future generations.

Epilogue

"Keep Stirring Up 'Good Trouble'"

*The only real revolutionary, people say, is a man
[or woman] who has nothing to lose. There are millions
of poor people in this country who have very little,
or even nothing to lose. If they can be helped to
take action together, they will do so with a freedom
and a power that will be a new and unsettling
force in our complacent national life.*

Martin Luther King Jr. (1967)[1]

*We can't begin to say how many times old people
that we meet in the street have compared the March
for Our Lives to the Civil Rights Movement and
the people that protested the Vietnam War. . . .
Courageous young people throughout history
have yelled so loud that it turned the country
upside down. Our goal is to do the same.*

John Barnitt, Sarah Chadwick, and Sofie Whitney
Stoneman Douglas High School, Parkland, Florida (2018)[2]

TIME MAGAZINE'S PERSON OF THE YEAR for 2019 was 16-year-old Greta Thunberg. "She is the youngest figure to receive this distinction in its 92-year history." *Time* editor in chief Edward Felsenthal added that Thunberg received this honor because "she became the biggest voice on the biggest issue facing the planet this year, coming from essentially nowhere to lead a worldwide movement. . . . She embodies youth activism."[3] Millions of high school students around the world, inspired by the Swedish teenager, marched in the streets, participating in "climate strikes." Fridays for Future is the global student movement that began in August 2018 after Greta Thunberg sat outside the Swedish parliament for three weeks to protest the lack of action on the climate crisis. Thunberg then decided to protest every Friday outside parliament, and other high school students began to join her. On May 24, 2019, and September 20 and 27, 2019, high school students in 131 countries participated in strikes and marched on government buildings demanding action on climate change, and they plan to continue their protests until meaningful action has been taken.[4]

On February 14, 2018, one of the worst mass shootings in US history took place at the Marjory Stoneman Douglas High School in Parkland, Florida. Seventeen students and teachers were killed and seventeen more were wounded. In the wake of that tragedy, students from Stoneman Douglas decided to organize a movement to challenge widespread access to guns, especially military-style assault weapons and the resulting violence in the United States. The Parkland students immediately gathered and began planning an anti-gun rally, which was held at the federal courthouse in Fort Lauderdale, Florida, on February 17, 2018. The students then mounted a social media campaign to generate awareness about the need to end gun violence and began meeting with state legislators to lobby for sensible gun legislation. Plans were made for a student walkout on March 14, 2019, "to demand that lawmakers pass legislation that addresses the epidemic of gun violence." Elementary and secondary school students in over twenty-five hundred schools in the United States participated in the walkout.[5]

Then, barely a month later, the Parkland students began making plans for a mass demonstration—the March for Our Lives—in Washington, DC, on Saturday, March 24, 2018. Stoneman Douglas student Jaclyn Corin recalled that "the whole month was a whirlwind; we worked day in and day out planning logistics, organizing talent and speakers, facilitating the sibling marches, and talking to volunteers." Corin distinctly remembered "the day [they] hit eight hundred sibling marches, some of which were being held in Mumbai, Japan, Australia, and all over Europe." In Washington, DC, that day it was estimated that over eight hundred thousand people participated. Stoneman Douglas student Alfonso Calderon recalled, "The one thing that shocked me is that I couldn't see the end of the crowd. I think 5'9" is not tall enough to see the end of 800,000 people in one street." Another student, Daniel Williams, declared, "It meant a lot to see so many high schoolers from around the country come to DC to support us. . . . This was truly a young people's march."[6]

March for Our Lives rallies in cities and towns brought hundreds of thousands of people into the streets. Reporters for the *New York Times* noted that the massive demonstration would not have taken place without "the fervor of the students." "From Pennsylvania Avenue in Washington to the streets of Salt Lake City to a small town in north Georgia," the March for Our Lives "ultimately represented twin triumphs: of organic, youthful grassroots energy and of sophisticated, experienced organizational muscle." Support from groups led by adults "was so helpful to the entire process," especially in the development of youth-led organizations seeking to stem gun violence.[7] Stoneman Douglas students John Barnitt, Sarah Chadwick, and Sofie Whitney reported, "We can't begin to say how many times old people that we meet in the street have compared the March for Our Lives to the Civil Rights Movement and the people that protested the Vietnam War. . . . Even the one and only John Lewis compared us to himself, and told us to keep stirring up 'good trouble.'"[8]

In fact, John Lewis was 17 years old in September 1957 when he arrived at American Baptist College, north of Nashville, Tennessee. In March 1959, he started participating in workshops on nonviolence offered by Rev. James Lawson, a pacifist who had studied Gandhian principles for social and political advancement while serving as a Methodist missionary in India. James Bevel, Diane Nash, and Bernard Lafayette also participated in Rev. Lawson's workshop, and all four moved to the forefront of the Nashville sit-in movement in 1960, and then became SNCC organizers in the South. Many SNCC activists went on to support the antiwar protests and the advocates of student rights and their efforts to engage in "good trouble" in the late 1960s.[9]

POST–CIVIL RIGHTS ERA YOUTH ACTIVISM

Children and teenagers continued to press demands for student rights and Black Power in the early 1970s, leading to the inclusion of lessons on the Black experience in US history courses and the introduction of Black History courses into public and private high school curricula. In some states this change was mandated by legislation.[10] Black and white student activism on college and university campuses in the late 1960s and 1970s led to the establishment of hundreds of Black/Africana Studies departments and programs, resulting in "the democratization of American higher education."[11] However, compared to the 1960s, children and teenagers were less involved in mass social movements. Political scientist Sekou M. Franklin points to the increased "political repression, movement fatigue, party realignment, and the triumph of the conservative agenda in the last three decades of the twentieth century."[12] In his book *After the Rebellion: Black Youth, Social Movement Activism, and the Post–Civil Rights Generation*, Franklin discusses the activities of youth-based protest groups that developed during that period, including the Student Organization for Black Unity, the Free South Africa campaign, the New Haven Youth Movement, the Black Student Leadership Network, and the juvenile justice reform movement. While these initiatives provided opportunities for young people's participation in social change, with the exception of the Free South Africa movement, they were "relatively low-risk, have been short-lived, and have had difficulty spreading beyond their initial locale."[13]

Wesley C. Hogan, in *On the Freedom Side: How Five Decades of Youth Activists Have Remixed American History*, examined youth-based groups seeking broad social change in the late twentieth and early twenty-first century. Hogan focused specifically on the example provided by Ella Baker and SNCC in the 1960s. She identifies Baker as "among the foremost experts in getting everyday people to the decision making table in twentieth-century America. Baker particularly excelled in activating young people." Ella Baker urged young activists to engage in collective decision making, and as has been discussed, SNCC organizers were successful not only in recruiting children and teenagers to become "young crusaders" and participate in civil rights protests, they also encouraged them to organize their own protests in cities and towns throughout the South. Hogan argues that youth activists in the 2000s are consciously or unconsciously "Ella Baker's children."[14]

Hogan devotes a chapter to Southerners on New Ground (SONG), founded in Durham, North Carolina, in 1993, by six LGBTQ activists interested in making the connections between race, gender, class, and sexual orientation. Through the creation of a resource center and holding workshops and retreats using "music, spoken word, poetry, theater, dance, food, and visual art," SONG promoted social change and cultural understanding. While these women organizers were past their twenties, "they laid the essential foundation for SONG's youth organizers in the second decade of the twenty-first century, who worked in collaboration with youth immigrant rights activists and the Movement for Black Lives in particular."[15]

On the Freedom Side includes a chapter on the "resistance citizenship" demonstrated by youthful activists who opposed the terrorist tactics of Immigration and Customs Enforcement (ICE) officers and organized rallies and marches in support of the passage of the DREAM Act to grant citizenship to undocumented youths brought to the United States as children. When the US Congress failed to pass the Development, Relief, and Education for Alien Minors (DREAM) Act, these teenagers not only continued their lobbying and advocacy within the political system but also launched sit-ins, hunger strikes, and street blockades, eventually leading to the Obama administration's Deferred Action for Childhood Arrivals (DACA) program. In the chapter on "The Movement for Black Lives," Hogan documents the activities of Black Lives Matter, Black Youth Project 100 (BYP100), the Dream Defenders, and other youth-oriented groups opposing police violence against African Americans and other people of color. BYP100 founder Charlene Carruthers declared, "From Ferguson to Chicago, Charlotte, and Baltimore, uprisings of young Blacks have put the world on notice that something is shifting in the United States."[16]

In July 2016, Native American youths organized a two-thousand-mile rally-run from the Standing Rock Sioux Reservation in North and South Dakota, to Washington, DC, to protest the construction of the Dakota Access Pipeline. The route covered eight hundred miles of unceded Lakota lands and sacred places, and some Indigenous elders were skeptical about this nonviolent direct-action protest, given past violations of treaties, attacks on their communities, and the failure to recognize their basic rights. Wesley Hogan quotes Jasilyn Charger of the Cheyenne River Lakota, 19 years old at the time, who understood that "it was important to make the adults see that if you're going to sit there and argue, we're gonna go wake up our brothers and sisters." The young people viewed themselves as "water protectors" and those who ran carried a petition with 144,000 signatures to stop the pipeline. When the young runners returned to Standing Rock, it was powerful to see thousands of people waiting to greet them. Hogan points out, "Similar to the 1960s sit-ins, youth putting their bodies on the line forced the rest of the country to take notice."[17]

Beginning on August 2016, when Indigenous youths and adults decided to mount their organized resistance at Standing Rock, they were supported by those in the Black Lives Matter movement. When asked why those in Black Lives Matter became involved, a member, Jumoke Emery-Brown, responded, "For us, the same law enforcement that's being employed to brutalize sovereign [Indigenous] nations is simply an extension of the forces being use to brutalize and terrorize [Black] communities. We do not believe that the history of stolen lands is separated from the history of stolen labor, so while we're not centered in this fight, it is absolutely something we are proud to be a part of because our histories are intertwined."[18]

YOUTH ACTIVISM AND REPARATORY JUSTICE IN THE TWENTY-FIRST CENTURY

The intertwined histories of African Americans and Native Americans means that both groups are pursuing *reparatory justice* in the twenty-first century. Reparatory justice refers to social and political activism aimed at repairing the damage that racist and homophobic laws, practices, and behaviors have done historically and currently to African Americans, to other people of color, and to sexual minorities; and to repairing damage to the air, water, and physical environment carried out in the past and currently by unrestrained corporate capitalists. Organized movements for reparations among African Americans can be traced to the late nineteenth century, and in the late 1960s and 1970s those who supported James Forman's "Black Manifesto" demanded and received modest reparations payments from various Protestant denominations and churches that benefited financially from slavery and slave trading.[19] The National Coalition of Blacks for Reparations in America (N'COBRA) was organized in 1987 following the US Congress legislation granting reparations to Japanese Americans who were placed in internment camps during World War II. In pursuit of reparatory justice, N'COBRA worked with political leaders to introduce legislation in city councils and state legislatures to grant reparations to African Americans to repair the remaining damage from slavery, slave trading, and legalized racial discrimination. This damage is readily apparent in the huge disparities in wealth and income between Black and white households. Working with N'COBRA, Detroit congressman John Conyers introduced HR 40 in the US House of Representatives in 1989 calling for the formation of a commission to study and make recommendations regarding reparations for African Americans. The bill was introduced into each session of Congress afterward, but did not move out of committee.[20]

More recently, the platforms and policies pursued by the youth-based Black Lives Matter (BLM), and the Black Youth Project 100 highlight antiracist activism and have included demands for reparations from the federal government, state governments that sanctioned slavery, and religious institutions, corporations, and other business enterprises that profited from slavery and legalized racial discrimination.[21] In August 2016, the leaders in Black Lives Matter issued *A Vision for Black Lives: Policy Demands for Black Power, Freedom, and Justice* and declared, "To address the past and current harms that slavery, Jim Crow, and mass incarceration have done to the black community, BLM is seeking reparations for the wealth extracted from our communities."[22] BYP100's *Agenda to Build Black Futures* called for the establishment of "budget lines for reparations at municipal, state, and federal government levels . . . as compensation for the economic, social, psychological, and political damage . . . to black people."[23]

The contemporary global reparations movement was launched in 2012 with the formation of the CARICOM Reparations Commission by the fifteen nations in the Caribbean Community. Reparations are being demanded from former colonial powers that granted independence to the peoples in the Caribbean region in the 1960s but failed to provide the financial support needed for economic development.[24] The chair of the

CARICOM Reparations Commission (CRC), Hilary McD. Beckles, has declared that reparatory justice will be the major social justice movement in the twenty-first century and has called upon the former colonial powers "to look at the past and its connection to the present, to recognize historic injustices, to eradicate the legacies of slavery, the slave trade, and colonialism ... to repair this damage."[25] The CRC has developed a Ten Point Program specifically outlining how the reparations funds are to be used.[26]

In 2019, an updated version of Congressman Conyers's HR 40, prepared by N'COBRA and the National African American Reparations Commission (NAARC), was introduced into the US Congress by Houston representative Sheila Jackson Lee with 125 cosponsors. It calls for the development of proposals for the implementation of reparations programs for African Americans, and the first hearings were held and televised in June 2019.[27] In the debates for the Democratic presidential nomination in 2020, the candidates were asked if they supported the new reparations bill and most agreed that if passed by Congress, as president they would sign it into law. At the same time, students at Georgetown University, Brown University, Virginia Theological Seminary, and other schools that benefited financially from slavery and slave trading pressed their administrators to develop reparations programs. In Chicago and Evanston, Illinois; Asheville, North Carolina; and other cities, political leaders have established "reparations funds" to financially assist impoverished Black residents. There have also been calls for the development of a national "Reparations Superfund," and economists William A. Darity Jr. and A. Kirsten Mullins declared that "the superfund strategy would meld public and private responsibility for American racial injustice in funding a program of black reparations."[28] In the 1950s and 1960s, the chant was "Freedom Now!" among young and older social activists; in the twenty-first century, given the long history of slavery and racism and legally protected predatory capitalist practices that have seriously damaged the physical environment globally, the chant should be "Reparations Now!"[29]

This should also be the chant among Native American youth. In the second half of the nineteenth century, Native Americans' lands in the Midwest and West were usurped by the US government and sold to settlers and large-scale agricultural interests. The funds were used to support the land-grant universities created by the 1862 Morrill Act. Land grant universities are found in every state, yet few Native Americans are enrolled. In pursuit of reparatory justice in the twenty-first century, Native American high school and college students should mobilize to seek reparations from land grant universities in the form of scholarships and other funds for higher education, especially from those institutions where Indigenous youths are significantly underrepresented in the student population.[30]

At the same time, elementary and secondary students victimized by the "tyranny of the tests" should mobilize and boycott standardized tests and demand reparations from the testing corporations that have promoted and lobbied for more and more testing in order to increase their profits. Parents, teachers, and students have complained bitterly about the damage to children's educational experiences due to "high stakes testing" and the huge amounts of classroom time lost to test preparation. Some upper-class parents have decided that their children will "opt out" of standardized testing altogether because they recognize the damage that the tests have done to their children's schooling and they refuse to continue to participate in "the testing charade."[31]

In the case of African Americans and other children of color, test results have been used historically to justify racial segregation in public education and the introduction of industrial and other nonacademic courses in all–African American or all–Mexican American schools. Currently, standardized testing prevents these youngsters from enrolling in highly specialized schools and educational programs that they would otherwise be prepared to attend.[32] The reintroduction of standardized testing in the wake of the COVID-19 pandemic should provide the opportunity for students, teachers, and school officials to renegotiate the terms of the testing regime with the testing corporations. And similar to the school strikes in Chicago, Boston, New York, and other cities for quality integrated education in the 1960s, children and teenagers should be prepared to "boycott on test day" to obtain reparations for the damage that testing corporations have done in the past, contributing mightily to the decline in the quality of schooling for elementary and secondary students in the United States. This would also allow teachers and administrators to focus attention on the development of alternative—teacher-student oriented—approaches for assessing educational outcomes.[33]

In the midst of the global coronavirus pandemic, national and international antiracist protests took place following the police murder of George Floyd in Minneapolis in May 2020 and have been compared to the mass demonstrations that brought hundreds of thousands of children, teenagers, and adults into the streets in the 1960s. In that turbulent decade, the precipitating events leading to far-reaching antiracist protests and demonstrations often were the unprovoked and unjustified incidents of police brutality. This was also the case in 2020, and thousands of children and teenagers not only participated in marches and demonstrations in large numbers; they also organized and led huge antiracist protests. In Savannah, Georgia, teenagers organized the marches and demonstrations; in New York City, Strategy for Black Lives was formed by teens and young adults to mount protests; and in Nashville, the largest gathering, with over ten thousand people, was organized by six teenagers—Jade Fuller, Nya Collins, Emma Rose Smith, Kennedy Green, Mikayla Smith, and Zee Thomas—who formed Teens4Equality to carry out their social activism. The teenagers were angered by the deaths of George Floyd, Breonna Taylor who was killed by police in her apartment in Louisville, and others at the hands of the police. "As teens, we are tired of waking up and seeing another innocent person being slain in broad daylight," declared Zee Thomas. "We're . . . dedicating our time to this to make sure things actually happen."[34]

The COVID-19 pandemic will be considered a watershed event globally in the early twenty-first century and has revealed significant flaws and deficiencies in health care, unemployment compensation, and wage-labor conditions in the United States. In the 1960s the urban uprisings and the revelations about the impoverished conditions in "The Other America" resulted in Lyndon Johnson's War on Poverty and the Great Society legislation.[35] The Elementary and Secondary Education Acts, 1966–68, led to the establishment of Head Start, Upward Bound, the funding for bilingual and special education programs, adult education, public and private school libraries, and to the Community Action Programs that required "maximum feasible participation" in policy decision making at the local level. Ford,

Rockefeller, and other philanthropic foundations funded scholarship and fellowship programs for minority undergraduate and graduate students. And the first major federal affirmative action program, the Philadelphia Plan, was promulgated in the construction trades industry following organized protests by the NAACP, CORE, and other civil rights groups at municipal building sites.[36]

The COVID-19 pandemic has made clear the need for far-reaching social and economic change in the United States. The pandemic has revealed the necessity of universal health care since employer-sponsored programs do not address the needs of the unemployed or the underemployed. The wage stagnation that strangled the economic advancement of lower- and middle-income workers over the previous four decades must be addressed by significant increases in salaries and the minimum wage. The absence of affordable housing in many cities needs to be addressed through government support for housing subsidies for families and incentives to builders to construct homes and apartments for moderate-income workers. In the trillion-dollar stimulus packages created in response to the pandemic, no provision was included to reduce or discharge student loan debt, especially for those newly unemployed. Children and teenagers must mobilize and demand that student loan debt be forgiven and that future generations of students leave college debt-free. If these needed changes are not forthcoming from the top down, then they must be pursued from the bottom up.

In his final statement to the young people, civil rights activist and political icon John Lewis declared, "In the last days of my life, you inspired me." In his youth, oppressed by the racial segregation and violence, he said, "Like so many young people today, I was searching for a way out, or a way in." Then he encountered the words and teachings of Dr. Martin Luther King Jr., who emphasized that "each of us has a moral obligation to stand up, speak up, and speak out. When you see something that is not right, you must say something, you must do something." Lewis also urged young people to "study and learn the lessons of history because humanity has been involved in this soul-wrenching, existential struggle for a long time."[37]

To obtain reparatory justice, it will require that the youth mobilize and advocate for redistributive policies aimed at correcting the extreme economic inequality in the United States and other late capitalist societies. In the past, civil rights and Black Power demands were realized through the willingness of children and teenagers to put their bodies on the line to support just causes. John Lewis understood that "ordinary people with extraordinary vision can redeem the soul of America by getting in what I call good trouble, necessary trouble": positive efforts to bring about the much-needed social, economic, and educational changes and improvements in the twenty-first century.

Acknowledgments

This book has been a long time coming. I began recognizing in the 1990s that children and teenagers had made significant contributions to civil rights campaigns while I was serving as a fellow in Temple University's Center for African American History and Culture and working with Bettye Collier-Thomas on *My Soul Is a Witness: A Chronology of the Civil Rights Era, 1954–1965*. In reading and collecting reports on civil rights activism throughout the United States found in the *New York Times, Jet* magazine, and the *Southern School News*, I began to identify where and when children and teenagers became important to the success of these protests. As part of the centennial celebration in 1998 of the birth of Paul Robeson, I was asked by Rae Alexander to develop a short social studies and language arts curriculum that could be used with secondary school students in Camden, New Jersey. *Better Be Ready: The Contributions of Children and Young People to the Civil Rights Movement* (1998) focused on Claudette Colvin, the 15-year-old arrested in Montgomery, Alabama, in March 1955 and who became a plaintiff, along with Rosa Parks, in *Browder v. Gayle*, the lawsuit that in 1956 struck down Alabama's transit segregation laws; the Little Rock Nine, who desegregated Central High School in Arkansas in 1957; the Children's Crusade in Birmingham, Alabama, in May 1963; and the teenage gang members who served as marshals in the demonstrations mounted by the NAACP to desegregate Girard College in Philadelphia in the 1960s.

After the publication of *My Soul Is a Witness* in 2000, I began examining children and teenagers' activism in Chicago, Boston, and other cities and published an article in 2001, "Black High School Student Activism: An Urban Phenomenon?" Most of the information I found at that point on civil rights activism came from large cities. Once I began to do more research,

I soon realized that the answer to that question was "no," because young-sters in small towns and rural areas participated in and organized civil rights demonstrations as well. However, that same year (2001), I agreed to accept the editorship of the *Journal of African American History* (*JAAH*). While I was able to publish the *JAAH* special issue in spring 2003, "The History of Black Student Activism," as editor, I no longer had time to conduct addi-tional research on children and teenagers' civil rights activism.

In 2011, after the *JAAH* had returned to its position as the leading schol-arly publication on African American life and history, I decided to work with my students at the University of California, Riverside (UCR), to pro-duce an exhibit to commemorate the fiftieth anniversary in May 2013 of the "Birmingham Children's Crusade." The students in the TRIO Mentor-ing Program volunteered to use the newspaper and magazine articles cited in *My Soul Is a Witness* to identify locations where children and teenagers were most active; and senior history majors in my research seminars in the Department of History gathered the photos, newspaper columns, school statistics, and other materials that were included in *Children, Youth, and Civil Rights, 1951–1965: A Student Exhibit* mounted at UCR's Rivera Library in May 2013, and *Children, Youth, and Civil Rights, 1951–1968: A Student Exhibit* displayed there in May 2014. The exhibit then traveled to Dillard University in New Orleans, Prince George's County Community College in Maryland, Drexel University in Philadelphia, the Association for the Study of African American Life and History's centennial convention in Atlanta, and the US Capitol Visitor Center in Washington, DC, in 2015. At exhibit openings, panel discussions and forums included interviews with individuals who participated in the civil rights activities in those locations as children and teenagers in the 1960s. The videotaped panel discussions and interviews served to guide my perspectives on the civil rights activism of the young crusaders.

I want to thank those who worked on the exhibits: Edward D. Col-lins, exhibit design; Kyle F. Anderson, graphic design; student assistants Viet N. Trinh and Juan Carlos Jauregui; and the student researchers Cait-lin Awrey, Harrison Buckley, Esmeralda Cano, Crystal Chambliss, David Chavez, Vincent Chrismon, Deborah Clark, Amee Covarrubias, Jonathan Dai, William Diermissen, Gabriel Flores, Eduardo Fornes, Reanna Gibbs,

Jessica Gutierrez, Kia Harris, Reyna Harvey, Ryan Hazinski, Shaino Ho, Tien Thuy Ho, Aiesha Khan, Charles Kim, Jade Kim, Nicholas Lam, Nikita Lau, Andres Lozano, Celina Lozano, Roslyn Ludden, Arman Makazi, Sean McElliott, Somailia Miller, Michael Morales, Ty Oberdank, Teresa Palafox, Jesus Peña, Victoria Phillips, Dario Puccini, Talia Ramirez, Jennifer Rener, Gessenia Rivas, Antonio Rodriguez, Cassiopeia Rogers, Veronica Sandoval, Jennifer Sayed, Gregory Schwab, Ieasha Serrat, Paul Sinkiewiez, Lila Sultan, Jin Sung, Fabiola Escobeda Torres, David Tran, Diana Vincenty, Brandon Walker, Briana White, Ed Wimpenny, and Sarah Wolk.

When I retired from UCR in 2015 and returned to New Orleans as a fellow at the Midlo Center for New Orleans Studies at the University of New Orleans, I worked with history department chair Robert Dupont and the center's codirectors, Connie Atkinson and Molly Mitchell, on the *JAAH* special issue "New Orleans at 300: The African American Experience, 1718–2018," published in fall 2018. By that time, it became clear that there was so much information available it would be possible to mount exhibits or write books and articles on youth activism for almost every state, especially in the South. As I continued to work on this manuscript defining the trends and patterns nationally, my colleagues at Xavier University in New Orleans, Sharlene Sinegal DeCuir and Cereci W. Olatungi, decided they wanted their students to research youth and civil rights activism in Louisiana and mount an exhibit. The result was *Children and Teenagers' Contributions to the Civil Rights Movement in Louisiana*, on display at Xavier University's Library, February–March 2018. At that exhibit opening, the videotaped panel discussion included interviews with Leona Tate, who desegregated McDonough 19 Elementary School in 1960, and Dr. Raphael Cassimere, Dr. Warren Ray, Kenneth Ferdinand, and Dodie Smith Simmons, who as teenagers in the 1960s organized NAACP youth council protests and were active in the New Orleans Congress of Racial Equality (CORE).

Over this long period of time, numerous friends and colleagues inspired me and kept me going, especially the late Sterling Stuckey and Tony Martin. Others include Walter R. Allen, Derrick P. Alridge, Monroe Anderson, Andrew Bond, Jillian Azevedo, Enora Brown, Nikki L. Brown, Barbara Dunn, Marne Campbell, Sundiata Keita Cha Jua, Melinda Chateauvert, Sylvia Cyrus, Pero G. Dagbovie, Bertis English, Lee Facincani, Garland

M. Franklin, LaShawn Harris, Robert L. Harris Jr., Karen May, Genna Rae McNeil, Yolanda Moses, Margaret Nash, Joyce Owens, Ann Patteson, June O. Patton, Linda M. Perkins, Gary Smalls, Clyde C. Robertson, Gloria Dumas Robinson, Michael Steele-Eytle, James B. Stewart, Lillian S. Williams, Thelma Williams, Francille Rusan Wilson, Stephanie Ann Wilms-Simpson, and Steven T. Zemke. I especially want to thank *JAAH* editorial assistant, Mindy Jarrett, who also conducted important research for this book. Gayatri Patnaik, Maya Fernandez, Susan Lumenello, and Marcy Barnes at Beacon Press provided comments and offered expertise in preparing the manuscript for publication.

Over these years, Mary Frances Berry, Edward D. Collins, Bettye Collier-Thomas, and Brenda E. Stevenson helped to sustain me, have been my sounding boards, and have read and commented on various chapters and versions of this work, and I am truly grateful. The driving sentiment in the movement from social studies curriculum to exhibit to published book has been to make more and more young people aware of the past struggles and achievements of children and teenagers to make a better world.

Image Credits

1. Library of Congress, Prints and Photographs Division, Visual Materials from the NAACP Records, [LC-USZ62-116731].
2. Library of Congress, Prints and Photographs Division, Visual Materials from the NAACP Records, [LC-USZ62-84483].
3. Library of Congress, Prints and Photographs Division, Visual Materials from the NAACP Records, [LC-USZ62-119154].
4. AP Photo/Bill Hudson.
5. AP Photo/Bill Hudson.
6. Northeastern University Libraries, Archives and Special Collections Department.
7. Northeastern University Libraries, Archives and Special Collections Department.
8. Photograph courtesy of the Milwaukee County Historical Society.
9. '63 Boycott/Kartemquin Films.
10. Patrick A. Burns/The New York Times/Redux.
11. Eddie Hausner/The New York Times/Redux.
12. The Cleveland Press Collection, Michael Schwartz Library, Cleveland State University.
13. The Cleveland Press Collection, Michael Schwartz Library, Cleveland State University.
14. Photograph courtesy of the Milwaukee County Historical Society.
15. Special Collections Research Center, Temple University Libraries, Philadelphia, PA; photo by Jack T. Franklin.
16. AP Photo/Bill Hudson.
17. Courtesy of the African American Museum in Philadelphia; photo by Jack T. Franklin.
18. Special Collections Research Center, Temple University Libraries, Philadelphia, PA.
19. Special Collections Research Center, Temple University Libraries, Philadelphia, PA; photo by Jack T. Franklin.

Notes

INTRODUCTION

1. Anne Moody, *Coming of Age in Mississippi* (New York: Random House, 1968), quote on 297.

2. *New York Times*, February 4, 1964.

3. Moody, *Coming of Age in Mississippi*, 294.

4. Edward M. Kennedy, "Review of *Coming of Age in Mississippi*," *New York Times Book Review*, January 9, 1969. The book became so popular, Anne Moody was interviewed on *The Merv Griffin Show* and the *Today* show. See Françoise N. Hamlin, "Historians and Ethics: Finding Anne Moody," *American Historical Review* 125 (April 2020): 487–97.

5. Gina Beavers, "Anne Moody," in *Black Women in America: An Historical Encyclopedia*, ed. Darlene C. Hine, Elsa Barkley Brown, and Rosalyn Terborg-Penn (Brooklyn, NY: Carlson, 1993), 2:809–10. There have been numerous studies of "The Movement"; see, for example, Vincent Harding, *The Other American Revolution* (Los Angeles: Center for African American Studies, 1980); Aldon Morris, *The Origins of the Civil Rights Movement: Black Communities Organizing for Change* (New York: Collier Macmillan, 1984); Taylor Branch, *Parting the Waters: America in the King Years, 1954–1963* (New York: Simon & Schuster, 1988); Taylor, *Pillar of Fire: America in the King Years, 1963–1965* (New York: Simon & Schuster, 1988); Taylor, *At Canaan's Edge: America in the King Years, 1965–1968* (New York: Simon & Schuster, 2006); Robert Weisbrot, *Freedom Bound: A History of America's Civil Rights Movement* (New York: Norton, 1989); Fred Powledge, *Free at Last? The Civil Rights Movement and the People Who Made It* (Boston: Little, Brown, 1991); Thomas Sugrue, *Sweet Land of Liberty: The Forgotten Struggle for Civil Rights in the North* (New York: Random House, 2008); and Brian Purnell, *The Strange Careers of Jim Crow North* (New York: New York University Press, 2019).

6. Moody, *Coming of Age in Mississippi*, quote on 290.

7. Moody, *Coming of Age in Mississippi*, quote on 296–97.

8. Moody, *Coming of Age in Mississippi*, quote on 298.

9. Moody, *Coming of Age in Mississippi*, quotes on 305–6.

10. Charles Payne, *I've Got the Light of Freedom: The Organizing Tradition and the Mississippi Freedom Struggle* (Berkeley: University of California Press, 1995), 285–90.

11. Autobiographies, memoirs, and personal narratives are the most important literary works in the African American intellectual tradition. See V. P. Franklin, *Living Our Stories, Telling Our Truths: Autobiography and the Making of the African American Intellectual Tradition* (New York: Scribner's, 1995), 11–20.

12. Charles Kellogg, *NAACP: A History of the National Association for the Advancement of Colored People, 1909–1920* (Baltimore; Johns Hopkins University Press, 1967); Richard Kluger, *Simple Justice: A History of Brown v. Board of Education and Black America's Struggle for Equality* (New York: Random House, 1976); Robert Zangrando, *The NAACP Crusade Against Lynching, 1909–1950* (Philadelphia: Temple University Press, 1980); Patricia Sullivan, *Lift Every Voice: The NAACP and the Making of the Civil Rights Movement* (New York: New Press, 2009).

13. Rebecca de Schweinitz, *If We Could Change the World: Young People and America's Long Struggle for Racial Equality* (Chapel Hill: University of North Carolina Press, 2009); and Thomas L. Bynum, *NAACP Youth and the Fight for Black Freedom, 1936–1965* (Knoxville: University of Tennessee Press, 2013).

14. Peter Irons, *Jim Crow's Children: The Broken Promise of the Brown Decision* (New York: Penguin Books, 2004); and Tracy Sugarman, *We Had Sneakers, They Had Guns: The Kids Who Fought for Civil Rights in Mississippi* (Syracuse, NY: Syracuse University Press, 2009).

15. Jo Ann Gibson, *The Montgomery Bus Boycott and the Women Who Started It* (Knoxville: University of Tennessee Press, 1987); Vicki L. Crawford, Jacqueline Rouse, and Barbara Woods, eds., *Women in the Civil Rights Movement: Trailblazers and Torchbearers, 1941–1965* (Brooklyn: Carlson, 1990); Kay Mills, *This Little Light of Mine: The Life of Fannie Lou Hamer* (New York: Dutton, 1993); Belinda Robnett, *How Long? How Long? African-American Women and the Struggle for Civil Rights* (New York: Oxford University Press, 1997); Cynthia Griggs Fleming, *Soon We Will Not Cry: The Liberation of Ruby Doris Smith Robinson* (Lanham, MD: Rowman & Littlefield, 1998); Peter J. Ling and Sharon Monteith, eds., *Gender and the Civil Rights Movement* (New York: Routledge, 1999); Chana Kai Lee, *For Freedom's Sake: The Life of Fannie Lou Hamer* (Urbana: University of Illinois Press, 2000); Lynne Olson, *Freedom's Daughters: The Unsung Heroines of the Civil Rights Movement from 1830 to 1970* (New York: Scribner's, 2001); Bettye Collier-Thomas and V. P. Franklin, eds., *Sisters in the Struggle: African American Women in the Civil Rights–Black Power Movement* (New York: New York University Press,

2001); Faith S. Holsaert, et al., eds., *Hands on the Freedom Plow: Personal Accounts by Women in SNCC* (Urbana: University of Illinois Press, 2010).

16. Rachel Devlin, *A Girl Stands at the Door: The Generation of Young Women Who Desegregated America's Schools* (New York: Basic Books, 2018).

17. For example, in *The March on Washington: Jobs, Freedom, and the Forgotten History of Civil Rights* (New York: Norton, 2013), William P. Jones did not mention the large youth marches on Washington, DC, in 1958 and 1959.

18. *Washington Post*, October 22, 1961.

19. Horace Huntley and John W. McKerley, eds., *Foot Soldiers for Democracy: The Men, Women, and Children of the Birmingham Civil Rights Movement* (Urbana: University of Illinois Press, 2009); and Nick Patterson, *Birmingham's Foot Soldiers: Voices from the Civil Rights Movement* (Charleston, SC: History Press, 2014).

20. Rufus Burrow Jr., *A Child Shall Lead Them: Martin Luther King Jr., Young People, and the Movement* (Minneapolis: Fortress Press, 2015), quotes on xvi, xxxii.

21. It would be quite possible to write informative articles and entire monographs on youth activism in each southern state. I am presenting an overview and select campaigns in this study. Future researchers should pursue this topic on a regional or state-by-state basis. For discussion, see V. P. Franklin, "Documenting Children and Teenagers' Contributions to the Civil Rights Movement: Special Report," *Journal of African American History* 100 (Fall 2015): 663–71; also Sharlene Sinegal DuCuir, Cirecie West Olatungi, and V. P. Franklin, *Children's and Teenagers' Contributions to the Civil Rights Movement in Louisiana*, exhibit, Xavier University Library, New Orleans, February–March 2018.

22. Moody, *Coming of Age in Mississippi,* quote on 317; on the protests in Canton, Mississippi, see Payne, *I've Got the Light of Freedom*, 199–200; 238–40.

23. Mary Frances Berry, *Black Resistance/White Law: A History of Constitutional Racism* (New York: Penguin Books, 1971); Mary Frances Berry and John W. Blassingame, *Long Memory: The Black Experience in America* (New York: Oxford University Press, 1981); V. P. Franklin, *Black Self-Determination: A Cultural History of African American Resistance* (Brooklyn, NY: Lawrence Hill Books, 1992); Mary Frances Berry, *History Teaches Us to Resist: How Progressive Movements Have Succeeded in Challenging Times* (Boston: Beacon Press, 2018); Robin D. G. Kelley, *Race Rebels: Culture, Politics, and the Black Working Class* (New York: Free Press, 1996); Robin D. G. Kelley, *Freedom Dreams: The Radical Black Imagination* (Boston: Beacon Press, 2002); Cornel West, *Prophesy Deliverance: An Afro-American Revolutionary Christianity* (Philadelphia: Westminster Press, 1982); Quinton Hosford Dixie and Cornel West, eds., *The Courage to Hope: From Black Suffering to Human Redemption* (Boston: Beacon Press, 1999); Gerald Horne, *Black*

Revolutionary: William Patterson and the Globalization of the African American Freedom Struggle (Urbana: University of Illinois Press, 2013); Gerald Horne, *White Supremacy Confronted: U.S. Imperialism and Anti-Communism v. the Liberation of Southern Africa from Rhodes to Mandela* (New York: International Publishers, 2019); Bettye Collier-Thomas, *Jesus, Jobs, and Justice: African American Women and Religion* (New York: Knopf, 2010); V.P. Franklin, "African Americans and Movements for Reparations: From Ex-Slave Pensions to the Reparations Superfund: Introduction," *Journal of African American History* 97 (Winter–Spring 2012): 1–12; Ta-Nehisi Coates, "The Case for Reparations," *Atlantic*, June 2014; and Keeanga-Yamahtta Taylor, *From #Black Lives Matter to Black Liberation* (Chicago: Haymarket Books, 2016).

CHAPTER 1: YOUTH AND CIVIL RIGHTS ACTIVISM
BEFORE THE *BROWN* DECISION

1. Juanita Jackson Mitchell, quoted in Katherine Kenny and Eleanor Randup, *Juanita Jackson Mitchell: Freedom Fighter* (Baltimore: PublishAmerica, 2005), 28.

2. Juanita Jackson Mitchell, "The Law in the Lives of People," *University of Pennsylvania Almanac* 28, no. 10 (1981): 2.

3. Mitchell, "Law in the Lives of People," 3; Genna Rae McNeil, "Youth Initiative in the African American Struggle for Racial Justice and Constitutional Rights: The City-Wide Young People's Forum of Baltimore, 1931–1941," in *African Americans and the Living Constitution*, ed. John Hope Franklin and Genna Rae McNeil (Washington, DC: Smithsonian Press, 1995), 56–62.

4. Mitchell, "The Law in the Lives of People," 2.

5. Richard Kluger, *Simple Justice: The History of* Brown v. Board of Education *and Black America's Struggle for Equality* (New York: Knopf, 1976), 72–73.

6. *Mobile Daily Register*, May 17, 1905, quoted in August Meier and Elliott Rudwick, "The Boycott Movement Against Jim Crow Streetcars in the South, 1900–1906," in *Along the Color Line: Explorations in the Black Experience* (Urbana: University of Illinois Press, 1976), 269.

7. Blair L. M. Kelley, *Right to Ride: Streetcar Boycotts and African American Citizenship in the Era of* Plessy v. Ferguson (Chapel Hill: University of North Carolina Press, 2010), 10.

8. Meier and Rudwick, "The Origins of Nonviolent Direct Action in Afro-American Protest," in *Along the Color Line*, 313–14.

9. Meier and Rudwick, "Origins of Nonviolent Direct Action," 316–20.

10. Meier and Rudwick, "Origins of Nonviolent Direct Action," 324–25.

11. Meier and Rudwick, "Origins of Nonviolent Direct Action," 324–25; McNeil, "Youth Initiative in the African American Struggle," 66.

12. Beth Tompkins Bates, "A New Crowd Challenges the Agenda of the Old Guard in the NAACP, 1933–1941," *American Historical Review* 102 (April 1997): 340–77.

13. Thomas L. Bynum, "'We Must March Forward!' Juanita Jackson and the Origins of the NAACP Youth Movement," *Journal of African American History* 94 (Fall 2009): 493–95.

14. Bynum, "'We Must March Forward!,'" 493–95.

15. Bynum, "'We Must March Forward!,'" 496.

16. Bynum, "'We Must March Forward!,'" 497–98; see also Thomas L. Bynum, *NAACP Youth and the Fight for Black Freedom, 1936–1965* (Knoxville: University of Tennessee Press, 2013), 3–23; Juan Williams, *Thurgood Marshall: American Revolutionary* (New York: Times Books, 1998), 79–81; and Rebecca de Schweinitz, *If We Could Change the World: Young People and America's Long Struggle for Racial Equality* (Chapel Hill: University of North Carolina Press, 2009), 166–68.

17. Patricia Sullivan, *Lift Every Voice: The NAACP and the Making of the Civil Rights Movement* (New York: New Press, 2009), 257–58.

18. Eric S. Gellman, *Death Blow to Jim Crow: The National Negro Congress and the Rise of Militant Civil Rights* (Chapel Hill: University of North Carolina Press, 2012), 24–29.

19. A. P. Randolph quoted in Gellman, *Death Blow to Jim Crow*, 28–29.

20. C. Alvin Hughes, "We Demand Our Rights: The Southern Negro Youth Congress, 1937–1949," *Phylon* 47, no. 1 (1987): 38–50; quote on 39.

21. Hughes, "We Demand Our Rights," 87–99.

22. Hughes, "We Demand Our Rights," 46; Gellman, *Death Blow to Jim Crow*, 120–22. It should be noted that teenagers participated in SNYC activities, but the leaders and the majority of the group's active members were in their twenties.

23. V. P. Franklin, *The Education of Black Philadelphia: The Social and Educational History of a Minority Community, 1900-1950* (Philadelphia: University of Pennsylvania Press, 1979), 119–21.

24. Meier and Rudwick, "The Origins of Nonviolent Direct Action," 326.

25. Sullivan, *Lift Every Voice*, quote on 194.

26. Sullivan, *Lift Every Voice*, quote on 195.

27. Bynum, *NAACP Youth*, 7–9; *Amsterdam News*, January 22, 1938, quoted in Meier and Rudwick, "The Origins of Nonviolent Direct Action," 343–44.

28. Bynum, "'We Must March Forward!,'" 494. Clarence Norris (19), Charles Weems (19), Andy Wright (19), and brother Roy Wright (13), Haywood Patterson (18), Olin Montgomery (17), Ozzie Powell (16), Willie Roberson (16), and Eugene Williams (13) were eventually exonerated after spending years in prison.

29. Bynum, "'We Must March Forward!,'" 503–4; Sullivan, *Lift Every Voice*, 145–51.

30. Bynum, *NAACP Youth*, 21; see also Kenny and Randrup, *Juanita Jackson Mitchell*, 35–39.

31. Peter Lau, *Democracy Rising: South Carolina and the Fight for Black Equality Since 1865* (Lexington: University of Kentucky Press, 2006), 108; Bynum, *NAACP Youth*, 29.

32. Lau, *Democracy Rising*, 109.

33. Bynum, *NAACP Youth*, 30–31.

34. De Schweinitz, *If We Could Change the World*, 186–87.

35. David Lucander, *Winning the War for Democracy: The March on Washington Movement* (Urbana: University of Illinois Press, 2014).

36. Louis Ruchames, *Race, Jobs, and Politics: The Story of the FEPC* (New York: Columbia University Press, 1953); Herbert Garfinkel, *When Negroes March: The March on Washington Movement in the Organizational Politics of the FEPC* (Glencoe, IL: Free Press, 1959); Paula F. Pfeffer, *A. Philip Randolph: Pioneer of the Civil Rights Movement* (Baton Rouge: Louisiana State University Press, 1990); Melinda Chateauvert, *Marching Together: Women of the Brotherhood of Sleeping Car Porters* (Urbana: University of Illinois Press, 1997).

37. Bynum, *NAACP Youth*, 33.

38. Franklin, *The Education of Black Philadelphia*, 173–74.

39. Bynum, *NAACP Youth*, 35; William D. Pierson, "Ruby Hurley, Civil Rights Activist and Organizational Leader," in *Notable Black American Women*, ed. Jessie Carney Smith (Detroit: Gale Research, 1992), 540–43.

40. De Schweinitz, *If We Could Change the World*, 184–85.

41. V. P. Franklin, "Introduction," *Cultural Capital and Black Education: African American Communities and the Funding of Black Schooling, 1856 to the Present*, ed. V. P. Franklin and Carter J. Savage (Greenwich, CT: Information Age, 2004), xi–xx.

42. Mary Hoffschwelle, *The Rosenwald Schools of the American South* (Gainesville: University Press of Florida, 2006); Peter M. Ascoli, *Julius Rosenwald: The Man Who Built Sears, Roebuck and Advanced the Cause of Black Education in the South* (Bloomington: Indiana University Press, 2006); and Susan Deutsch, *You Need a Schoolhouse: Booker T. Washington, Julius Rosenwald, and the Building of Schools for the Segregated South* (Evanston, IL: Northwestern University Press, 2011).

43. Ada F. Coleman, "The Salary Equalization Movement," *Journal of Negro Education* 16 (Spring 1947): 235–41; Bruce Beezer, "Black Teachers' Salaries and the Federal Courts before *Brown v. Board of Education*: One Beginning for

Equality," *Journal of Negro Education* 55 (Spring 1986): 200–13; Scott Baker, "Testing Equality: The National Teacher Examination and the NAACP's Legal Campaign to Equalize Teachers' Salaries in the South, 1936–1963," *History of Education Quarterly* 35 (Spring 1995): 49–64; and John Kirk, "The NAACP's Campaign for Teachers' Salary Equalization: African American Women Educators and the Early Civil Rights Struggle," *Journal of African American History* 94 (Fall 2009): 529–52.

44. Sarah C. Thueson, *Greater Than Equal: African American Struggles for Schools and Citizenship in North Carolina, 1919–1965* (Chapel Hill: University of North Carolina Press, 2013), 168–69.

45. Thueson, *Greater Than Equal*, quote on 175.

46. Thueson, *Greater Than Equal*, quotes on 175, 176, 179.

47. Rachel Devlin, *A Girl Stands at the Door: The Generation of Young Women Who Desegregated America's Schools* (New York: Basic Books, 2018), 171–81.

48. Jill Titus, *Brown's Battleground: Students, Segregationists, and the Struggle for Justice in Prince Edward County, Virginia* (Chapel Hill: University of North Carolina Press, 2011), 23–35.

49. Titus, *Brown's Battleground*; Kluger, *Simple Justice*, 469.

50. Belinda Rochelle, *Witnesses to Freedom: Young People Who Fought for Civil Rights* (New York: Penguin Books, 1993), quote on 4.

51. Kluger, *Simple Justice*, 468–75.

52. Rochelle, *Witnesses to Freedom*, 5.

53. Devlin, *A Girl Stands at the Door*, quote on 179.

54. Kluger, *Simple Justice*, quote on 478.

CHAPTER 2: GRACE UNDER PRESSURE

1. Ernest Green, "The Untold Story of Little Rock: Had Many Unseen Supporters; Racists Were in the Minority," *Jet*, June 19, 1958, 24.

2. Carlotta Walls LaNier, *A Mighty Long Way: My Journey to Justice at Little Rock Central High School* (New York: Random House, 2009), 32.

3. *New York Times*, May 29, 1955.

4. George Lewis, *The White South and the Red Menace: Segregationists, Anti-Communism, and Massive Resistance, 1945–1965* (Gainesville: University Press of Florida, 2004); and George Lewis, *Massive Resistance: The White Response to the Civil Rights Movement* (London: Bloomsbury Academic, 2006).

5. Bettye Collier-Thomas and V. P. Franklin, *My Soul Is a Witness: A Chronology of the Civil Rights Era, 1954–1965* (New York: Henry Holt, 2000), 5–19; Neil McMillen, *The Citizens' Council: Organized Resistance to the Second Reconstruction, 1954–1964* (Urbana: University of Illinois Press, 1971); Stephanie R.

Rolph, *Resisting Equality: The Citizens' Council, 1954–1989* (Baton Rouge: Louisiana State University Press, 2018).

6. Richard Kluger, *Simple Justice: The History of* Brown v. Board of Education *and Black America's Struggle for Equality* (New York: Knopf, 1976), 600–618; Brett V. Gadsden, "'He Said He Wouldn't Help Me Get a Jim Crow Bus': The Shifting Terms of Challenge to Segregated Public Education, 1950–1954," *Journal of African American History* 90 (Winter 2005): 9–18; and Brett V. Gadsden, *Between North and South: Delaware, Desegregation, and the Myth of American Sectionalism* (Philadelphia: University of Pennsylvania Press, 2013).

7. *New York Times,* September 21, 1954.

8. *New York Times,* September 23, 1954.

9. *New York Times,* September 27, 1954.

10. *New York Times,* September 30, 1954, and October 2, 1954.

11. Milton Bracker, "School Desegregation: Lessons from Milford," *New York Times,* October 24, 1954.

12. George Lewis, *Massive Resistance,* 76–78.

13. Claudette Colvin quoted in Ellen Levine, *Freedom's Children: Young Civil Rights Activists Tell Their Own Stories* (New York: Penguin Books, 1993), 23.

14. Colvin quoted in Levine, *Freedom's Children,* 25.

15. Colvin quoted in Levine, *Freedom's Children,* 22. For information on the arrest and electrocution of Jeremiah Reeves, see Gary Younge, "She Would Not Be Moved," *Guardian,* December 16, 2000.

16. Colvin quoted in Levine, *Freedom's Children,* 21, 23. See also Rufus A. Burrow Jr., *A Child Shall Lead Them: Martin Luther King Jr., Young People, and the Movement* (Minneapolis: Fortress Press, 2014), 31–43.

17. Rebecca de Schweinitz, *If We Could Change the World: Young People and America's Long Struggle for Racial Equality* (Chapel Hill: University of North Carolina Press, 2009), 214.

18. Anne Moody, *Coming of Age in Mississippi* (New York: Random House, 1968), 132.

19. De Schweinitz, *If We Could Change the World,* 217.

20. *New York Times,* August 27, 1956.

21. *New York Times,* December 5, 1956.

22. *New York Times,* December 6, 1956.

23. *New York Times,* May 26, 1957.

24. *New York Times,* May 19, 1957.

25. Martin Luther King Jr., "Give Us the Ballot—We Will Transform the

South," in *A Testament of Hope: The Essential Writings*, ed., James M. Washington (New York: Harper & Row, 1986), 197–200.

26. King, "Give Us the Ballot," 197–200; Christina Greene, *Our Separate Ways: Women and the Black Freedom Movement in Durham, North Carolina* (Chapel Hill: University of North Carolina Press, 2005), 26.

27. The campaigns to desegregate Girard College in Philadelphia will be discussed in detail in chapter 8.

28. *New York Times*, May 26 and 27, 1957; Thomas Bynum, *NAACP Youth and the Fight for Black Freedom, 1936–1965* (Lexington: University of Tennessee Press, 2015), 84, 176.

29. Ernest Green, quoted in Levine, *Freedom's Children*, 42–43. See also John A. Kirk, "The NAACP Campaign for Teachers' Salary Equalization: African American Women Educators and the Early Civil Rights Struggle," *Journal of African American History* 94 (Fall 2009): 529–52.

30. LaNier, *A Mighty Long Way*, 42.

31. LaNier, *A Mighty Long Way*, 74.

32. LaNier, *A Mighty Long Way*, quotes on 45, 51–52.

33. Elizabeth Huckaby, *Crisis at Central High, Little Rock, 1957–58* (Baton Rouge: Louisiana State University Press, 1980).

34. Minnijean Brown, "What They Did to Me in Little Rock," *Look*, June 1958, 30–39.

35. LaNier, *A Might Long Way*, quotes on 69, 96, 118.

36. Melba Pattillo Beals, *Warriors Don't Cry: A Searing Memoir of the Battle to Integrate Little Rock's Central High* (New York: Washington Square Press, 1993), 64–65.

37. Beals, *Warriors Don't Cry*, quotes on 192.

38. Beals, *Warriors Don't Cry*, quotes on 246, 270, 296.

39. Green, "The Untold Story of Little Rock," 20–24.

40. Bettye Collier-Thomas and V. P. Franklin, *My Soul Is a Witness: A Chronology of the Civil Rights Era, 1954–1965* (New York: Henry Holt, 2000), 90–91; LaNier, *A Mighty Long Way*, 145–47.

41. James Baldwin, "A Hard Kind of Courage," *Harper's Magazine*, October 1958; reprinted as "A Fly in Buttermilk," in *The Price of the Ticket: Collected Nonfiction, 1948–1985* (New York, 1985), 161–70. See also Davidson M. Douglas, *Reading, Writing, and Race: The Desegregation of the Charlotte Schools* (Chapel Hill, NC, 1995).

42. *New York Times*, September 13, 2019; Collier-Thomas and Franklin, *My Soul Is a Witness*, 70.

43. Sarah C. Thuesen, *Greater Than Equal: African American Struggles for Schools and Citizenship in North Carolina, 1919–1965* (Chapel Hill: University of North Carolina Press, 2013), 222.

44. Bynum, *NAACP Youth*, 87–88; and Rachel Devlin, *A Girl Stands at the Door: The Generation of Young Women Who Desegregated America's Schools* (New York: Basic Books, 2018), 202.

45. Devlin, *A Girl Stands at the Door*, 203; for discussion, see also McMillen, *Citizens' Council*; and Rolph, *Resisting Equality*.

46. Collier-Thomas and Franklin, *My Soul Is a Witness*, 76–87.

47. Herbert Wright to NAACP youth and college units, October 25, 1958, quoted in Bynum, *NAACP Youth*, 88.

48. Herbert Wright to NAACP youth and college units, October 25, 1958, quoted in Bynum, *NAACP Youth*, 88–89; *New York Times*, October 27, 1958; *Pittsburgh Courier*, November 1, 1958; *Chicago Defender*, October 27, and November 1, 1958.

49. Quotes from Lloyd Weaver, "A Teen Viewpoint," *New York Amsterdam News*, November 8, 1958.

50. *New York Times*, October 31, 1958.

51. Collier-Thomas and Franklin, *My Soul Is a Witness*, 91; see also Andrew B. Lewis, "Emergency Mothers: Basement Schools and the Preservation of Public Education in Charlottesville"; and James H. Hershman, "Massive Resistance Meets Its Match," in *The Moderates' Dilemma: Massive Resistance to School Desegregation in Virginia*, ed. Matthew D. Lassiter and Andrew B. Lewis (Charlottesville: University Press of Virginia, 1998), 72–103, 104–33.

52. Bynum, *NAACP Youth*, 91–92; David Halberstam, *The Children* (New York: Random House, 1998), 52–54; and Sonya Ramsey, *Reading, Writing, and Segregation: A Century of Black Women Teachers in Nashville* (Urbana: University of Illinois Press, 2008), 55–84.

53. *New York Times*, April 19, 1959; Bynum, *NAACP Youth*, 89–90.

54. Bynum, *NAACP Youth*, 90; Halberstam, *The Children*, 54–70.

CHAPTER 3: HIGH SCHOOL STUDENTS AND NONVIOLENT DIRECT-ACTION PROTESTS

1. Joanne Grant, "The Time Is Always Now," *Freedomways* 2 (Spring 1962): 150.

2. Ronald W. Walters, "Standing Up in America's Heartlands: Sitting In Before Greensboro," *American Vision* 8 (February 1993): 20. See also Thomas L. Bynum, *NAACP Youth and the Fight for Black Freedom, 1936–1965* (Chapel Hill: University of North Carolina Press, 2014), 95–97.

3. Walters, "Standing Up in America's Heartlands," 23.

4. Walters, "Standing Up in America's Heartlands," 25; Bynum, *NAACP Youth*, 96.

5. Walters, "Standing Up in America's Heartlands," 26; and Ronald W. Walters, "The Great Plains Sit-In Movement, 1958–1960," *Great Plains Quarterly* 16 (Winter 1996): 85–94. Ronald W. Walters, a noted scholar-activist, wrote numerous books and articles on Black national and international political activities.

6. Aldon Morris, *The Origins of the Civil Rights Movement: Black Communities Organizing for Change* (New York: Free Press, 1984), 124–25.

7. *New York Times*, August 22, 1958; *Chicago Defender*, August 30, 1958.

8. *New York Times*, August 24, 1958.

9. *New York Times*, August 25, 1958.

10. *Cleveland Call and Post*, August 30, 1958.

11. *New York Times*, August 26, 1958.

12. *Philadelphia Tribune*, August 30, 1958.

13. *Chicago Defender*, August 30, 1958.

14. *New York Times*, September 2, 1958; *Chicago Tribune*, September 2, 1958.

15. Bynum, *NAACP Youth*, 97.

16. Clayborne Carson, *In Struggle: SNCC and the Black Awakening of the 1960s* (Cambridge, MA: Harvard University Press, 1981), 9.

17. Bynum, *NAACP Youth*, 100–101.

18. Deirdre B. Flowers, "The Launching of the Student Sit-In Movement: The Role of Black Women at Bennett College," *Journal of African American History* 90 (Winter–Spring 2005): 52–63.

19. Walters, "Standing Up in America's Heartlands," 23; Gilbert Jonas, *Freedom's Sword: The NAACP and the Struggle against Racism in America, 1909–1969* (New York: Routledge, 2005), 104–7.

20. Morris, *The Origins of the Civil Rights Movement*, 195–228.

21. Bynum, *NAACP Youth*, 104–5.

22. William H. Chafe, *Civilities and Civil Rights: Greensboro, North Carolina, and the Black Freedom Struggle* (New York: Oxford University Press, 1980), 122–23.

23. Juan Williams, *Eyes on the Prize: America's Civil Rights Years, 1954–1965* (New York: Penguin Books, 1987), quote on 129.

24. Bobby Lovett, *The Civil Rights Movement in Tennessee* (Knoxville: University of Tennessee Press, 2005), 149–50.

25. Lovett, *The Civil Rights Movement in Tennessee*, 151–52.

26. *Times-Picayune* (New Orleans), March 29, 1960.

27. *Times-Picayune*, March 30, 1960.

28. *Times-Picayune*, March 31, 1960.

29. *Times-Picayune*, April 1, 1960.

30. *Times-Picayune*, April 4, 1960.

31. Carson, *In Struggle*, 19–22.

32. Lovett, *The Civil Rights Movement in Tennessee*, 137–39. For a detailed account based on interviews of the Nashville college students who participated in the sit-ins and other civil rights protests, see David Halberstam, *The Children* (New York: Random House, 1998).

33. *New York Times*, April 20, 1960.

34. *New York Times*, April 12, 1960.

35. *New York Times*, April 9, 1960.

36. *New York Times*, April 10, 1960.

37. *New York Times*, May 9, 1960.

38. *Jet*, April 28, 1960.

39. *Louisiana Weekly* (New Orleans), September 17, 1960.

40. Raphael Cassimere, Kenneth Ferdinand, and Warren Ray, members of the NAACP youth council in New Orleans who participated in the Canal Street protests, described what occurred at the exhibit and public forum *Children and Teenagers' Contributions to the Civil Rights Movement in Louisiana*, Xavier University, February 28, 2018.

41. *Louisiana Weekly*, September 17, 1960.

42. *Louisiana Weekly*, September 24, 1960.

43. Rodney L. Hurst Sr., *It Was Never About a Hot Dog and a Coke! A Personal Account of the 1960 Sit-In Demonstrations in Jacksonville, Florida and Ax Handle Saturday* (Livermore, CA: WingSpan Press, 2008), 58–60.

44. Hurst, *It Was Never About a Hot Dog and a Coke*, 70–72. See also Abel A. Bartley, *Keeping the Faith: Race, Politics, and Social Development in Jacksonville, Florida* (New York: Praeger Books, 2000), 97–120.

45. Kim Lacey Rogers, *Righteous Lives: Narratives of the New Orleans Civil Rights Movement* (New York: New York University Press), 69–74.

46. Bettye Collier-Thomas and V. P. Franklin, *My Soul Is a Witness: A Chronology of the Civil Rights Era, 1954–1965* (New York: Henry Holt, 2000), 124–25, 129.

47. *New York Times*, November 15, 1960.

48. Robert Coles, *Children of Crisis: A Study of Courage and Fear* (Boston: Little, Brown, 1967); Donald E. DeVore and Joseph Logsdon, *Crescent City Schools: Public Education in New Orleans, 1841–1991* (Lafayette: University of South Louisiana Press, 1991), 216–51; Rogers, *Righteous Lives*: 49–77; Adam Fairclough, *Race and Democracy: The Civil Rights Struggle in Louisiana, 1915–1972* (Athens: University of Georgia Press, 1995), 234–54.

49. Rachel Devlin, *A Girl Stands at the Door: The Generation of Young Women Who Desegregated America's Schools* (New York: Basic Books, 2018), 214–15.

50. Devlin, *A Girl Stands at the Door*, 217.

51. *New York Times*, May 10, 1960.

52. *New York Times*, May 18, 1960.

53. *New York Times*, October 20 and 21, 1960.

54. *New York Times*, October 23–26, 1960. It should be noted that at this point, negotiations began between store owners and local Black leaders, college presidents, and student activists, but Dr. King was not among those released from jail. Judge J. Oscar Mitchell refused to release King and remanded him to Reidsville Penitentiary, a maximum security prison, accusing him of violating the terms of his probation after he was arrested earlier that year for driving in Georgia with an Alabama driver's license. Coretta Scott King got in touch with John Kennedy and Robert Kennedy, who contacted Judge Mitchell and asked him to release King on bond. Mitchell agreed, and when Martin Luther King Sr. met his son at the airport upon his release from prison, King Sr. told the reporters, "If I had a suitcase full of votes, I'd dump as many of them as he could hold right in John Kennedy's lap." Considered one of the most decisive events in the extremely close 1960 presidential election, the Kennedy campaign created a pamphlet quoting "Daddy King's" endorsement and distributed it in Black neighborhoods in northern cities. Historians attribute Kennedy's small margin of victory to Black voters in key northern states. See Collier-Thomas and Franklin, *My Soul Is a Witness*, 131; V. P. Franklin, *Martin Luther King Jr.: A Biography* (New York: Park Lane Press, 1998), 66–69.

55. *New York Times*, December 12–14, 1960.

56. Bynum, *NAACP Youth*, 105–6.

57. *New York Times*, February 9, 1961.

58. *New York Times*, February 2, 7, and 9, 1961; Collier-Thomas and Franklin, *My Soul Is a Witness*, 142.

59. *New York Times*, February 8–11, 1961.

60. *New York Times*, February 19, 20, and 23, 1961; Collier-Thomas and Franklin, *My Soul Is a Witness*, 142.

61. James Collins, "Taking the Lead: Dorothy Williams, NAACP Youth Councils, and Civil Rights Protests in Pittsburgh, 1961–1964," *Journal of African American History* 88 (Spring 2003): 129.

62. Collins, "Taking the Lead," quotes on 130.

63. *New York Times*, August 25, 1961; Eric Burner, *And Gently Shall He Lead Them: Robert Parris Moses and Civil Rights in Mississippi* (New York: New York

University Press, 1994), 50–51; and Laura Visser-Maessen, *Robert Parris Moses: A Life in Civil Rights and Leadership at the Grassroots* (Chapel Hill: University of North Carolina Press, 2016), 71–73.

64. Carson, *In Struggle*, 48–49; Robert Baker, "Negroes to Boycott Stores Owned by Whites," *Washington Post*, October 22, 1961; Burner, *And Gently Shall He Lead Them*, 57–58.

65. Baker, "Negroes to Boycott Stores"; Bob Zellner and Constance Curry, *The Wrong Side of Murder Creek: A White Southerner in the Freedom Movement* (Montgomery, AL: New South Books, 2008), 150–72.

66. Baker, "Negroes to Boycott Stores"; Visser-Maessen, *Robert Parris Moses*, 84–85.

67. *New York Times*, October 21, 1961.

68. Baker, "Negroes to Boycott Stores"; *Jet*, November 2, 1961.

69. August Meier and Elliott Rudwick, *CORE: A Study of the Civil Rights Movement* (Urbana: University of Illinois Press, 1975), 135.

70. For a listing of the names and ages of those who participated in the Freedom Rides between May and December 1961, see Raymond Arsenault, *Freedom Riders: 1961 and the Struggle for Racial Justice* (New York: Oxford University Press, 2007), chapter 1, "You Don't Have to Ride Jim Crow," 11–55, and the appendix, "Roster of Freedom Riders," 533–87.

71. Meier and Rudwick, *CORE*, 135–37.

72. Meier and Rudwick, *CORE*, 135–37; Arsenault, *Freedom Riders*, 533–87.

73. Taylor Branch, *Parting the Waters: America in the King Years, 1954–63* (New York: Simon and Shuster, 1988), 422–23.

74. Arsenault, *Freedom Riders*, quote on 150.

75. Arsenault, *Freedom Riders*, 177–82.

76. Arsenault, *Freedom Riders*. See also Sharlene Sinegal DeCuir, "Nothing Is to Be Feared: Norman Francis, Civil Rights Activism, and the Black Catholic Movement," *Journal of African American History* 101 (Summer 2016): 321–24.

77. Arsenault, *Freedom Riders*, 225–29.

78. Collier-Thomas and Franklin, *My Soul Is a Witness*, 150; Arsenault, *Freedom Riders*, 229–42.

79. Burner, *And Gently He Shall Lead Them*, 89–107; *New York Times*, January 11, 1962.

80. Collier-Thomas and Franklin, *My Soul Is a Witness*, 150; Carson, *In Struggle*, 31–45; Arsenault, *Freedom Riders*, 439.

81. *Atlanta Daily World*, November 2, 1961.

82. *New York Times*, December 4, 1961.

83. *Atlanta Daily World*, November 25, 1961.

84. *Atlanta Daily World*, November 25, 1961.

85. *Atlanta Daily World*, November 28, 1961.

86. *New York Times*, December 11, 1961.

87. *New York Times*, December 13, 1961.

88. *New York Times*, December 14, 1961.

89. "Freedom Singing: An Interview with Bernice Johnson Reagon," in Williams, *Eyes on the Prize*, 177.

90. "Freedom Singing," 177.

91. *New York Times*, December 15, 1961.

92. *New York Times*, December 16 and 17, 1961.

93. *New York Times*, December 18, 1961.

94. Collier-Thomas and Franklin, *My Soul Is a Witness*, 172.

95. Adam Fairclough, *To Redeem the Soul of America: The Southern Christian Leadership Conference and Martin Luther King Jr.* (Athens: University of Georgia Press, 1987), 88–89.

96. *New York Times*, July 10, 1962.

97. *New York Times*, July 12, 1962.

98. *New York Times*, July 13, 1962.

99. *New York Times*, July 14, 1962.

100. *New York Times*, July 17, 1962.

101. Carson, *In Struggle*, 63–65.

102. Stephen G. N. Tuck, *Beyond Atlanta: The Struggle for Racial Equality in Georgia, 1940–1980* (Athens: University of Georgia Press, 2001), 178.

103. Tuck, *Beyond Atlanta*, 184–85.

CHAPTER 4: THE BIRMINGHAM CHILDREN'S CRUSADE AND SOUTHERN STUDENT ACTIVISM

1. Gloria Washington Lewis-Randell, "I Remember I Couldn't" (2005), in Nick Patterson, *Birmingham Foot Soldiers: Stories from the Front Line of the Civil Rights Battle* (Charleston, SC: The History Press, 2014), 58.

2. Larry Russell's testimony on the "Children's Crusade," in Ellen Levine, *Freedom's Children: Young Civil Rights Activists Tell Their Own Story* (New York: Puffin Books, 1993), 83–84.

3. Robert Hudson and Bobby Houston, *Mighty Times: The Children's March* (Montgomery, AL: Southern Poverty Law Center, Teaching Tolerance, 2004), compact disc & kit.

4. Some historians have suggested that there was a "long civil rights movement" that began in the nineteenth century (or even earlier) and extended into the 1970s. However, this study documents civil rights activism from the 1930s that eventually

culminated in what sociologists and most historians consider a "social movement" only in the 1950s with the launching of the Montgomery bus boycott. It was followed by the Black Power Movement from 1966 to 1975. See Charles Tilly et al., *Social Movements, 1768–2018*, 4th ed. (New York: Routledge, 2019); Sundiata Keita Cha-Jua and Clarence Lang, "The 'Long Movement' as Vampire: Temporal and Spatial Fallacies in Black Freedom Studies," *Journal of African American History* 92 (Spring 2007): 265–88; V. P. Franklin, "Introduction—New Black Power Studies: National, International, and Transnational Perspectives," *Journal of African American History* 92 (Fall 2007): 463–66; and Jeffrey Helgeson, "Beyond a Long Civil Rights Movement," *Journal of African American History* 99 (Fall 2014): 442–55.

5. Robert D. Loevy, *The Civil Rights Law of 1964: The Passage of the Law That Ended Racial Segregation* (Albany: State University of New York Press, 1997); William P. Jones, *The March on Washington: Jobs, Freedom, and the Forgotten History of Civil Rights* (New York: William Norton, 2013).

6. *New York Times*, December 18, 1962.

7. Andrew A. Manis, *A Fire You Can't Put Out: The Civil Rights Life of Birmingham's Reverend Fred Shuttlesworth* (Tuscaloosa: University of Alabama Press, 1999), 68–78.

8. Manis, *A Fire You Can't Put Out*, 168–79.

9. Manis, *A Fire You Can't Put Out*, 168–79; Robert Arsenault, *Freedom Riders: 1961 and the Struggle for Racial Justice* (New York: Oxford University Press, 2011), chap. 4.

10. Manis, *A Fire You Can't Put Out*, 162–75.

11. V. P. Franklin, *Martin Luther King Jr.: A Biography* (New York: Park Lane Press, 1998), 81–93; Adam Fairclough, *To Redeem the Soul of America: The Southern Christian Leadership Conference and Martin Luther King Jr.* (Athens: University of Georgia Press, 1987), 111–40; Glenn T. Eskew, *But for Birmingham: The Local and National Movements in the Civil Rights Struggle* (Chapel Hill: University of North Carolina Press, 1997), 221–28; Taylor Branch, *Pillar of Fire: America in the King Years, 1963–1965* (New York: Simon & Schuster, 1999), 75–85.

12. Bernita Roberson's testimony in Levine, *Freedom's Children*, 82–83; see also, Rufus Burrow Jr., *A Child Shall Lead Them: Martin Luther King Jr., Young People, and the Movement* (Minneapolis: Fortress Press, 2014), 105–6; "Oral Testimony of Jonathan McPherson," in *Foot Soldiers for Democracy: The Men, Women, and Children of the Birmingham Civil Rights Movement*, ed. Horace Huntley and John W. McKerley (Urbana: University of Illinois Press, 2009), 86–87, 102–3.

13. "Letter from a Birmingham Jail" in *A Testament of Hope: The Essential Writings of Martin Luther King, Jr.*, ed. James M. Washington (New York: Harper & Row, 1986), 289–302.

14. For discussion, see Jonathan Rieder, *Gospel of Freedom: Martin Luther King Jr.'s Letter from a Birmingham Jail and the Struggle That Changed a Nation* (New York: Bloomsbury Press, 2013).

15. Burrow, *A Child Shall Lead Them*, 109–11.

16. "Oral Testimony of Annetta Streeter Gary," in Huntley and McKerley, *Foot Soldiers for Democracy*, 120–21.

17. "Mary Gadson Testimony," in Levine, *Freedom's Children*, 84–85.

18. "Myrna Carter Testimony," in Levine, *Freedom's Children*, 86–88.

19. "Oral Testimony of Willie A. Casey," in Huntley and McKerley, *Foot Soldiers for Democracy*, 126–27.

20. "Oral Testimony of Gwendolyn Sanders Gamble," in Huntley and McKerley, *Foot Soldiers for Democracy*, 146–47.

21. Carolyn Maull McKinstry, *While the World Watched: A Birmingham Bombing Survivor Comes of Age during the Civil Rights Movement* (Carol Stream, IL: Tyndale House, 2011), 140–41.

22. McKinstry, *While the World Watched*, 143.

23. "Birmingham Truce Agreement" in David Garrow, *Bearing the Cross: Martin Luther King, Jr., and the Southern Christian Leadership Conference* (New York: Harper Collins, 1986), 259.

24. Martin Luther King, quoted in Burrow, *A Child Shall Lead Them*, 137.

25. Burrow, *A Child Shall Lead Them*, 144.

26. See Fairclough, *To Redeem the Soul of America*. This phrase became SCLC's motto.

27. Thomas Bynum, *NAACP Youth and the Fight for Black Freedom, 1935–1965* (Lexington: University of Kentucky Press, 2013), quote on 120.

28. Christina Greene, *Our Separate Ways: Women and the Black Freedom Struggle in Durham, North Carolina* (Chapel Hill: University of North Carolina Press, 2005), 262n8.

29. Greene, *Our Separate Ways*, 127–28; see also Timothy B. Tyson, *Radio Free Dixie: Robert F. Williams and the Roots of Black Power* (Chapel Hill: University of North Carolina Press, 1999).

30. Bynum, *NAACP Youth*, 128–30.

31. Bynum, *NAACP Youth*, quote on 129.

32. Bynum, *NAACP Youth*, 130.

33. Bynum, *NAACP Youth*, 131.

34. *New York Times*, June 16, 1963.

35. *New York Times*, June 18, 1963.

36. *New York Times*, June 19, 1963.

37. For the Durham Plan, see Greene, *Our Separate Ways*, 63–65, 83–95.

38. *New York Times*, June 20, 1963.

39. Bynum, *NAACP Youth*, quotes on 133.

40. Charles Euchner, *Nobody Turn Me Around: A People's History of the 1963 March on Washington* (Boston: Beacon Press, 2010); Jones, *The March on Washington*.

41. Euchner, *Nobody Turn Me Around*, quotes on 111.

42. Euchner, *Nobody Turn Me Around*, 112.

43. Euchner, *Nobody Turn Me Around*, 133–34.

44. Belinda Rochelle, *Witnesses to Freedom: Young People Who Fought for Civil Rights* (New York: Puffin Books, 1993), 68–69.

45. *New York Times*, August 20, 1963; *Times-Picayune*, August 21, 1963; Collier-Thomas and Franklin, *My Soul Is a Witness*, 193.

46. *New York Times*, August 30, 1963.

47. Adam Fairclough, *Race and Democracy: The Civil Rights Struggle in Louisiana, 1915–1972* (Athens: University of Georgia Press, 1995), 265–97.

48. *New York Times*, August 25, 1963.

49. *New York Times*, August 20, 1963; *Times-Picayune*, August 22, 1963.

50. James Farmer, *Lay Bare the Heart: An Autobiography of the Civil Rights Movement* (New York: Arbor House, 1985), 244.

51. *Times-Picayune*, August 22, 1963; *New York Times*, August 25, 1963.

52. *New York Times*, August 26, 1963.

53. *New York Times*, August 30, 1963.

54. *New York Times*, September 2, 1963.

55. *New York Times*, September 4, 1963.

56. Farmer, *Lay Bare the Heart*, 249.

57. Farmer, *Lay Bare the Heart*, 249. Unfortunately, Farmer does not include the funeral director's name in his account.

58. Farmer, *Lay Bare the Heart*, quotes on 252–53.

59. *Greenwood (MS) Commonwealth*, October 4, 1963; Greta de Jong, *A Different Day: African Americans and the Struggle for Justice in Rural Louisiana, 1900–1970* (Chapel Hill: University of North Carolina Press, 2002), 178–82.

60. *Times-Picayune*, September 6, 1963.

61. *Greenwood Commonwealth*, October 4, 1963; *Lake Charles (LA) American Press*, September 7, 1963.

62. *Lake Charles American Press*, September 9, 1963.

63. Fairclough, *Race and Democracy*, 379.

64. Anne Moody, *Coming of Age in Mississippi* (New York: Random House, 1968), 294–95.

65. Eskew, *But for Birmingham*, 259–99.

66. *New York Times*, September 17, 1963.

67. *Philadelphia Tribune*, September 17 and 26, 1963.

68. *Times-Picayune*, September 6, 1963.

69. *Times-Picayune*, October 5, 1963; *New York Times*, October 5, 1963.

70. *Times-Picayune*, October 6, 1963; *New York Times*, October 6, 1963.

71. *Times-Picayune*, October 8, 1963; *Enterprise-Journal* (McComb, MS), October 7, 1963; *New York Times*, October 8, 1963; *Lake Charles American Press*, October 8, 1963; *Monroe (LA) Morning World*, October 8, 1963.

72. *Times-Picayune*, October 10, 1963; *New York Times*, October 10, 1963; *Lake Charles American Press*, October 10, 1963.

73. *Lake Charles American Press*, October 10, 1963; *New York Times*, October 11, 1963.

74. *Enterprise-Journal*, October 11, 1963.

75. *Times-Picayune*, October 11, 1963.

76. *Lake Charles American Press*, October 11, 1963; *Times-Picayune*, October 12, 1963; *Monroe Morning World*, October 12, 1963.

77. *Lake Charles American Press*, October 15, 1963; *Times-Picayune*, October 15 and 16, 1963; *Pittsburgh Courier*, October 19, 1963.

78. *Times-Picayune*, October 17, 1963; Fairclough, *Race and Democracy*, 328–30.

79. August Meier and Elliott M. Rudwick, *CORE: A Study in the Civil Rights Movement* (Urbana: University of Illinois Press, 1975), 263–64.

80. *Times-Picayune*, October 13, 1963.

81. *Times-Picayune*, October 13, 1963.

82. *Times-Picayune*, October 18, 1963.

83. Meier and Rudwick, *CORE*, 263.

84. Meier and Rudwick, *CORE*, 266.

85. *New York Times*, August 29, 1961.

86. *New York Times*, October 4, 1961.

87. *Jet*, July 12, 1962.

88. *New York Times*, September 2, 1963. Events in Memphis in 1967 and 1968 are discussed in chapter 8.

89. Bynum, *NAACP Youth*, 107–8; Peter Lau, *Democracy Rising: South Carolina and the Fight for Black Freedom Since 1865* (Lexington: University Press of Kentucky, 2006), 215.

90. Barbara Woods, "Working in the Shadows: Southern Women and Civil Rights," in *Southern Women at the Millennium: A Historical Perspective*, ed. Melissa Walker, Jeanette Dunn, and Joe P. Dolan (Columbia: University of Missouri Press, 2003), 92–93.

91. Lau, *Democracy Rising*, 216–17.

92. *New York Times*, October 9, 1963; Woods, "Working in the Shadows," 103–4.

93. *New York Times*, October 9, 1963.

94. *New York Times*, October 16, 1963; Woods, "Working in the Shadows," 104.

95. *New York Times*, October 20, 1963.

96. *New York Times*, October 24, 1963.

97. Woods, "Working in the Shadows," 95–97; and James L. Felder, *Civil Rights in South Carolina: From Peaceful Protests to Groundbreaking Rulings* (Charleston, SC: The History Press, 2012), 91–97.

CHAPTER 5: FREEDOM DAY BOYCOTTS

1. James R. Ralph, *Northern Protests: Martin Luther King, Jr., Chicago, and the Civil Rights Movement* (Cambridge, MA: Harvard University Press, 1993), 14; Elizabeth Todd-Breland, *A Political Education: Black Politics and Education Reform in Chicago Since the 1960s* (Chapel Hill: University of North Carolina Press, 2018), 22.

2. Ralph, *Northern Protests*, 15.

3. Ralph, *Northern Protests*, 22–23; Alan B. Anderson and George W. Pickering, *Confronting the Color Line: The Broken Promise of the Civil Rights Movement in Chicago* (Athens: University of Georgia Press, 1986), 80–81.

4. Arvarh E. Strickland, *History of the Chicago Urban League* (Urbana: University of Illinois Press, 1966), 235–38.

5. Strickland, *History of the Chicago Urban League*, 87.

6. Ralph, *Northern Protests*, 14–16; Todd-Breland, *A Political Education*, 19–23.

7. Anderson and Pickering, *Confronting the Color Line*, 86.

8. David J. Garrow, *Bearing the Cross: Martin Luther King, Jr., and the Southern Christian Leadership Conference* (New York: Quill, 1999), 530. The idea that Dr. King's campaign in Chicago was "a failure" is also found in Adam Fairclough, *To Redeem the Soul of America: The Southern Christian Leadership Conference and Martin Luther King Jr.* (Athens: University of Georgia Press, 1987), see chapter 11, "Defeat in Chicago."

9. Anderson and Pickering, *Confronting the Color Line*, 89.

10. Anderson and Pickering, *Confronting the Color Line*, 90; Ralph, *Northern Protest*, 17–18.

11. Ralph, *Northern Protest*, 17–19; Anderson and Pickering, *Confronting the Color Line*, 89–90.

12. Anderson and Pickering, *Confronting the Color Line*, 92.

13. Anderson and Pickering, *Confronting the Color Line*, 94–95.

14. Anderson and Pickering, *Confronting the Color Line*, 96; August Meier and Elliott M. Rudwick, *CORE: A Study in the Civil Rights Movement* (Urbana: University of Illinois Press, 1975), 193; Bettye Collier-Thomas and V. P. Franklin, *My Soul Is a Witness: A Chronology of the Civil Rights Era, 1954-1965* (New York: Henry Holt, 2000), 122.

15. US Commission on Civil Rights, *Civil Rights, 1962*, quoted in Anderson and Pickering, *Confronting the Color Line*, 96.

16. Anderson and Pickering, *Confronting the Color Line*, quote on 109.

17. Anderson and Pickering, *Confronting the Color Line*, 111; *Chicago Daily Defender*, June 17, 19, 1963; Thomas J. Sugrue, *Sweet Land of Liberty: The Forgotten Struggle for Civil Rights in the North* (New York: Random House, 2008), 298.

18. *Chicago Tribune*, June 20, 1963.

19. *Chicago Daily Defender*, June 20, 1963.

20. *Chicago Sun-Times*, July 11, 1963; *Chicago Tribune*, July 11 and 13, 1963.

21. *Chicago Tribune*, July 23, 1963.

22. *Chicago Tribune*, August 3, 1963.

23. *Chicago Tribune*, August 13, 1963.

24. *Chicago Tribune*, August 13, 1963; Meier and Rudwick, *CORE*, 247–48; Anderson and Pickering, *Confronting the Color Line*, 111.

25. Charles Euchner, *Nobody Turn Me Around: A People's History of the 1963 March on Washington* (Boston: Beacon Press, 2010), 185–86.

26. Anderson and Pickering, *Confronting the Color Line*, 117.

27. Ralph, *Northern Protest*, 20–21; Anderson and Pickering, *Confronting the Color Line*, 118–20.

28. Jeanne Theoharis, "'I'd Rather Go to School in the South': How Boston's School Desegregation Complicates the Civil Rights Paradigm," in *Freedom North: Black Freedom Struggles Outside the South, 1940–1980*, ed. Jeanne Theoharis and Komozi Woodard (New York: Palgrave Macmillan, 2003), quote on 130. See also Audrea Jones Dunham, "Boston's 1960s Civil Rights Movement: A Look Back," *Open Vault from WGBH*, www.openvault.wgbh/exhibits/boston_civil_rights/article.

29. Jonathan Kozol, *Death at an Early Age* (Boston: Houghton Mifflin, 1967).

30. Ronald Batchelor and V. P. Franklin, "Freedom Schooling: A New Approach to Federal-Local Cooperation in Public Education," *Teachers College Record* 80 (December 1978): 225–48; V. P. Franklin, "From Freedom Schools to Freedom Schooling," in *Using the Past as Prologue: Contemporary Perspectives on African American Educational History*, ed. Dionne Danns, Michele Y. Purdy, and Christopher M. Span (Charlotte, NC: Information Age, 2015), 353–60.

31. *New York Times*, June 19, 1963.

32. *New York Times*, June 19, 1963; see also Jeanne F. Theoharis, "'We Saved the City': Black Struggles for Equality in Boston, 1960–1976," *Radical History Review,* no. 81 (2001): 68–69.

33. *New York Times*, February 26 and 27, 1964.

34. Theoharis, "I'd Rather Go to School in the South," quote on 132. See also Jeanne Theoharis, "'They Told Us Our Children Were Stupid': Ruth Batson and the Educational Movement in Boston," in *Groundwork: Local Black Freedom Movements in America*, ed. Jeanne Theoharis and Komozi Woodard (New York: New York University Press, 2005), 27–28.

35. The high school student boycotts in Chicago in 1967 and 1968 are documented in chapter 8.

36. *New York Times*, October 23, 1963; *Chicago Daily Defender*, October 22, 1963.

37. Robert B. McKersie, *A Decisive Decade: An Insider's View of the Chicago Civil Rights Movement in the 1960s* (Carbondale: Southern Illinois University Press, 2013), 55–56. See also the documentary film *'63 Boycott*, prod. Rachel Dickson, Tracye A. Matthews, and Gordon Quinn (Chicago: Kartemquin Films, 2017).

38. *Chicago Tribune*, October 23, 1963; *Chicago Daily Defender*, February 27, 1964; Anderson and Pickering, *Confronting the Color Line*, 118–20; Dionne Danns, *Something Better for Our Children: Black Organization in the Chicago Public Schools, 1963–1971* (New York: Routledge, 2002), 36–37.

39. McKersie, *A Decisive Decade*, quote on 58.

40. *New York Times*, February 5, 1964.

41. *New York Times*, February 23, 1963; Anderson and Pickering, *Confronting the Color Line*, 118; Danns, *Something Better for Our Children*, 38–40.

42. *New York Times*, February 5, 1964.

43. *New York Times*, February 25, 1964.

44. *New York Times*, February 26, 1964.

45. *Chicago Tribune*, February 26, 1964.

46. *Chicago Tribune*, February 26, 1964; McKersie, *A Decisive Decade*, quote on 63–64. The *Chicago Tribune* on February 26, 1963, published the official statistics: on October 22, 1963, there were 179,559 elementary students, and 49,752 high school students absent; and 134,690 elementary students and 37,660 high school students were absent on February 25, 1964.

47. *Chicago Defender*, May 28, 1964.

48. Ralph, *Northern Protest*, 92–130; Anderson and Pickering, *Confronting the Color Line*, 150–208.

49. Mary Lou Finley and James R. Ralph Jr., "In Their Own Voices: The Story

of the Movement as Told by the Participants," in *The Chicago Freedom Movement: Martin Luther King Jr. and Civil Rights Activism in the North*, ed. Mary Lou Finley et al. (Lexington: University Press of Kentucky, 2016), 17–33.

50. See chapter 8.

51. Adina Back, "Blacks, Jews, and the Struggle to Integrate Brooklyn's Junior High School 258: A Cold War Story," *Journal of American Ethnic History* 20 (Winter 2001): quote on 57.

52. Adina Back, "Exposing the 'Whole Segregation Myth': The Harlem Nine and New York City's School Desegregation Battles," in Theoharis and Woodard, *Freedom North*, quote on 74.

53. Clarence Taylor, *Knocking at Our Own Door: Milton A. Galamison and the Struggle to Integrate New York City Schools* (New York: Columbia University Press, 1997), 91–92.

54. Taylor, *Knocking at Our Own Door*, 108–9.

55. Taylor, *Knocking at Our Own Door*, quote on 113.

56. Taylor, *Knocking at Our Own Door*, 113–15.

57. Taylor, *Knocking at Our Own Door*, quote on 122.

58. *Amsterdam News*, December 21, 1963.

59. *Amsterdam News*, December 14, 1963.

60. *Amsterdam News*, January 4, 1964.

61. *Amsterdam News*, January 26, 1964.

62. Taylor, *Knocking at Our Own Door*, 138.

63. Taylor, *Knocking at Our Own Door*, 141–42; *New York Times*, February 4, 1964.

64. *Amsterdam News*, February 8, 1964.

65. Taylor, *Knocking at Our Own Door*, 143; *New York Times*, February 5, 1964.

66. *New York Times*, February 5, 1964.

67. *Amsterdam News*, February 8, 1964.

68. *New York Times*, February 5, 1964.

69. *New York Times*, February 5, 1964.

70. *New York Times*, February 5, 1964.

71. *New York Times*, March 11, 1964; Taylor, *Knocking at Our Own Door*, 162.

72. *New York Times*, March 17, 1964.

73. *New York Times*, March 17, 1964; Clarence Taylor, *Knocking on Our Own Door*, 161–62.

74. *New York Times*, May 13, 1964.

75. Taylor, *Knocking on Our Own Door*, quotes on 167.

76. *New York Times*, March 12 and 21, 1964.

77. *New York Times*, September 14 and 15, 1964.

78. *New York Times*, September 15 and 16, 1964.

79. *New York Times*, January 20, 1965; Taylor, *Knocking at Our Own Door*, 172–73.

80. Taylor, *Knocking at Our Own Door*, quote on 175.

CHAPTER 6: EVERY CHILD A FREEDOM SOLDIER

1. Clarence Taylor, *Knocking at Our Own Door: Milton A. Galamison and the Struggle to Integrate New York City Schools* (New York: Columbia University Press, 1997), quote on 174.

2. Leonard N. Moore, "The School Desegregation Crisis of Cleveland, Ohio, 1963–1964: The Catalyst for Black Political Power in a Northern City," *Journal of Urban History* 28 (January 2002): 135–57.

3. For background information, population statistics, and educational issues for African Americans in Cleveland, see Todd M. Michney, *Surrogate Suburbs: Black Upward Mobility and Neighborhood Change in Cleveland, 1900–1980* (Chapel Hill: University of North Carolina Press, 2017), 14–24; Moore, "The School Desegregation Crisis," and Leonard N. Moore, *Carl Stokes and the Rise of Black Political Power in Cleveland* (Urbana: University of Illinois Press, 2002), 26–45.

4. Moore, "The School Desegregation Crisis," 136–37.

5. Moore, "The School Desegregation Crisis," quotes on 138.

6. Moore, "The School Desegregation Crisis," quotes on 140.

7. Moore, "The School Desegregation Crisis," 141–42; *Cleveland Plain Dealer*, September 27, 1963.

8. Moore, "The School Desegregation Crisis," 144–45.

9. Moore, "The School Desegregation Crisis," 144–45; August Meier and Elliott Rudwick, *CORE: A Study of the Civil Rights Movement* (Urbana: University of Illinois Press, 1975), 248–49.

10. Moore, "The School Desegregation Crisis," 146–47.

11. Gene Roberts and Hank Klibanoff, *The Race Beat: The Press, the Civil Rights Struggle, and the Awakening of a Nation* (New York: Knopf, 2006), 159–207.

12. The Kerner commission report on the rioting in the 1960s devoted an entire section to "media unfairness" and the "distrust and dislike of the media" among urban African Americans. See Otto Kerner et al., *Report of the National Advisory Commission on Civil Disorders* (New York: E. P. Dutton, 1968), 374–77.

13. Moore, "The School Desegregation Crisis," 147–48.

14. Moore, "The School Desegregation Crisis," quote on 148; *Cleveland Plain Dealer*, February 27, 1964.

15. *New York Times*, February 12, 1964; Meier and Rudwick, *CORE: A Study in the Civil Rights Movement*, 248.

16. *Cleveland Plain Dealer*, February 29, 1964; Moore, "The School Desegregation Crisis," quote on 150.

17. *Cleveland Plain Dealer*, March 10, 1964.

18. Moore, "The School Desegregation Crisis," 151–52.

19. *Cleveland Plain Dealer*, April 8, 1964.

20. *Cleveland Plain Dealer*, April 11, 1964.

21. Moore, "The School Desegregation Crisis," 152.

22. Moore, "The School Desegregation Crisis," quote on 153.

23. *Cleveland Plain Dealer*, April 21, 1964.

24. Moore, "School Desegregation Crisis," 154.

25. Moore, "School Desegregation Crisis," quote on 154.

26. *Milwaukee Journal*, February 4, 1964.

27. Jack Dougherty, *More Than One Struggle: The Evolution of Black School Reform in Milwaukee* (Chapel Hill: University of North Carolina Press, 2004), 75–80.

28. Jack Dougherty, "'That's When We Were Marching to Gain Jobs': Black Teachers and the Early Civil Rights Movement in Milwaukee," *History of Education Quarterly* 38 (Summer 1998): 121–41.

29. Dougherty, *More Than One Struggle*, quote on 88.

30. *Milwaukee Journal*, July 29, 1962.

31. Dougherty, *More Than One Struggle*, quote on 67.

32. Dougherty, *More Than One Struggle*, quote on 69. See also Edmund Gordon and Doxey A. Wilkerson, *Compensatory Education for the Disadvantaged: Programs and Practices, Pre-School through College* (Princeton, NJ: College Board, 1966); Helen E. Rees, *Deprivation and Compensatory Education: A Consideration* (Boston: Houghton Mifflin, 1968); California Department of Education, *Instructional Materials Developed Under the Auspices of the Elementary and Secondary Education Act, Title I* (Sacramento, CA: Department of Education, 1969).

33. For analyses of the reception and impact of the Moynihan Report, see James T. Patterson, *Freedom Is Not Enough: The Moynihan Report and America's Struggle over Black Family Life from LBJ to Obama* (New York: Basic Books, 2012); Susan Greenbaum, *Blaming the Poor: The Long Shadow of the Moynihan Report on Cruel Images of Poverty* (New Brunswick: Rutgers University Press, 2015); and Daniel Geary, *Beyond Civil Rights: The Moynihan Report and Its Legacy* (Philadelphia: University of Pennsylvania Press, 2015).

34. See also William Ryan, *Blaming the Victim* (New York: Vintage Press, 1970); Douglass Massey et al., eds., *The Moynihan Report Revisited: Lessons and Reflections after Four Decades* (Thousand Oaks, CA: Sage Publications, 2009).

35. Dougherty, *More Than One Struggle*, 74–75.

36. Dougherty, *More Than One Struggle*, quote on 71.

37. Dougherty, *More Than One Struggle*, 78–79.

38. Dougherty, *More Than One Struggle*, quote on 88–89.

39. Jack Dougherty suggests that Barbee and some other Black leaders in Milwaukee "rejected compensatory education as only 'half a loaf'" and did not fully endorse Barbee's commitment to integration, but the evidence offered does not support that conclusion.

40. *Milwaukee Journal*, October 22 and 23, 1963; Dougherty, *More Than One Struggle*, 87.

41. *Milwaukee Journal*, March 26 and 28, 1963; Dougherty, *More Than One Struggle*, 89–90.

42. *Milwaukee Journal*, January 28, 1964; Dougherty, *More Than One Struggle*, quote on 101.

43. Dougherty, *More Than One Struggle*, quote on 94.

44. *Milwaukee Journal*, January 22, 1964.

45. *Milwaukee Journal*, January 28, 1964; *Milwaukee Star*, February 1, 1964.

46. *Milwaukee Journal*, February 3, 1964.

47. Dougherty, *More Than One Struggle*, 111.

48. Dougherty, *More Than One Struggle*, quotes on 111–13.

49. Dougherty, *More Than One Struggle*, 120. Black high school students' demands in the late 1960s for the teaching of Black History are detailed in chapter 8.

50. *Milwaukee Journal*, May 18, 1964.

51. *Milwaukee Journal*, May 18 and 19, 1964.

52. *Milwaukee Journal*, May 19, 1964.

53. *Milwaukee Journal*, June 18, 1965.

54. Patrick D. Jones, "'Not a Color, But an Attitude': Father James Groppi and Black Power Politics in Milwaukee," in *Groundwork: Local Black Freedom Movements in America*, ed. Jeanne Theoharis and Komozi Woodard (New York: New York University Press, 2005), 266–67.

55. Dougherty, *More Than One Struggle*, 125–27; Patrick D. Jones, *The Selma of the North: Civil Rights Insurgency in Milwaukee* (Cambridge, MA: Harvard University Press, 2009); and Paul Geneen, *Civil Rights Activism in Milwaukee: South Side Struggles in the '60s and '70s* (Charleston, SC: History Press, 2014).

56. Laura Visser-Maessen, *Robert Parris Moses: A Life in Civil Rights and Leadership at the Grassroots* (Chapel Hill: University of North Carolina Press, 2016), 95–96.

57. Eric R. Burner, *And Gently He Shall Lead Them: Robert Parris Moses and*

Civil Rights in Mississippi (New York: New York University Press, 1994), quote on 125–26.

58. Clayborne Carson, *In Struggle: SNCC and the Black Awakening of the 1960s* (Cambridge, MA: Harvard University Press, 1981), 114–15.

59. Bruce Watson, *Freedom Summer: The Savage Season That Made Mississippi Burn and Made America a Democracy* (New York: Viking Press, 2010), 78–104, 205–11; *New York Times*, August 6 and 7, 1964.

60. Moses hoped for four hundred thousand, then lowered his projection to one hundred thousand, and got sixty-three thousand participants in the Freedom Vote. Watson, *Freedom Summer*, 235.

61. Jon N. Hale, "The Student as a Force for Social Change: The Mississippi Freedom Schools and Student Engagement," *Journal of African American History* 96 (Summer 2011): quotes on 330–31.

62. Hale, "The Student as a Force for Social Change," quote on 334–35; see also Watson, *Freedom Summer*, 67, 105–6. For an investigation of the impact of the SNCC 1964 Mississippi project on the subsequent lives of the northern students who participated, see Doug McAdam, *Freedom Summer* (New York: Oxford University Press, 1988).

63. Thelma Eubanks quoted in Ellen Levine, *Freedom's Children: Young Civil Rights Activists Tell Their Stories* (New York: Puffin Books, 1993), 94.

64. Hale, "The Student as a Force for Social Change," quote on 335; see also William Sturkey and Jon N. Hale, eds., *To Write in the Light of Freedom: The Newspapers of the 1964 Mississippi Freedom Schools* (Oxford: University Press of Mississippi, 2015).

65. Hale, "The Student as a Force for Social Change," 336–38.

66. Levine, *Freedom's Children*, 150.

67. Hale, "The Student as a Force for Social Change," quote on 340.

68. Hale, "The Student as a Force for Social Change," quote on 341. See also Jon N. Hale, *The Freedom Schools: Student Activists in the Mississippi Civil Rights Movement* (New York: Columbia University Press, 2016).

CHAPTER 7: POLICE BRUTALITY, BLACK SELF-DEFENSE, AND STUDENT ACTIVISM

1. Ellen Levine, *Freedom's Children: Young Civil Rights Activists Tell Their Stories* (New York: Puffin Books, 1993), quote on 135.

2. Lynda Blackmon Lowery, with Elspeth Leacock and Susan Buckley, *Turning 15 on the Road to Freedom: My Story of the 1965 Selma Voting Rights March* (New York: Penguin Random House, 2016), quote on 74.

3. Taylor Branch, *Pillar of Fire: America in the King Years, 1963–65* (New York: Simon & Schuster, 1998), 81–85.

4. Amelia P. Boynton, "Early Attempts at Betterment," in *Eyes on the Prize Civil Rights Reader*, ed. Clayborne Carson et al. (New York: Penguin Books, 1991), quote on 209.

5. Bernard Lafayette, "Selma, Alabama," in Carson, *Eyes on the Prize Civil Rights Reader*, quote on 211–12. See also David J. Garrow, *Protest at Selma: Martin Luther King, Jr., and the Voting Rights Act of 1965* (New Haven, CT: Yale University Press, 1978), 39–40; Clayborne Carson, *In Struggle: SNCC and the Black Awakening of the 1960s* (Cambridge, MA: Harvard University Press, 1981), 157–58.

6. Adam Fairclough, *To Redeem the Soul of America: The Southern Christian Leadership Conference and Martin Luther King Jr.* (Athens: University of Georgia Press, 1987), quote on 229.

7. Lowery, *Turning 15 on the Road to Freedom*, 26.

8. Sheyann Webb and Rachel West, with Frank Sikora, *Selma, Lord, Selma: Girlhood Memories of Civil Rights Days* (Tuscaloosa: University of Alabama Press, 1980), 25–26. See also *Selma, Lord, Selma*, made for television drama, Charles Burnett, dir. (1999).

9. Webb and West, *Selma, Lord, Selma*, 28–29.

10. Webb and West, *Selma, Lord, Selma*, 32–33.

11. Webb and West, *Selma, Lord, Selma*, 37; Branch, *Pillar of Fire*, 563–64.

12. Rachel West, in Webb and West, *Selma, Lord, Selma*, 39–40.

13. Webb and West, *Selma, Lord, Selma*, 48–49.

14. *New York Times*, February 2 and 3, 1965.

15. Branch, *Pillar of Fire*, 577–78.

16. Sheyann Webb, in Webb and West, *Selma, Lord, Selma*, 62; *New York Times*, February 4, 1965.

17. Rachel West, in Webb and West, *Selma, Lord, Selma*, 67–68.

18. Branch, *Pillar of Fire*, 588.

19. Lowery, *Turning 15 on the Road to Freedom*, 38–39.

20. *New York Times*, February 18, 1965.

21. *New York Times*, February 19, 1965; Branch, *Pillar of Fire*, 592–93.

22. Lowery, *Turning 15 on the Road to Freedom*, 46.

23. Lowery, *Turning 15 on the Road to Freedom*, 47.

24. Branch, *Pillar of Fire*, quote on 599–600; *New York Times*, March 4, 1965.

25. Taylor Branch, *At Canaan's Edge: America in the King Years, 1965–68* (New York: Simon & Schuster, 2006), 32–43.

26. Sheyann Webb, in Webb and West, *Selma, Lord, Selma*, 106.

27. Sheyann Webb, in Webb and West, *Selma, Lord, Selma*, 93–94.

28. Lowery, *Turning 15 on the Road to Freedom*, 53, 56.

29. Lowery, *Turning 15 on the Road to Freedom*, 60.

30. Rachel West, in Webb and West, *Selma, Lord, Selma*, 100–101. Taylor Branch in *At Canaan's Edge* said that Frank Soracco "collapsed bruised and gassed in the upstairs bathroom of his host family, locking the door" (53). But there is no mention of Soracco saving Rachel West from the police on horseback. And she had never met Soracco before; he was just "this white guy" (100).

31. Sheyann Webb, in Webb and West, *Selma, Lord, Selma*, 106.

32. *New York Times*, March 9, 1965.

33. Lowery, *Turning 15 on the Road to Freedom*, 100; *New York Times*, March 12, 1965.

34. *New York Times*, March 22–26, 1965. The march was front-page news in the *Times* each of these days. See also Branch, "Selma: The Last Revolution," part 1 in *At Canaan's Edge*, 5–204.

35. Martin Luther King Jr., "Our God Is Marching On!" in *A Testament of Hope: The Essential Writings of Martin Luther King Jr.*, ed. James M. Washington (New York: Harper & Row, 1986), quotes on 229.

36. Lowery, *Turning 15 on the Road to Freedom*, 102.

37. *New York Times*, March 15 and 16, 1965.

38. Lance Hill, *The Deacons for Defense: Armed Resistance and the Civil Rights Movement* (Chapel Hill: University of North Carolina Press, 2004), quote on 65. See also Bettye Collier-Thomas and V. P. Franklin, *My Soul Is a Witness: A Chronology of the Civil Rights Era* (New York: Henry Holt, 2000), 241.

39. Christopher Strain, *Pure Fire: Self-Defense as Activism in the Civil Rights Era* (Athens: University of Georgia Press, 2005); Hasan Kwame Jeffries, *Bloody Lowndes: Civil Rights and Black Power in Alabama's Black Belt* (New York: New York University Press, 2010); and Akinyele Omowale Umoja, *We Will Shoot Back: Armed Resistance in the Mississippi Freedom Movement* (New York: New York University Press, 2013).

40. Simon Wendt, *The Spirit and the Shotgun: Armed Resistance and the Struggle for Civil Rights* (Gainesville: University Press of Florida, 2007), quote on 59; see also Simon Wendt, "God, Gandhi, and Guns: The African American Freedom Struggle in Tuscaloosa, Alabama, 1964–1965," *Journal of African American History* 89 (Winter 2004): 36–56.

41. Hill, *The Deacons for Defense*, 31–33.

42. Hill, *The Deacons for Defense*, quote on 66; see also Adam Fairclough, *Race and Democracy: The Civil Rights Struggle in Louisiana, 1915–1972* (Athens: University of Georgia Press, 1995), 357–58.

43. Hill, *The Deacons for Defense*, quote on 68.

44. Hill, *The Deacons for Defense*, quote on 69.

45. *New York Times*, March 15, 1965.

46. *New York Times*, March 15, 1965.

47. See Elliott Jaspin, *Buried in the Bitter Waters: The Hidden History of Racial Cleansing in America* (New York: Basic Books, 2007); and Isabel Wilkerson, *The Warmth of Other Suns: The Epic History of America's Great Migration* (New York: Vintage Books, 2011).

48. Mayor Fiorella La Guardia Commission, *The Complete Report on the Harlem Riot of March 19, 1935*, quoted in Janet L. Abu-Lughod, *Race, Space, and Riots in Chicago, New York, and Los Angeles* (New York: Oxford University Press, 2007), 142–43.

49. Abu-Lughod, *Race, Space, and Riots*, 149–50.

50. C. Eric Lincoln, *The Black Muslims in America* (Boston: Beacon Press, 1961); E. U. Essien-Udom, *Black Nationalism: The Search for an Identity in America* (Chicago: University of Chicago Press, 1962); and Malcolm X with Alex Haley, *The Autobiography of Malcolm X* (New York: Grove Press, 1965).

51. Historians have documented the ideological impact of Malcolm X's speeches on African American youths in the cities and on college and university campuses, emphasizing Black self-defense against racial violence. See Charles Jones, ed., *The Black Panther Party Reconsidered* (Baltimore: Black Classics Press, 1998); Scot Brown, *Fighting for Us: Maulana Karenga, the US Organization, and Black Cultural Nationalism* (New York: New York University Press, 2005); Martha Biondi, *Black Revolution on Campus* (Berkeley: University of California Press, 2012); Manning Marable, *Malcolm X: A Life of Reinvention* (New York: Penguin Books, 2011); Ibram H. Rogers (Kendi), "'People All Over the World Are Supporting You': Malcolm X, Ideological Formations, and Black Student Activism, 1960–1972," *Journal of African American History* 96 (Winter 2011): 14–38; and Ibram H. Rogers (Kendi), *The Black Campus Movement: Black Students and the Racial Reconstitution of Higher Education, 1965–1972* (New York: Palgrave, 2012).

52. J. Herman Blake, "Black Nationalism," in "Protest in the Sixties," *Annals of the American Academy of Political and Social Sciences* 382 (March 1969): 15–25, quote on 20.

53. The massive resistance campaign to prevent the implementation of the *Brown* decision in the 1950s and early 1960s consisted not just of legislation and litigation but also of mob violence, arson, bombings, murder, and police brutality. See George Lewis, *Massive Resistance: The White Response to the Civil Rights Movement* (London: Bloomsbury Academic, 2006); Clive Webb, ed., *Massive Resistance: Southern Opposition to the Second Reconstruction* (New York: Oxford University Press, 2005); John Kyle Day, *The Southern Manifesto: Massive Resistance*

and the Fight to Preserve Segregation (Oxford: University Press of Mississippi, 2015); and Elizabeth G. McRae, *Mothers of Massive Resistance: White Women and the Politics of White Supremacy* (New York: Oxford University Press, 2018).

54. *New York Times*, March 25 and 26, 1964.

55. See chapter 6.

56. Abu-Lughod, *Race, Space, and Riots*, quotes on 170.

57. Abu-Lughod, *Race, Space, and Riots*, 173.

58. *New York Times*, July 19–23, 1964.

59. Fred C. Shapiro and James W. Sullivan, *Race Riots: New York 1964* (New York: Crowell, 1964), 172.

60. Matthew J. Countryman, *Up South: Civil Rights and Black Power in Philadelphia* (Philadelphia: University of Pennsylvania Press, 2006), 154–55.

61. Countryman, *Up South*, quote on 156; *New York Times*, August 30 and 31, 1964; September 1 and 2, 1964.

62. *New York Times*, August 14–15, 1965; Collier-Thomas and Franklin, *My Soul Is a Witness*, 236.

63. *New York Times*, August 12–14, 1965; see also Gerald Horne, *Fire This Time: The Watts Uprising and the 1960s* (Charlottesville: University Press of Virginia, 1975).

64. V. P. Franklin, *Martin Luther King, Jr.: A Biography* (New York: Park Lane Press, 1998), quotes on 133.

65. John McCone et al., *Violence in the City: An End or Beginning? A Report by the Governor's Commission in the Los Angeles Riots, December 2, 1965*, quoted in Abu-Lughod, *Race, Space, and Riots*, 214.

66. McCone et al., *Violence in the City*, in Abu-Lughod, *Race, Space, and Riots*, 214–15.

67. Thomas R. Brooks, "Necessary Force—Or Police Brutality?" *New York Times Magazine*, December 5, 1965, 61.

68. Brooks, "Necessary Force—Or Police Brutality?," quotes on 66.

69. Countryman, *Up South*, quotes on 160.

70. Otto Kerner et al., *Report of the National Advisory Commission on Civil Disorders* (New York: E. P. Dutton, 1968), quotes on 1, 11.

71. Kerner et al., *Report of the National Advisory Commission on Civil Disorders*, quotes on 40, 284. The ages and percentages of those arrested during the riots are found on 127–35.

72. Kerner et al., *Report of the National Advisory Commission on Civil Disorders*, quotes on 288, 311–12.

73. Kerner et al., *Report of the National Advisory Commission on Civil Disorders*, quotes on 205–6.

74. The literature on Black Power has become voluminous. See, for example, Stokely Carmichael and Charles Hamilton, *Black Power: The Politics of Liberation* (New York: Vintage Press, 1968); William Van Deberg, *New Day in Babylon: The Black Power Movement and American Culture, 1966–1975* (Chicago: University of Chicago Press, 1993); Sundiata Keita Cha-Jua and Clarence Lang, "The 'Long Movement' as Vampire: Temporal and Spatial Fallacies in Black Freedom Studies," *Journal of African American History* 92 (Spring 2007): 265–88; V. P. Franklin, "Introduction—The New Black Power Studies," *Journal of African American History* 92 (Fall 2007): 463–67, 468–575; Peniel E. Joseph, "Introduction: Toward a Historiography of the Black Power Movement," in *The Black Power Movement: Rethinking the Civil Rights—Black Power Era* (New York, 2006), 1–15; Peniel E. Joseph, *Waiting for the Midnight Hour: A Narrative History of Black Power in America* (New York: Henry Holt, 2007); Russell Rickford, *We Are an African People: Independent Education, Black Power, and the Radical Imagination* (New York: Oxford University Press, 2016); Stefan Bradley, *Upending the Ivory Tower: Civil Rights, Black Power, and the Ivy League* (New York: New York University Press, 2018).

75. For discussion of the teenagers and young adults who joined the Black Panther Party and the US organization, see Jones, ed., *The Black Panther Party Reconsidered*; Brown, *Fighting for US*; V. P. Franklin, "Jackanapes: Reflections on the Legacy of the Black Panther Party for the Hip Hop Generation," *Journal of African American History* 92 (Fall 2007): 553–60; Donna Jean Murch, *Living for the City: Migration, Education and the Rise of the Black Panther Party in Oakland, California* (Chapel Hill: University of North Carolina Press, 2010); Robyn C. Spencer, *The Revolution Has Come: Black Power, Gender, and the Black Panther Party in Oakland* (Durham, NC: Duke University Press, 2016); Joshua Bloom and Waldo Martin, *Black Against Empire: The History and Politics of the Black Panther Party* (Berkeley: University of California Press, 2016); and Bobby Seale and Stephen Shames, *Power to the People: The World of the Black Panthers* (New York: Harold Abrams, 2016).

CHAPTER 8: CIVIL RIGHTS, BLACK POWER,
AND INCREASING YOUTH MILITANCY

1. James Brown, "The Black Athlete," in *High School Revolutionaries*, ed. Marc Liberle and Tom Seligson (New York: Random House, 1970), 50.

2. Bettye Collier-Thomas and V. P. Franklin, *A Chronology of the Civil Rights Era in the United States and in Philadelphia, 1954–1975* (Philadelphia: Packard Press, 1994), 54–55.

3. *Philadelphia Bulletin*, November 18, 1968; Matthew J. Countryman, *Up South:*

Civil Rights and Black Power in Philadelphia (Philadelphia: University of Pennsylvania Press, 2006), 223–28.

4. Bettye Collier-Thomas and V.P. Franklin, *My Soul Is a Witness: A Chronology of the Civil Rights Era, 1954–1965* (New York: Henry Holt, 2000), 12; *New York Times*, September 25, 1954; David A. Canton, *Raymond Pace Alexander: A New Negro Lawyer Fights for Civil Rights in Philadelphia* (Jackson: University Press of Mississippi, 2010), 125–31.

5. *New York Times*, April 30, 1957.

6. *New York Times*, October 5, 1957.

7. *New York Times*, January 25, 1958; July 1, 1958.

8. Collier-Thomas and Franklin, *A Chronology of the Civil Rights Era*, 41–44. Matthew Countryman suggested that the consumer boycotts, protests at construction sites, and Girard College protests "reveal[ed] the failure of civil rights liberalism in Philadelphia" and "the limitations of protest as a strategy for creating substantive economic opportunity for poor and working class blacks"; *Up South*, 178–79. Yet each of these direct action campaigns brought educational and employment advances for Black children and workers. Indeed, the federal government's first affirmative action directives aimed at the building trades and construction companies were in response to NAACP and CORE protests at construction sites in Philadelphia, New York, Cleveland, and other cities. The directive was named the "Philadelphia Plan." See Hugh Davis Graham, *The Civil Rights Era: Origins and Development of National Policy, 1960–1972* (New York: Oxford University Press, 1990), chap. 1–2.

9. V. P. Franklin, "Operation Street Corner: The Wharton Centre and the Juvenile Gang Problem in Philadelphia, 1945–1958," in *W. E. B. Du Bois, Race, and the City: The Philadelphia Negro and Its Legacy*, ed. Michael B. Katz and Thomas J. Sugrue (Philadelphia: University of Pennsylvania Press, 1998), 195–216.

10. *Philadelphia Tribune*, May 8, 1965.

11. *Philadelphia Tribune*, May 8, 1965.

12. *Philadelphia Tribune*, August 2, 1965; Collier-Thomas and Franklin, *A Chronology of the Civil Rights Era*, 42–43; Countryman, *Up South*, 176–78.

13. Countryman, *Up South*, quote on 210.

14. Countryman, *Up South*, quote on 211.

15. Countryman, *Up South*, quote on 211.

16. Collier-Thomas and Franklin, *A Chronology of the Civil Rights Era*, 46.

17. *Philadelphia Tribune*, September 6, 1966.

18. *Philadelphia Tribune*, September 14, 1968. Fatherless girls were enrolled at Girard College beginning in 1983.

19. Pam Smith, "Youth and Nonviolence: Then and Now," in *The Chicago*

Freedom Movement: Martin Luther King Jr. and Civil Rights Activism in the North, ed. Mary Lou Finley et al. (Lexington: University Press of Kentucky, 2016), quote on 294; see also Sherrillyn J. Bevel, "Roots of the Environmental Justice Movement: A Community Mobilizes to End Childhood Lead Poisoning," in Finley et al., *Chicago Freedom Movement*, 274–91.

20. Taylor Branch, *At Canaan's Edge: America in the King Years, 1965–68* (New York: Simon & Schuster, 2006), quotes on 296–97.

21. Branch, *At Canaan's Edge*, quotes on 321.

22. Smith, "Youth and Nonviolence," quotes on 298.

23. Smith, "Youth and Nonviolence," quotes on 300.

24. Smith, "Youth and Nonviolence," quotes on 301.

25. Otto Kerner et al., *Report of the National Advisory Commission on Civil Disorders* (New York: E. P. Dutton, 1968), quote on 39.

26. Branch, *At Canaan's Edge*, 507–11.

27. Smith, "Youth and Nonviolence," quote on 305.

28. For information on the affirmative action directives in the construction trades, see Graham, *The Civil Rights Era*, chap. 2; Countryman, *Up South*, 130–48.

29. C. T. Vivian, quoted in James R. Ralph Jr. and Mary Lou Finley, eds., "In Their Own Voices: The Story of the Movement as Told by Participants," in Finley et al., *The Chicago Freedom Movement*, 74–75.

30. James R. Ralph, *Northern Protest: Martin Luther King Jr., Chicago, and the Civil Rights Movement* (Cambridge, MA: Harvard University Press, 1993), 228–29.

31. Simon Balto, quoted in Smith, "Youth and Nonviolence," 309; see also Simon Balto, *Occupied Territory: Policing Black Chicago from Red Summer to Black Power* (Chapel Hill: University of North Carolina Press, 2019).

32. *New York Times*, October 25, 1964.

33. *New York Times*, May 15, 1966; V. P. Franklin, "Black High School Student Activism: An Urban Phenomenon?," *Journal of Research in Education* 10 (Fall 2000): 3–8; and Jonathan Zimmerman, *Whose America? Culture Wars in the Public Schools* (Cambridge, MA: Harvard University Press, 2002), 107–10.

34. *New York Times*, August 24, 1966.

35. *New York Times*, August 26, 1966.

36. *New York Times*, September 3, 1966.

37. Dionne Danns, "Chicago High School Students' Movement for Quality Public Education, 1966–1971," *Journal of African American History* 88 (Spring 2003): 141.

38. Kerner et al., *Report of the National Advisory Commission on Civil Disorders*, 47–73, 84–108.

39. *Chicago Daily Defender*, November 20, 1968.

40. *Chicago Daily Defender*, November 21, 1968.

41. *Chicago Daily Defender*, November 22, 1968.

42. *Chicago Daily Defender*, November 22, 1968; *Chicago Tribune*, November 22 and 23, 1967.

43. Danns, "Chicago High School Students' Movement," quote on 142.

44. *Chicago Daily Defender*, April 3, 1968.

45. *Chicago Daily Defender*, April 4, 1968.

46. Shirletta J. Kinchen, *Black Power in the Bluff City: African American Youth and Student Activism in Memphis, 1965–1975* (Knoxville: University of Tennessee Press, 2016), quotes on 54–55.

47. Kinchen, *Black Power in the Bluff City*, quote on 62.

48. V. P. Franklin, *Martin Luther King Jr.: A Biography* (New York: Park Lane Press, 1998), quote on 161.

49. Franklin, *Martin Luther King Jr.*, 165–66; *New York Times*, April 5 and 6, 1968.

50. *New York Times*, April 6 and 7, 1968. See also Jason Sokol, "The World Stands Aghast: The Death of Martin Luther King in Global Perspective," *Journal of African American History* 103 (Summer 2018): 343–68; and Jason Sokol, *The Heavens Might Crack: The Death and Legacy of Martin Luther King Jr.* (New York: Basic Books, 2018).

51. Jakobi Williams, *From the Bullet to the Ballot: The Illinois Chapter of the Black Panther Party and Racial Coalition Politics in Chicago* (Chapel Hill: University of North Carolina Press, 2013), quote on 70.

52. "The Mayor's Riot Study Report," August 1, 1968, quoted in Janet L. Abu-Lughod, *Race, Space, and Riots in Chicago, New York, and Los Angeles* (New York: Oxford University Press, 2007), 95.

53. Dwayne C. Wright, "Black Pride Day, 1968: High School Student Activism in York, Pennsylvania," *Journal of African American History* 88 (Spring 2003): 151–62; quotes on 155–56.

54. Wright, "Black Pride Day, 1968," quote on 158; the entire list of demands is reprinted on 157.

55. Wright, "Black Pride Day, 1968," 159–62.

56. Danns, "Chicago High School Students," quote on 140.

57. Danns, "Chicago High School Students," quote on 143; see also *Chicago Daily Defender*, October 8, 1968; *Chicago Sun-Times*, October 8, 1968.

58. *Chicago Daily Defender*, October 8 and 9, 1968.

59. *Chicago Tribune*, October 6, 1968.

60. *Chicago Daily Defender*, October 9, 1968.

61. *Chicago Tribune*, October 10, 1968.

62. *Chicago Tribune*, October 14, 1968. The groups represented at the meeting included the Afro-American Student Association, the Black Student Congress, and Black Students for Defense.

63. *Chicago Tribune*, October 14, 1968; *Chicago Daily Defender*, October 14, 1968.

64. *Chicago Daily Defender*, October 15, 1968; *Chicago Tribune*, October 16, 1968.

65. *Chicago Tribune*, October 16, 1968.

66. *Chicago Tribune*, October 22, 1968.

67. *Chicago Tribune*, October 23, 1968.

68. *Chicago Tribune*, October 22 and 23, 1968; *Chicago Daily Defender*, October 22, 1968.

69. *Chicago Tribune*, October 29, 1968; *Chicago Daily Defender*, October 29, 1968.

70. *Chicago Tribune*, October 31, 1968.

71. *Chicago Tribune*, November 1, 1968.

72. *Chicago Tribune*, November 5, 1968; *Chicago Daily Defender*, November 5, 1968.

73. *Chicago Tribune*, November 5, 1968.

74. *Chicago Tribune*, December 22, 1968.

75. Danns, "Chicago High School Students," quote on 147; and Dionne Danns, *Something Better for the Children: Black Organization in the Chicago Public Schools* (New York: Routledge, 2002), 71–88.

76. Beatrice Gudridge, *High School Student Unrest* (Washington, DC: National Public Relations Association, 1969), 1–2.

77. Kenneth Fish, *Conflict and Dissent in the High School* (New York: Bruce Publishing, 1970), quotes on i–ii.

78. Fish, *Conflict and Dissent in the High School*, quotes on ii, 9.

79. Fish, *Conflict and Dissent in the High School*, 9–10.

80. John H. Harrington, "L.A.'s Student Blowouts," in *Student Dissent in the Schools*, ed. Irving G. Hendrick and Reginald L. Jones (Boston: Houghton Mifflin, 1970), 239–47; and Ian F. Haney Lopez, *Racism on Trial: The Chicano Fight for Justice* (Cambridge, MA: Harvard University Press, 2003), 15–24.

81. Haney Lopez, *Racism on Trial*, quotes on 21.

82. Haney Lopez, *Racism on Trial*, 21–22.

83. *Los Angeles Times*, December 13, 1968.

84. Gael Graham, *Young Activists: American High School Students in the Age of Protest* (DeKalb: Northern Illinois University Press, 2006), quote on 78.

85. Graham, *Young Activists*, quote on 77.

86. Graham, *Young Activists*, 6–7.

87. Graham, *Young Activists*, quotes on 80–81.

88. *New York Times*, September 28, 1968.

89. Gladis Williams, quoted in Ellen Levine, *Freedom's Children: Young Civil Rights Activists Tell Their Own Stories* (New York: Penguin, 1993), 68.

90. Robert Baker, "Negroes to Boycott Stores Owned by Whites," *Washington Post*, October 22, 1961.

91. The school boycotts for quality integrated education even spread to small cities such as Riverside, California, in September 1965. See V. P. Franklin, foreword to Arthur L. Littleworth, *No Easy Way: Integrating Riverside Schools— A Victory for Community* (Riverside, CA: Inlandia Institute, 2014), iv–vi. Additional photos and educational materials are available at www.youngcrusaders.org.

EPILOGUE: "KEEP STIRRING UP 'GOOD TROUBLE'"

1. Martin Luther King Jr., "Non-Violence and Social Change," in *Triumph of Conscience*, reprinted in *A Testament of Hope: The Essential Writings of Martin Luther King Jr.* (New York: Harper & Row, 1986), 650–51.

2. Founders of March for Our Lives, *Glimmer of Hope: How Tragedy Sparked a Movement* (New York: Razorbill & Dutton, 2018), quote on 141.

3. *Time*, December 11, 2019.

4. *New York Times*, May 25, September 21, and 28, 2019.

5. Founders of March for Our Lives, *Glimmer of Hope*, quote on 141.

6. Founders of March for Our Lives, *Glimmer of Hope*, quotes on 147, 149, 153.

7. *New York Times*, March 26, 2018. With support from Michael Bloomberg's nonprofit Everytown for Gun Safety, the Parkland students went on to found Students Demand Action, because they believe "gun violence is a symptom of other things, like poverty, racism, housing insecurity, domestic violence." By 2020, there were four hundred chapters. See *New York Times*, August 4, 2020.

8. Founders of March for Our Lives, *Glimmer of Hope*, quotes on 47–48.

9. David Halberstam, *The Children* (New York: Random House, 1998), 67–68, 97–98; John Lewis and Michael D'Orso, *Walking with the Wind: A Memoir of the Movement* (New York: Simon & Schuster, 1998), 57–90; and *John Lewis: Good Trouble*, dir. Dawn Porter, Magnolia Pictures, 2020.

10. Jonathan Zimmerman, *Whose America? Culture Wars in the Public Schools* (Cambridge, MA: Harvard University Press, 2002), 107–34.

11. Charles P. Henry, *Black Studies and the Democratization of American Higher Education* (New York: Palgrave Macmillan, 2017). See also Abdul Alkalimat,

Introduction to Afro-American Studies (Breckenridge, CO: Twenty-First Century Books, 1986); James B. Stewart, *Flight: In Search of a Vision* (Trenton, NJ: Africa World Press, 2004); Noliwe Rooks, *White Money/Black Power: The Surprising History of African American Studies* (Boston: Beacon Press, 2006); Dolores Alridge and E. Lincoln James, eds., *Africana Studies: Philosophical and Theoretical Paradigms* (Pullman: Washington State University Press, 2007); and Fabio Rojas, *From Black Power to Black Studies: How a Radical Social Movement Became an Academic Discipline* (Baltimore: Johns Hopkins University Press, 2007).

12. Sekou M. Franklin, *After the Rebellion: Black Youth, Social Movement Activism, and the Post–Civil Rights Generation* (New York: New York University Press, 2014), 2.

13. Franklin, *After the Rebellion*, 255–56.

14. Wesley C. Hogan, *On the Freedom Side: How Five Decades of Youth Activists Have Remixed American History* (Chapel Hill: University of North Carolina Press, 2019), 10.

15. Hogan, *On the Freedom Side*, quotes on 39, 49.

16. Hogan, *On the Freedom Side*, quotes on 105, 154.

17. Hogan, *On the Freedom Side*, quotes on 158–59.

18. Hogan, *On the Freedom Side*, quote on 184.

19. V.P. Franklin, "African Americans and Movements for Reparations: From Ex-Slave Pensions to the Reparations Superfund: Introduction," *Journal of African American History* 97 (Winter–Spring 2012): 1–12; and Elaine Allen Lechtreck, "'We Are Demanding $500 Million for Reparations': The Black Manifesto, Mainline Religious Denominations, and Black Economic Development," *Journal of African American History* 97 (Winter–Spring 2012): 1–12, 39–71.

20. Adjoa A. Aiyetoro, "The National Coalition for Blacks for Reparations in America (N'COBRA): Its Creation and Contributions to the Reparations Movement," in *Should America Pay? Slavery and the Raging Debate on Reparations*, ed. Raymond A. Winbush (New York: HarperCollins Publishers, 2003), 209–25.

21. Keeanga-Yamahtta Taylor, *From #Black Lives Matter to Black Liberation* (Chicago: Haymarket Books, 2014); Christopher J. Lebron, *The Making of Black Lives Matter: A Brief History of an Idea* (New York: Oxford University Press, 2017); and Barbara Ransby, *Making All Black Lives Matter: Reimagining Freedom in the Twenty-First Century* (Berkeley: University of California Press, 2018).

22. Black Lives Matter, *A Vision for Black Lives: Policy Demands for Black Power, Freedom, and Justice*, August 2016, https://policy.m4bl.org.

23. Black Youth Project 100, *Agenda to Build Black Futures* (2018), 15–16.

24. Ron Daniels, "CARICOM Initiative Could Provide the Spark:

Revitalizing the U.S. Reparations Movement" (October 2012), in *Still on This Journey: The Vision and Mission of Dr. Ron Daniels* (New York: State of the Black World Press, 2019), 233–36.

25. Hilary McD. Beckles, *Britain's Black Debt: Reparations for Caribbean Slavery and Native Genocide* (Kingston, Jamaica: University of the West Indies Press, 2013), 174.

26. See CARICOM Reparations Commission, "Ten Point Reparation Plan," http://caricomreparations.org/caricom/caricom-tenpoint-reparation-plan/; V.P. Franklin, "Reparations as a Development Strategy: The CARICOM Reparations Commission," *Journal of African American History* 98 (Summer 2013): 363–66; and Nicola Frith and Joyce Hope Scott, "Introduction: National and International Perspectives on Movements for Reparations," *Journal of African American History* 103 (Winter–Spring 2018): 1–18.

27. *New York Times*, June 19, 2019. For information on the formation of the National African American Reparations Commission (NAARC), see Ron Daniels, "The National/International Summit: Seizing the Moment to Galvanize the U.S. and Global Reparations Movement," in *Still on This Journey*, 237–41.

28. William A. Darity Jr. and A. Kirsten Mullen, *From Here to Equality: Reparations for Black Americans in the Twenty-First Century* (Chapel Hill: University of North Carolina Press, 2020), quote on 266. See also Franklin, "African Americans and Movements for Reparations," 1–12.

29. Evan Gerstmann, "Will America's Universities Point the Way Towards Reparations for Slavery?," *Forbes*, November 2, 2019; Tracy Scott Forson, "Enslaved Labor Built These Universities. Now They Are Starting to Repay the Debt," *USA Today*, February 12, 2020; and Darity and Mullen, *From Here to Equality*, 207–38.

30. Margaret A. Nash, "Entangled Pasts: Land Grant Colleges and American Indian Dispossession," *History of Educational Quarterly* 59 (November 2019): 437–67; and "The Dark History of Land Grant Universities," *Washington Post*, November 8, 2019.

31. Daniel Koretz, *The Testing Charade: Pretending to Make Schools Better* (Chicago: University of Chicago Press, 2017). See also Alfie Kohn, *The Case Against Standardized Testing: Raising the Scores, Ruining the Schools* (Portsmouth, NH: Heinemann, 2000); and Diane Ravitch, *Reign of Error: The Hoax of the Privatization Movement and the Danger to America's Public Schools* (New York: Vintage Books, 2013). For information on the "Opt-Out Movement," see Jeanette Deutermann, "Long Island Opts Out: My Story of Resistance," and Dao X. Tran, "Forget Teaching to the Test: Castle Bridge Boycotts It," in *More Than a*

Score: The New Uprising Against High Stakes Testing, ed. Jesse Hagopian (Chicago: Haymarket Press, 2014), 195–204, 211–18; and Diane Ravitch, *Slaying Goliath: The Passionate Resistance to Privatization and the Fight to Save America's Public Schools* (New York: Knopf, 2020), 97–102.

32. V. P. Franklin, "Black Social Scientists and the Mental Testing Movement, 1920–1940," in *Black Psychology*, 2nd edition, ed. Reginald Jones (New York: Harper and Row, 1980), 201–15; and "The Tests Are Written for the Dogs: *The Journal of Negro Education*, African American Children, and the Intelligence Testing Movement in Historical Perspective," *Journal of Negro Education* 76 (Summer 2007): 216–29; Brian Jones, "Standardized Testing and Children of Color," in Hagopian, *More Than a Score*, 71–76; and Diane Ravitch, *The Death and Life of the Great American School System: How Testing and Choice Are Undermining Education* (New York: Basic Books, 2010).

33. For approaches to alternative schooling, see Clyde C. Robertson, "Blueprints for the Development of African American Youth," *Journal of African American History* 97 (Winter–Spring 2012): 163–73; Joyce E. King, "A Reparatory Justice Curriculum for Human Freedom: Rewriting the Story of African American Dispossession and the Debt Owed," *Journal of African American History* 102 (Spring 2017): 213–31; and Bettina L. Love, *We Want to Do More Than Survive: Abolitionist Teaching and the Pursuit of Educational Freedom* (Boston: Beacon Press, 2019).

34. Lena Felton, "Teen Girls Organized Nashville's Largest Protest," *The Lily*, June 8, 2020. See also Desia Moore, "Young People Have the Megaphone: Here's What They Want Everyone Else to Hear," *Boston Globe*, June 13, 2020; Jessica Bennett, "Teen Girls Fighting for a More Just Future," *New York Times*, June 28, 2020; and Ibram X. Kendi, *How to Be an Antiracist* (New York: One World, 2019).

35. Michael Harrington, *The Other America: Poverty in the United States* (New York: Simon & Schuster, 1962); see also N. A. Naples, *Grassroots Warriors: Activist Mothering, Community Work, and the War on Poverty* (New York: Routledge, 1997); Thomas F. Jackson, *From Civil Rights to Human Rights: Martin Luther King Jr. and the Struggle for Economic Justice* (Philadelphia: University of Pennsylvania Press, 2007); Annelise Orleck and Lisa Gayle Hazirjian, *The War on Poverty: A New Grassroots History, 1964–1980* (Athens: University of Georgia Press, 2011); Gordon K. Mantler, *Power to the Poor: Black-Brown Coalition and the Fight for Economic Justice, 1960–1974* (Chapel Hill: University of North Carolina Press, 2013); Sylvie Laurent, *King and the Other America: The Poor People's Campaign and the Quest for Economic Equality* (Berkeley: University of California Press, 2018).

36. James Jennings, ed., *National Issues in Education: Elementary and Secondary Act* (New York: Phi Delta Kappa, 1995); Hugh Davis Graham, *The Civil Rights Era: Origins and Development of National Policy, 1960–1972* (New York: Oxford

University Press, 1990); Sidney L. Milkis and Jerome M. Mileur, *The Great Society and the High Tide of Liberalism* (Amherst: University of Massachusetts Press, 2005); Noel Cazenave, *Impossible Democracy: The Unlikely Success of the War on Poverty Community Action Programs* (Albany: State University of New York Press, 2007); Gavin Wright, *Sharing the Prize: The Economics of the Civil Rights Revolution in the South* (Cambridge, MA: Harvard University Press, 2013); Julian E. Zelizer, *The Fierce Urgency of Now: Lyndon Johnson, Congress, and the Battle for the Great Society* (New York: Penguin Press, 2015).

37. John Lewis, "Together, You Can Redeem the Soul of Our Nation," *New York Times*, July 30, 2020.

Index